ANDRÉ GIDE and ROMAIN ROLLAND:

Two Men Divided

ANDRÉ GIDE and
ROMAIN ROLLAND:
Two Men Divided

FREDERICK JOHN HARRIS

RUTGERS UNIVERSITY PRESS
New Brunswick, New Jersey

Permission to reprint, in the original French or in English translation, has been kindly granted by the following:

Albin Michel (Paris), from Romain Rolland's *Correspondance entre Louis Gillet et Romain Rolland*, 1949; *Deux Hommes se rencontrent*, 1964; *L'Esprit libre*, 1953; *Jean-Christophe*, 1956; *Journal des années de guerre*, 1952; *Mémoires*, 1956; *Printemps romain*, 1954; *Retour au Palais Farnèse*, 1956; *Le Voyage intérieur*, 1959.

Alfred A. Knopf (New York), from Justin O'Brien's translation of Gide's *Journal*.

Editions Gallimard (Paris), from André Gide's *Correspondance André Gide-Roger Martin du Gard*, edited by Jean Delay, 1968; *Journal*, Pléiade edition, 1951–1954; *Littérature engagée*, 1950; *Retour de l'U.R.S.S.*, 1950; and from Louis Guilloux's "D'un voyage en U.R.S.S.," *La Nouvelle Revue Française*, 1951; and from Jean Schlumberger's *Œuvres complètes*, 1958–1961.

Library of Congress Cataloging in Publication Data

Harris, Frederick John, 1943–
    André Gide and Romain Rolland: two men divided.

    Bibliography: p.
    1. Gide, André Paul Guillaume, 1869–1951.
    2. Rolland, Romain, 1866–1944. I. Title.
PQ2613.I2Z635   848'.9'1209   73–5991
ISBN 0–8135–0716–2

Contents

Preface

This book is a study of two men, André Gide and Romain Rolland. It is a study of the attitudes they adopted toward each other and of the impressions they formed of each other as persons and as artists, as revealed in their mutual correspondence, in their letters and statements to others, and in their written works. To some extent it is also a history, as they viewed it, of the time in which they lived, especially of World War I and the growing awareness of communism that followed the Russian Revolution.

In preparing the book I received valuable assistance both from specialists in contemporary French literature and from the heirs of the writers under discussion. The late Justin O'Brien of Columbia University inspired my work and, together with his colleague Leon S. Roudiez, afforded much helpful advice. In Paris, Mme Marie Romain Rolland, the widow of Romain Rolland and the administrator of the Archives Romain Rolland, gave me access to an extensive portion of Rolland's unpublished correspondence, works, and notes, which have been copied and collected in the Archives.

I wish to express my sincere thanks to Mme Rolland, to Mme Catherine Gide, and to Mme Marie-Hélène Dasté for their kind interest in my work. I am also indebted to Jacques Naville, director of the Comité Gide, and François Chapon, director of the Bibliothèque Doucet, for their guidance on Gide documents. Professor Claude Martin of Lyon offered not only generous advice but also constant moral support, both at Columbia and in France. Through William Scott Willis, chairman of the committee that administered the Bourse Romain Rolland, I was able to spend many months in Paris gathering my sources.

Mme Catherine Gide, Mme Marie Romain Rolland, and Mme Marie-Hélène Dasté have kindly granted me permission to reproduce various as yet unpublished texts of André Gide, Romain Rolland, and Jacques Copeau in this book. All rights to these materials are reserved, and it is clearly understood that no part of them may be reproduced elsewhere for any reason, either in the original French or in English translation, without the express permission of Mme Gide, Mme Rolland, or Mme Dasté.

To my great regret, however, Mme Rolland declined to allow me to quote verbatim from some of Rolland's unpublished literary remains.* In these instances I have supplied a paraphrase of the original text.

* Romain Rolland's unpublished letters to André Gide; the unpublished passages from Romain Rolland's "Journal intime" relating to the meeting between Rolland and Gide in 1934; Rolland's unpublished record, dated January 3, 1937, of an interview he had with a certain "X" who was on assignment with *Europe* to write an article on Gide's *Retour de l'U.R.S.S.;* those passages relating to the visit of Mme Gabrielle Duchêne dated January 4, 1937; and the passages of June 29, 1937, from the "Journal intime" relating to Louis Aragon and Gide; also Rolland's letters to Pierre Abraham of July 26, 1932; to René Arcos of November 27, 1936; to Jean-Richard Bloch of August 26, 1935, and February 24, 1936; to Jacques Copeau of Easter Monday, 1912, and October 13, 1912; to Maxim Gorki of July 30, 1935; to Mme E. Marchand of January 28, 1931; to Marcel Martinet of November 15, 1930; to Jean Paulhan of January 12, 1932; and to Thérèse Pottecher of December 10, 1936.

The French texts from which the English translations were made will be found in a section following the notes. At the request of Alfred A. Knopf, Inc., I used Justin O'Brien's translation of Gide's *Journal*. All other English translations are my own.

Frederick John Harris

New York, New York
March, 1973

ANDRÉ GIDE and
ROMAIN ROLLAND:
Two Men Divided

I The Two Men

In 1907 a loose and rather unlikely association came into being between the writers André Gide and Romain Rolland. Though it spanned some thirty years in all, it was in many ways an improbable association from the start. The two men shared many common interests and often pursued similar intellectual endeavors, occasionally even in an atmosphere of mutual cooperation. But Gide and Rolland were different in nature. Their temperaments were different, and so was their *manière d'être*.

Gide was thoroughly the artist; Rolland aspired to be many other things besides, and his preoccupations with socio-political questions reached an intensity that Gide never knew. Their conceptions of art were not the same. Both were seekers of truth, as they said time and again; and yet they did not look in the same place to find it. Jean Paulhan, editor of the *Nouvelle Revue Française* from 1925 until his death in 1968, responded in precise terms to my inquiry on their association: "Rolland and Gide could not bear each

3

other." As to their opinions of each other as artists: " 'that hypocrite,' said one of the other, 'that sham artist.' " [1]

The two men clearly did not always understand each other. They wrote seldom and sporadically, only when circumstances made it imperative for them to communicate; and their entire correspondence consists of only eleven letters, six from Gide to Rolland, five from Rolland to Gide. They knew each other personally, but they met only twice, and how much each knew of the other's work is a debatable question.

They belonged to the same generation, the generation that grew to manhood between the Franco-Prussian War and World War I. Romain Rolland was born on January 29, 1866, and André Gide slightly less than four years later on November 22, 1869. Their experience of the world they lived in and their reactions to it were often strikingly similar. The Dreyfus affair shook France when both were quite young, and neither actively took sides. Both had contacts with Mallarmé, though Gide was much closer to him; both witnessed the decline of symbolism, and, as artists, both rejected the movement for themselves. In the case of Gide, however, the allure was far more powerful and the influence a more lasting one. Both were in their own way religious men, though the emphasis of their thinking on religion was somewhat different. They shared a deep love of music, this being one of Rolland's greatest passions in life, a passion to which his work gave enduring homage.

While Gide was asserting himself as a novelist in *L'Immoraliste* in 1902, *La Porte étroite* in 1909, and *Les Caves du Vatican* in 1914, Rolland's *Jean-Christophe* (1903 to 1912) dominated fiction in France. By turns admiring and highly critical of *Jean-Christophe*, Gide began his *Dostoïevsky* before 1914 in imitation of "ces belles monographies de Romain Rolland" on Michelangelo and Beethoven.

Gide and Rolland lived at a time when the destiny of

France was riveted with that of Germany. Their lives encompassed three major wars, two of them world wars, and all of them fought against Germany. Though theirs was an age when things German were detested and scorned in France, both were internationalists in their thinking and their influence, and the world *outre-Rhin* exerted a powerful fascination on them. Both rejected narrow chauvinism, but the intensity of their convictions and the means they used to express them were quite different.

Sometime after the war while Rolland was publishing *L'Âme enchantée,* Gide was engaged with *Les Faux-Monnayeurs;* and the role he played in the monthly *Nouvelle Revue Française* from 1909 until 1940 was paralleled to a degree, especially during the 1920's, by Rolland's role in the periodical *Europe.*

The advent of Russian communism after the revolution of 1917 together with Gide's own "conversion" to communism in the 1930's channeled the thinking of the two men onto a common meeting ground. But they were not politicians, and their commitment to the Communist party, especially in the case of Gide, was more often than not rhetorical or theoretical in nature, consisting of statements of support, both oral and written, and participation in various communist-affiliated meetings. At this time their names appeared even frequently on the same programs and at the same congresses, both communist-inspired and other. But with Gide's "defection" from communism, the gulf that had separated them widened again. Yet there had been a period when they had found each other, so to speak, when they had been able to communicate, at least to some extent, on the same wave lengths.

During the period of their rapprochement Gide and Rolland seem to have asked themselves if for all their differences, hurt, and even envy, they were not made to work and fight together to advance the same causes. In his last letter to

Gide dated February 5, 1936, from the Villa Olga at Villeneuve in the canton Vaud in Switzerland, where he lived
from 1922 to 1937, Rolland spoke of his great joy in knowing
that finally, toward the end of their lives, he and Gide were
able to come together. This joy had been refused to so many
of their predecessors, who, though made to be allies, died
estranged. The rapprochement with André Gide was simply
one more reason for him to show gratitude toward communism, to which he referred as "mankind's great cause," whose
servants both he and Gide had become.[2]

Before the end of the same year, however, they were again
estranged, never more to be reconciled. Romain Rolland
died on December 30, 1944, Gide on February 19, 1951.

At the present moment the figure of André Gide looms
large on the French literary horizon. He has succeeded in
remaining *actuel,* whereas the person and, even more especially, the work of Romain Rolland have long since entered
an eclipse. Whether that eclipse will be of long duration or
whether it will indeed prove to be permanent is of little importance to the considerations at hand. This book is intended
solely as a study of the interrelations between Gide and Rolland on a personal and on an intellectual level.

The attitudes and conceptions of the two men in regard to
art and literature have been of central concern in this book.
That Gide's influence in literature has been greater than Rolland's is of course unquestioned. However, consideration
has also been given to that very important part of their lives
that both devoted to improving the social order. In the case
of Romain Rolland, perhaps this accounted for the most
significant portion of his life. But the question of influences,
whether of influences that converged on the two authors
from without or of influences that emanated from them, in
the literary or in the sociopolitical sphere, is beyond the
scope of this investigation.

In order to appreciate the full import of the data avail-

able in the Gide-Rolland correspondence, in the encounters
the two men had, and in the remarks they made about each
other in writing to others, it has seemed essential to treat
such broad subjects as art, religion, individualism, and communism in some detail. One cannot, for example, understand as well as one ought, Gide's conversion to communism
without some prior understanding of his ideas on religion
and Christianity. One cannot really understand his defection
from communism if one does not appreciate his passion for
individualism. And one can far less understand the feelings of hostility, misunderstanding, and probably even frus-
tration, that arose at various points in the lifetimes of Gide
and Rolland without first understanding the basic differences
that existed in their conceptions of art.

The present treatment of such broad areas does not pre-
tend to be the final word on each subject. Each of the areas
mentioned could be examined in greater detail in a separate
treatment of each author, and some of these areas have been
so treated.

That Gide and Rolland differed so frequently is perhaps
more interesting than their similarity. Any comparison made
between them can only gain therefrom in precision and interest. The fact that they were at once similar and different
should afford a more comprehensive study of the era in which
they lived, as well as a more penetrating analysis of their
thinking.

II First Contacts

André Gide and Romain Rolland first met late in 1907. From 1904, when a chair in the history of music was created for Rolland until he resigned in 1912, he lectured at the Sorbonne. It was there that he was introduced to Gide, who, with Emile Verhaeren, had come to hear him. Verhaeren had made the arrangements for the meeting and informed Gide thereof in a letter dated December 2, 1907, at Saint-Cloud.

> Next Thursday at 4:15 Romain Rolland will see you in his office at the Amphithéâtre Turgot. In his letter he has indicated the way to get there. Please be under the Galeries de l'Odéon at 3:30. We shall meet there and go together to the Sorbonne. Looking forward to seeing you soon again.[1]

When the two writers recorded this first encounter some twenty years later, their recollections were no longer precise. In his as yet unpublished "Journal intime" for September, 1933, to June, 1934, Rolland remembered having seen Gide

8

before 1910 when Gide had come with Verhaeren to hear
one of his lectures at the Sorbonne.[2] Gide's recollections
were more detailed. On the evening of January 31, 1936, he
presided at a *soirée d'hommage* held in Rolland's honor at
the large assembly hall in the Quartier Latin called the Mutualité. The text of his address had been printed in the
weekly *Vendredi* on January 24.

> I recall the day on which I made his acquaintance. It was
> a number of years before the war. Romain Rolland was then
> giving a course on ancient music at the Collège de France. I
> wanted to see and hear him and gladly allowed myself to be
> taken along by Verhaeren, who was a close friend of mine.
> Together we listened reflectively, as did the large audience,
> to the warm and vibrant voice of the master, who was still
> young but already renowned, whose sedate and gracious
> authority made itself felt, as though involuntarily, by the
> simple effect of his profound conviction and his natural dig-
> nity. His lecture was interspersed with examples that he
> himself played on the piano with grave and persuasive elo-
> quence. No personal concern for turning himself to account
> but rather for the musician (I no longer know which one)
> he was interpreting. At the end of the lecture, Verhaeren
> and I approached him. He spoke to us with the same sim-
> plicity that had made his lecture a kind of friendly chat.[3]

Gide has confused in his memory the exact place of the
meeting, and the parenthetical "I no longer know which
one" in reference to the musician Rolland had been discussing is sincere, human, amusing, and very typical. At
those times when he did not take himself too seriously, Gide
often seemed incapable of taking anyone or anything seriously, and in this he differed radically from Rolland. Gide
could be playful, where Rolland remained earnest. In response to the question "Pourquoi écrivez-vous?" asked in a
survey of writers in 1919, Gide gave the following answer:

You can classify writers according to whether their answer
to your survey begins with "so that," "in order to," or
"because."

There will be those for whom literature is above all an
end, and those for whom it is above all a means.

As for me, I write because I have a good pen, and in order
to be read by you... But I never answer surveys.[4]

This is not the kind of answer Rolland would have given,
nor is it the only kind of response Gide gave to such basically
serious questions. However, it might be said that the answer
highlights a certain quality of temperament, and that in it
lies the key to a thousand differences and misunderstandings
that were to separate the two writers throughout the course
of their lives, the key to what might be called Gide's artistic
temperament.

The earliest correspondence between Gide and Rolland
of which there is any record was dated Thursday, July 8,
1909. Rolland wrote from his apartment at 162 boulevard
Montparnasse to thank Gide for a book Gide had sent him.
It seems logical to assume that the book in question was one
Gide had just completed; and so, very likely, it was *La Porte
étroite,* which appeared in 1909. The letter, with a salutation of "cher Monsieur," was polite, but brief and correct.
Rolland congratulated Gide. He found the book to be beautiful from the first to the last pages, and the last pages to be
most beautiful of all. The letter ended with a simple statement assuring Gide of Rolland's congenial friendship for
him.[5] That was all. A good beginning, one might say. And
a good choice on the part of Gide. There was much in the
Porte étroite that might appeal to the character of Romain
Rolland. The themes of friendship, love, and sacrifice in
love were themes akin to those found in his own novels. And
it was precisely at this time that Rolland was writing what
has become the best known of his novels, *Jean-Christophe.*

Despite his complimentary letter of 1909, Rolland chose less than two years later to criticize severely Gide's work and the literature of contemporary Paris in general. In a letter to Jean-Richard Bloch [6] on February 3, 1911, he advised the young *agrégé* in history and geography to avoid involving himself too deeply with this literature which breathed forth a certain *malaise*. Gide, among others, such as the writer Remy de Gourmont and the socialist Léon Blum, not only perceived this state of *malaise* but was one of the causes of it, Rolland contended. But in a letter postmarked two days later, he recognized that this position was a bit too hastily taken and harsh. [7] "Forget my letter," he told Bloch. "It was only one of those friendly discussions in which, without wanting to, one exaggerates one's thought a bit." Still he felt that the basis of his criticism had to stand.

> except for its form—there is much less to be learned from the literature of Paris today than from the literature of the rest of Europe; and there is less to be learned from European literature than from all the other things that go to make up the lives of Europeans. Art was once upon a time prophetic, but it is today outdistanced by life. [8]

Again on January 14, 1912, and again in a letter to Bloch, Rolland attacked Gide as an artist. Bloch had been associated with the founding of the literary and artistic review *L'Effort* and as of June, 1910, had undertaken to keep Rolland informed of his activities on behalf of the magazine. Rolland now saw fit to admonish Bloch to keep distinct a literature that was creative and constructive from one that was not. To attempt to combine the two could only result in *L'Effort's* becoming a review "de grand dilettantisme." [9]

> I sincerely do not see how a love of Tolstoy and Whitman can be reconciled with love of art in the style of Gide or Duhamel. I am expressing no criticism against them. But if,

in a strict sense, they can all harmonize together in a purely critical, contemplative, and static intelligence, they cannot harmonize (to my way of thinking) in a creative and constructive spirit.[10]

The known Gide-Rolland correspondence contains only one more letter before World War I; it is dated Tuesday, February 25, 1913.[11] Again it was from Romain Rolland thanking Gide for receipt of a book. Given Rolland's feelings about Gide's work as stated in his correspondence with Bloch, this letter was surprisingly and even deceptively cordial. The tone was far more relaxed here than in the first letter, and Rolland now addressed Gide by name, dropping from the salutation the more formal "Monsieur" of the earlier letter. As in the previous letter, Rolland again called the book Gide had sent him "beautiful," adding that he had more than once recognized the "donor in the corner of the painting" and associated himself with the donor's moral anguish and intellectual joy. Rolland now became specific. More than anything else, *L'Enfant prodigue* and *El Hadj* had moved him. He saw their wisdom and perception as the product of a calm and tragic mind.[12]

Before the outbreak of the war Rolland's own *Jean-Christophe* had made its appearance in the pages of the *Cahiers de la Quinzaine,* the literary and socialist discussion forum published by the poet Charles Péguy. The biographies Rolland wrote of Beethoven, Michelangelo, Händel, and Tolstoy had also been published, and his career as a dramatic writer, too, was long since under way. Though Gide never referred to Rolland's efforts in the theater, he did mention in a lecture on Dostoevsky that before the war he was preparing a life of the Russian novelist in imitation of the lives of Beethoven and Michelangelo, "those beautiful monographs of Romain Rolland."[13] He was also familiar with *Jean-Christophe,* or at least became familiar with it before the end of the war, and much of his harshly adverse criticism of the novel must be viewed in light of the times that produced it.

Late in 1913 Rolland had praise for Gide's translation of Rabindranath Tagore's *Gitanjali,* which had appeared in that year, and gave a veritable, if concise, eulogy of Gide, "who is one of our best writers. The fragments by him that I have read in the *Nouvelle Revue Française* seemed very beautiful to me." [14] Rolland himself in succeeding years established a relatively substantial correspondence with Tagore, to whose internationalism in thought he was very much attracted.

World War I marked a drastic turning point in the relations of Rolland and Gide. Neither was required to serve in the military forces, and so each sought another outlet for his energies, Rolland working at the Agence Internationale des Prisonniers de Guerre with the Red Cross in Geneva, Gide trying to aid refugees from the occupied territories at the Foyer Franco-Belge in Paris. For both, the war was a time of strain, and especially of mental strain. It lasted long enough to accentuate certain traits of character in each one that made them incompatible either as friends or as artists.

III War

From the outset of World War I Romain Rolland was grief-stricken, and declared the war a catastrophe for Western civilization. Beginning on July 31, 1914, he meticulously kept a diary, the *Journal des années de guerre,* in which he recorded the events of the war, his own activities during the war, and the reaction that these activities occasioned in different parts of the world, especially in Europe's two principal opposing camps. The diary comprises some eighteen hundred pages covering the war and beyond, the last entry being dated Monday, June 23, 1919.

From the first pages, Rolland expressed his horror of the war and his commitment to humanity. The entry for August 3–4, 1914, reads:

"I am overwhelmed. I wish I were dead. It is a horrible thing to live in the midst of this demented humanity, to witness helplessly the bankruptcy of civilization. This European war is the greatest catastrophe of history that has occurred in centuries; it dashes our most sacred hopes for human brotherhood." [1]

Gide took a different position. The words "human brotherhood" were not without meaning for him; but he was far less ready than Rolland to sacrifice his patriotism for a higher ideal. The entry in Gide's *Journal* for the first day of August, 1914, established a tone quite unlike Rolland's: "A day of painful waiting. Why don't we mobilize? Every moment we delay is that much more advantage for Germany." [2]

Characteristic of Rolland was the tone he adopted in the article entitled "Au-dessus de la mêlée," since published as part of the larger volume *L'Esprit libre*. Love of one's fatherland did not require one to hate others who loved their own countries, but rather for all to unite to attain the common good.[3] Rolland saw it as essential for man to free himself from the concept of the national fatherland, which he called half-beast and half-God in *Clerambault*,[4] a novel published shortly after the war. The instinct to love one's country was not a bad one, but needed proper channeling, and the concept of the national fatherland must be replaced by that of the human fatherland encompassing the entire world. The dimensions of this *patrie* became even larger for Rolland as his life progressed. Concerned first for the friendship of the peoples of France and Germany, he extended his thesis to include all Europe by the end of the war, and when asked for his adherence to the Pan-Europe movement, refused, saying that Europe had now become too small a fatherland or homeland for him.[5] "Europe, broaden your horizons or die," he wrote in 1930.[6] Through later contacts with leaders of Eastern thought such as Gandhi, Ramakrishna, and Vivekananda, he gave further testimony to the global quality of his own patriotism.

The ideal that is on its way out is that of a national fatherland that wishes to be and to remain first and foremost. . . .
The incoming ideal is that of the human Fatherland that asks all other fatherlands to consent to mutual sacrifice in

order to harmonize and cooperate in the great common effort: the mastery of Nature by the human species.[7]

Between these two ideals, a choice must be made: "We must break with a past which certainly is venerable but which has given sufficient proof of its wrongdoing and of its deadly incapacity." [8]

Rolland was opposed not so much to patriotism, as such, as to the horrors that patriotism could produce when it became tinged with fanaticism. In this he was not far removed from Gide, who recognized that "toute obéissance comporte un aveuglement," [9] and that once the blind spots had been removed, man's power to love was capable of infinite extension.[10]

If Romain Rolland actively condemned the immoderate workings of patriotism as he saw them everywhere manifested from his wartime refuge in Switzerland, he did not by any means renounce his country, as Henri Massis would have us believe. Massis's pamphlet *Romain Rolland contre la France* had expounded a patriotism that refused to yield to the force of reason, and it was this type of patriotism that aroused Rolland's active protest. France was, for Massis, the "land of humanity and land of the Spirit, land of Sacrifice and of Light," the land that in spite of its errors and blasphemies was the one God chose whenever he wished something great to be accomplished on this earth.[11] Massis accused Romain Rolland of fleeing to take refuge in Switzerland while his brothers were dying in France, and of being a "dilettante" in refusing to choose sides.

Romain Rolland did not refuse to choose sides. His choice was unequivocally with France. Nonetheless, he remained clear-sighted enough to perceive that in this war both sides in some way shared the blame. He could objectively look at his own France where patriotism had reached such a height of delirium that it was forbidden to say that the prisoners

were tall and had blue eyes,[12] where certain people attempted
to preach to the nation that the Germans had no soul and
that therefore there was no wrong in killing them. And he
felt obliged to tell France the truth. He had to maintain, if
no one else would, the ideal of humanity and raise it above
the cry of combat. How much more sane and noble Rolland's
own type of patriotism now appears as set forth in his comments to an unidentified German who had told him of the
stupendous moral victory he thought France had obtained
during this war: the sympathy of the world was hers to
command.

> We must all want her to preserve this moral victory until
> the end, we must want her to remain until the end just,
> lucid, and human. I have never been able to distinguish the
> cause of France from that of humanity. . . . I want France
> to be loved, I want her to be victorious not only by force,
> not only by right . . . but by the superiority of her own great
> and generous heart. I want her to be strong enough to fight
> without hatred and to see, even in those she is forced to
> vanquish, brothers who have gone astray and who are to be
> pitied, after they have been rendered incapable of doing
> harm.[13]

Rolland's move to Switzerland was certainly not flight.
Nor was it an escape. As had become his annual custom,
Rolland went to Switzerland in the spring of 1914. Some two
months later war was declared. There he remained, in the
hope of keeping himself free from hatred, and in the hope
of writing with greater freedom than would have been possible in France. More than ten years later, he recalled in his
"Journal intime" the determining reasons for his decision
to remain in Switzerland.

> it was not only the heart of France I wanted to hear. But
> the heart of my true fatherland: Europe. Had I remained

in France, the throbbings of that heart would never have reached me. In Switzerland, and only in Switzerland, could I directly receive the confidences of both sides. Only in Switzerland could I judge impartially: for there, and only there, could I bring together all the elements of the case.[14]

Rolland complained on several occasions of the censorship imposed on him, and as late as January 20, 1919, he noted in his *Journal des années de guerre:* "It is useless for the war to have ended, as I am told, three months ago. Never has the constraint on thought been worse. The censorship of letters is intolerable. Half of my correspondence from France is suppressed altogether; the rest is thoroughly cut up with censor blocks." [15]

It is ironic that the passages from "Au-dessus de la mêlée" that Massis quoted in his pamphlet against Rolland were in print before any other portion of the text was released in France.[16]

Although Gide was no proponent of the war, his efforts to reduce the hatred it had generated pale beside the gigantic effort of Romain Rolland. In addition to his openly political writings and enormous correspondence, two of Rolland's novels, *Clerambault* and *Pierre et Luce,* and one play, *Liluli,* were all three born directly of the war. If Gide made little or no open propaganda to end the war, however, his refusal, and perhaps inability, to do any creative writing during the crisis was noteworthy. The fact is that André Gide did not look upon the war in the same way as his outspoken contemporary. Gide's basic dislike of war is clear from a response elicited by René Gillouin [17] many years later in 1935 at a meeting of the Union pour la Vérité.[18] Gide had consented to answer questions on his affiliation with communism at this meeting, and Gillouin was one of his interviewers. Gillouin had remarked that a non-Christian might deplore the fact of war and seek to limit it, but would have no right to justify its abolition. The Christian, too, might associate himself with any serious effort against war, but the Christian exists simultaneously on a higher plane, and on that plane war loses its importance. Gide's response: "To come to the point of believing that is dangerous." [19] To relegate the problem to the spiritual domain was not to solve it, and Gide was far too much concerned with the here and now to accept such an explanation.

That Gide's statement is separated in time from the period now under consideration does not negate its relevance. His own deep-rooted sense of humanity assured him a certain consistency on the subject of war, and though he might accept war he could never condone it per se and without reserve. In certain instances war might prove to be a necessary evil, but it remained an evil nonetheless.

Neither Gide nor Rolland harbored any profound dislike of Germany. In fact, both had an abiding interest in Germany. (How much they were influenced by German culture is beyond the scope of this book.) Both were on friendly terms with many members of the rather substantial colony of German and Austrian writers established in Paris, but both apparently made conversation with them in French. Both had been exposed to Germany and the German language at a relatively early age, Gide by his Scottish governess Anna Shackleton while he was yet a child in his mother's home,[20] and Rolland in his long association with Malwida von Meysenbug,[21] which began in his twenty-second year. She shared with him many of the treasures of the German cultural heritage.[22] Both Gide and Rolland had studied German literature, and the names of Goethe and Nietzsche occur over and over in their writings. Both were extremely fond of and well-versed in German music. Though Gide very definitely disliked Wagner, he, like Rolland, greatly esteemed Bach, Mozart, and Beethoven.

Rolland's passion for Beethoven was lifelong. He saw in Beethoven not only the artist but the revolutionary and was drawn to him on both levels. His slim one-volume *Vie de Beethoven,* published in 1903 in the *Cahiers de la Quinzaine,* was supplemented in later years by many more related books, now bound together in one large volume entitled simply *Beethoven.* Rolland said that through music he had penetrated the German soul and that music had made of him a *Weltbürger.*[23] So imbued was he with the spirit of Germany and its music that he made the hero of his first novel, *Jean-Christophe,* a German and a musician.

Rolland's background, then, disposed him favorably to Germany, but because he loved Germany, the course she was following caused him deep personal grief. When the same Germany that had given him so much in an esthetic way invaded Belgium, laying in ruins the old town of Louvain, he cried out in protest to the great German dramatist Gerhart Hauptmann in an open letter dated August 29, 1914, and first published in the *Journal de Genève* on September 2.

> I am not, Gerhart Hauptmann, among those Frenchmen who treat Germany as a barbarian. I know the intellectual and moral greatness of your powerful race. I am aware of all that I owe to the thinkers of old Germany; and even at the present hour, I call to mind the example and the words of *our* Goethe—he belongs to all of humanity—repudiating all national hatred. . . . I have worked all my life to bring together the minds of our two nations; and the atrocities of the ungodly war that sets them against each other for the ruination of European civilization will never lead me to sully my mind with hatred.
>
> Whatever reasons I may then have for suffering today on account of your Germany and for judging as criminal, German politics and the methods it uses, I in no way hold responsible the people who submit to these politics and who have become their blind instrument.[24]

Rolland was now forced to recognize another Germany, no longer the *vieille Allemagne* of whose culture he felt a part.

He viewed this new Germany as unfaithful to its past, and by his letter to Hauptmann he hoped to make German intellectuals aware of this. But this was a time when patriotism was reaching the same heights of delirium in Germany as in France, and Hauptmann repudiated Rolland's attempt, scornfully alluding to the word "barbare" that French intellectuals had already used more than once in reference to his country.[25]

Where did Rolland stand amid all this hysteria? A man not without a country, as Massis would have us believe, but a man wanted by no country. In the early part of 1916 Rolland's war diary reads: "A Frenchwoman who is in Russia reproaches me with being a bad Frenchman. A German at Saint-Moritz reproaches me with being a Frenchman blinded by national feeling. The two letters arrive in the same mail delivery." [26]

André Gide recognized the danger in the policy Rolland was pursuing. At no time did he minimize Rolland's efforts; rather he seemed to understand that there was grandeur in them. But it was a dangerous time requiring not only tact but also unity so that France might emerge victorious.

When Jacques Copeau, the founder of the Vieux-Colombier Theater, learned that Rolland was working at the Prisoner of War Agency, he immediately took advantage of the opportunity to request information on his friend Jacques Rivière, who had disappeared while serving in arms. Copeau and Gide were among the founders of the *Nouvelle Revue Française,* and Rivière was its secretary. In a letter of October 16, 1914, Rolland promised to do all he could. Four days later Gide wrote to him.

Dear Romain Rolland,
    Since I was living with Copeau at the home of mutual friends and was as anxious as he in regard to Jacques Rivière, it was natural for Copeau to show me your letter. You will

understand without difficulty, I trust, and with what emotion I read it: More than once already since the start of this abominable struggle I have been at the point of writing to you—and especially after having read your letter to Hauptmann in the papers. I beg you to forget for a moment what may displease you in my books; I am talking to you as a man of good faith, a man the events of the times have brought closer to you; someone who, like yourself, had friends in Germany whom he cannot bring himself to hate.

You seem to hold on to some hope, if not of convincing them, at least of informing them. You say they are ignorant of all the cruelty perpetrated by their army... But what strange result do you expect in unmasking these horrors for them? To make them take a dislike to their country? No, they need to defend it with all their heart, they need to delude themselves on all its monstrous faults.

Ah! how I would like to talk with you about these things! If you should return to Paris, kindly let me know—and be assured of my warm *sympathie*.

André Gide

I was going to close my letter when I received word from one of my best friends, Paul Laurens, whose brother must have fallen into the hands of the enemy. He must have telegraphed Monsieur Ador [27] yesterday, but would be profoundly thankful to you if you could see to it from your side that the necessary steps are taken to obtain some information about *Sergeant Pierre Laurens*—25th infantry reg Co. 8, wounded on the 26th or 27th of Sept. in the region around Arras and presumed to be missing.

Do you know anything about Bachelin? [28]

A.G. [29]

Gide was fully aware that Rolland's hopes would be dashed. Though sympathetic to Rolland, he made no attempt to join him in his campaign; rather he tried politely to dissuade him.

Gide's allusion to the fact that Rolland did not appreciate his work does not come as a surprise, for Rolland had taken occasion before the war to criticize Gide's art, but it is the first hint in the letters exchanged between them that there were differences separating them.

Romain Rolland's answer was not slow in coming. On October 26, 1914, he wrote from Geneva and the first paragraph is simply a response to Gide's inquiries about Jacques Rivière and Pierre Laurens. Rolland promised to do all he could to try to locate them, and in the case of Rivière he was taking advantage of personal contacts outside the Red Cross. That very morning he had received a note from a German intellectual whom he did not identify, but described as one of the most "megalomaniacal" of those with whom he had contacts. The German was deeply moved by what Rolland had written him of Jacques Rivière, for he recognized a moral debt to the *Nouvelle Revue Française* and associated himself with all that concerned those who were part of it. The German added that he and many of his friends also mourned the death of Charles Péguy, and he ended by thanking Rolland for coming to him with the task of locating Rivière. He had many friends in Stuttgart who would help him find Rivière if he was in that area.[30]

The remainder of Rolland's letter has in large part been published in the *Journal des années de guerre* (and, unlike the foregoing, can be reproduced verbatim here).

> Your letter moved me, my dear Gide. There is at least one good thing about this abominable war: it is bringing together many minds that used to live somewhat apart from one another. —Shall I tell you? The war has even brought me closer to some of our "enemies" from Germany. It is opening up the depths of our hearts.
> You ask me what I expect from these discussions. I expect by enlightening others that they will enlighten me. I am not trying to make them feel contempt for their homeland but to give them the means to make it liked. They must be made aware of the crimes imputed to it, and they must condemn

these crimes, or submit to me evidence that they have been
invented by a deceitful press or by witnesses living in a state
of hallucination. France, my dear friend, is enveloped in
almost as many lies as Germany. It is like a sea of mist. And
Europe is covered with mist.

In the unpublished text of the letter Rolland remarked
at this point that one had to scale mountain peaks to find
any light in these times. But the light must be made to
penetrate down below and the question was precisely how
to accomplish this? The lies that were being spread were
having a poisonous effect on the war.

How can a Richepin [31] possibly be allowed to write in the
Petit Journal that the Germans have cut off the right hands
of 4,000 young boys between the ages of fifteen and seventeen, and other vile nonsense of this kind! Isn't there a risk
that such words will bring on real cruelty from our side?
Since the start of the war, each barbaric deed . . . has been
amplified a hundred times; and it naturally gives rise to
others. There comes a succession of reprisals. How far will
these reprisals go . . . ?

What indeed would be the extent of the reprisals if no effort
were made to contain the spread of hatred?

Men like us must vigorously disengage themselves from this
deadly atmosphere, in the high interest not only of the spirit
of Europe but of their own people. We, who have the privi-
lege of knowing the best of the German intellectuals and
of being known by them, must maintain close relations with
them; we must make use of the confidence they still have
in us. . . .

A parenthetical observation referred to the letters Rolland
had been receiving for a month now, attesting to the con-

fidence German intellectuals had in their French counter-
parts.

> We must try to hear them faithfully: official *Addresses*
> stamped with the endorsement of the Prussian police do not
> express their true thinking; this is expressed in their let-
> ters . . . ; it would be expressed even better in discussion,
> if I could, as I am striving to do, have a certain number of
> them come to Geneva . . . to explain themselves. I might
> possibly succeed. . . .

Another parenthetical remark made note of a curious fact:
the most outspoken of Rolland's letters to Germany had all
reached their destinations. As to the meetings Rolland was
planning, whether in Geneva or another Swiss city, he held
fast to the hope that Gerhart Hauptmann, the Austrian
writer and critic Hermann Bahr, or others, free men from
still other countries, would answer his call.

> I would like to see the moral unity of Europe's elite recon-
> stituted at the very eye of the storm. At least I would like
> to try. . . .

Such a dream was worth trying.

> In any case, I, for my part, shall never compromise with
> hatred. I know it to be wrong. What we now suffer does not
> come from Germany alone.

A postscript to the letter spoke of many things Rolland
wanted to tell Gide and could not by letter. He feared that
Gide would not believe him, for they were living in different
moral atmospheres in Paris and Geneva. And furthermore,
there would be too much to write and insufficient time to
write it. Rolland concluded by saying he knew nothing of
Henri Bachelin.

Thus Rolland, too, alluded to the fact that there had been differences between himself and Gide. Although the war brought them together momentarily, it seems rather to have alienated them in the long run.

Another item of importance in this letter: the German people were not alone in being asked to swallow the lies that their government and press deemed appropriate at the moment; this practice existed in France as well. It has sometimes been difficult for a people to recognize that its own government can perpetrate gross falsehood, but for Rolland there was no hesitation on this point. He was convinced that the peoples on both sides had been duped and that the people themselves were not the principal culprits. The average soldier fought for what he believed to be right; and for the German, as well as for the Frenchman, the war was in that sense a holy war fought to uphold his ideals.[32] Nevertheless, all must bear responsibility for this holocaust: the average or "good" people, their governments and their press, the intellectuals, and even the Church. On November 2, 1916, All Souls Day, Rolland wrote:

In today's disaster we all have our share: some through an act of the will, others through weakness; and weakness is not the least of the unpardonables. The apathy of the majority, the timidity of the honest, the skeptical selfishness of weak governments, the ignorance or cynicism of the press, greedy mouths of gangsters, fearful servility of thinkers who have become the message-bearers of deadly prejudices which it was their mission to destroy; ruthless pride of those intellectuals who believe in their ideas more than in the life of their neighbor and would have 20 million men perish, simply to satisfy their own need to be right; political prudence of a too Roman Church, where Saint Peter the fisherman has become the boatsman of diplomacy; pastors with souls as dry and cutting as a knife, sacrificing their flock to purify it; doltish fatalism of these poor sheep— Who among us is not guilty?

Who among us has the right to wash his hands of the blood
of an assassinated Europe? [33]

Governments concerned not with the welfare of their people
but only with their own power, religious leaders on both
sides who supported these governments and counseled their
"faithful" to go and fight to destroy another "flock" counseled
to go and do the same: the situation was odious and absurd.
For Romain Rolland one fact alone dominated: "Europe is
not free. The voice of her peoples is stifled." [34]

Rolland was convinced that the greatest share of the guilt
for the war must fall on Germany: "I have never doubted it,"
he wrote in the latter part of 1916. "She carries everything
to excess. Imbalance is her constant characteristic, in bad as
well as in good." [35] Yet he did not spare France his criticism
either. The attack he leveled against the rulers of France in
a letter to the poet Pierre-Jean Jouve on August 14, 1915,
and recorded in the *Journal des années de guerre,* was
particularly harsh. There was no doubt, he wrote, that peace
would soon be established if France wanted it as much as
Germany. But she did not want it, or rather her leaders
would not allow her to want it.[36] Toward the end of the war
he wrote in a similar vein, commenting on the speech
Clemenceau delivered in the Chamber of Deputies on June 5,
1918. Rolland classified the speech as sinister and went on
to say, first quoting Clemenceau:

" *'Let me complete the work of the dead'* (that is to say,
kill all of France). 377 votes against 110. A heroism that is
murderous, murderous of itself. Heroism taken as an end,
when it should never be anything but the instrument to an
end, serving the task at hand. This always was France's error
of ideal. She is dying because of it. A people always dies of
the error of its virtues." [37]

Statements such as these written by Rolland throughout
the four years of the war made André Gide extremely wary.

On November 15, 1914, he took special note in his *Journal* of the Jean Richepin article Rolland had alluded to in his letter of October 26, in which Richepin told of four thousand children whose right hands had been amputated by the German barbarians.[38] The statement was without proof, and Gide appeared to understand Rolland's indignation. At this time, however, he did not even hint at his own possible indignation against the excesses alleged in the press simply to malign the Germans. But on December 27, 1915, he again referred to the incident, which he said Henri Ghéon [39] had now incorporated into a play on Romain Rolland. "I deplore the fact that his long play on Romain Rolland makes use of arguments that are often dubious." Gide noted that America had promised a huge reward to anyone who might be able to bring confirmation of such atrocities, and he said that the Foyer Franco-Belge had conducted inquiries everywhere in an attempt to uncover proof of one single such barbarism committed by the Germans. All the inquiries made led only to denials.[40]

Gide could write against the kind of slander Richepin was perpetrating, but he could not follow the open-mindedness of someone like Rolland to its conclusion. Their views on war and country were simply not the same. Discussing the meaning of the concept of fatherland or *patrie* in 1941 in an interview he might well have given during World War I, Gide reflected that *patrie* might not have the same meaning, or include the same terrain for the peasant in the north of France as for the peasant of the Midi. The farmer and the intellectual, the poor and the rich, think of different things when they hear this word. But "it is a rallying cry. And when we hear that 'the Fatherland is in danger,' the important thing is for us to rise and unite to defend it." It mattered little that what the peasant defended was his farm, the intellectual French culture, the worker and the businessman French industry, the retired their pensions. The word *patrie* meant all of these; it appealed to mind and heart simultaneously.[41]

War was not long a reality before Gide took occasion to warn Romain Rolland of the dangers of trying to be neutral and French at the same time. From Cuverville he wrote on November 10:

Dear Romain Rolland

Overburdened with work at the Foyer Franco-Belge, I have regretfully had to give up on the long letter I wanted to write you in answer to the article from the *Journal de Genève* that you so kindly sent me. Another of your articles, read since then, in the same journal (Oct. 12) answers in advance several objections I was preparing to make to you. I have the joy of being able to associate myself fully with this second article and of no longer having to make the reservations that the first one demanded of me. In this first article, the generosity of your thinking seemed to me alas! too unreal, and the desire to remain, if I may put it this way, at one and the same time neutral and French, too dangerous. Yes, indeed, our newspapers do explain events (and in a general way, the whole face of the war) with a systematic partiality that sometimes makes reading them very disturbing to me; don't think I am taken in by them. But the important thing today is to create and maintain a state of mind that will allow us to win. I know nothing of the people I used to know in Germany— not even of Rainer Maria Rilke, of whom I was very fond and whose translation of my *Enfant prodigue* was supposed to come out in October at the . . . [sic] Verlag. I cannot believe that he has withdrawn his affection any more than I have withdrawn mine.

I had occasion to read this article of Oct. 12, and to have it read by several people who had been able to get acquainted with your thinking only through the quotations skillfully cut by certain newspapers in such a way as to distort it treacherously. Unfortunately I have had to return this issue of the *Journal de Genève* to the friend who lent it to me. Would

it not be possible for you to get me another copy? And if some
other article of yours comes out, kindly send it to me—for I
find it repugnant to hear you misjudged; so give me all the
arms to defend you—but act in such a way that I can defend
you to the hilt and talk no more about expatriating yourself
the day France begins to live under an oppressive regime;
for then especially the presence of a mind like yours would
become necessary. As to that . . . [*sic*] secret meeting you
tell me in your letter you hope for, which would bring together on I know not what mountain peak in Switzerland the
superior minds of the enemy countries... no, already I am sure
that you no longer think it possible. You see quite clearly
that *they* have refused to recognize the United States' commission. Discussion with them will be possible only after
they have been conquered. Today we must not even try to
shorten the duration of the war: it would only start up
again tomorrow, more terrible.

Escorting Belgian refugees here, I have left Paris for two
days; I was waiting for this moment to write you and the
wisdom of the open countryside is quieting. If I were staying
here longer, I would have written you at greater length and
my letter would have taken another form, so as to be able
to be published in the *Journal de Genève* or elsewhere, but
I am overtaxed and too tired to give good expression to my
thought. I await you at the other side of the tunnel; it will
be good to talk things over then. But even now, be assured
of my heartfelt attention.

André Gide

I know that Copeau has corresponded with you regarding
Rivière; but I, too, want to thank you for the zeal you are
showing in this matter. You undoubtedly know that Mme
Rivière has received a second letter from her husband. Perhaps we shall soon be able to have assurance that his captivity
isn't too trying [? preceding word illegible], for his health
was delicate and I don't know how he will bear the winter—
Still nothing from Pierre Laurens.[42]

Rolland did not shirk his chosen task of remaining neutral and French. He recorded Gide's admonition in his *Journal des années de guerre* without comment,[43] and his attitude remained unchanged.

The first of Rolland's articles discussed in Gide's letter Rolland himself identified in the *Journal des années de guerre* [44] as "Au-dessus de la mêlée." It appeared in the *Journal de Genève* on September 15, 1914. Addressed to "la jeunesse héroïque du monde," to those who were actually fighting the war, it was a condemnation of the war, a condemnation of imperialism, that "monster with a hundred heads," [45] of socialism and Christianity, both of which had failed in his eyes, and a condemnation of the priests who, although part of the one holy and Catholic church, had joined in the war effort. It was a condemnation of Pius X, who was said to have died of sorrow. "Il s'agissait bien de mourir," exclaimed an infuriated Rolland, hoping that God would inspire a new Pontiff to wash the Church of its silence. You will conquer, he told the young soldiers, and could not refrain from adding that if France should lose the war, her death would be the most beautiful of which a "race" could dream.[46] Hatred banished from his mind, he called on his brothers in both camps: "brothers of France, brothers of England, brothers of Germany, let us not hate one another. I know you, I know us. Our peoples asked only for peace and freedom." [47]

Rolland's second article was different in tone, and with it Gide felt he could associate himself to the full extent. Entitled "De deux maux le moindre: pangermanisme ou panslavisme?" and since published in the collection *L'Esprit libre,* it was sent originally to the *Journal de Genève* on October 9 and appeared in the issue of October 12. It stated flatly that for France, England, and the whole Western world the worst enemy was Prussian imperialism. Rolland had mentioned this point in the first article also, but now it fell into center stage. He recalled to the Germans the glories of their cultural past and asked rhetorically: What do we owe to today's Germany, what has it created since Wagner? Rolland detested Czarist imperialism, observing that the intellectual élite in Russia had consistently been hostile to it, but he concluded that pan-Germanism was the worse of the two evils.[48]

The war was bringing to the fore attitudes, convictions, and weaknesses, and mutual understanding was becoming more and more difficult. Gide could not always comprehend Rolland's insistence on the bold and demonstrative position he had taken, and Rolland could not always comprehend Gide's reticence. On April 1, 1915, Rolland took dismal note of the burst of patriotism that animated the composer Vincent d'Indy, and associated Gide with him:

"He is wildly gleeful. War (who would have thought so!) is his element. According to his words, this is the natural state. . . . This state of bellicose glee is giving him health as never before. He eats and drinks for four. Curiously enough, Gide has gotten close to him and shares his exuberance." [49]

Much later on September 13, 1934, Gide sought to explain his wartime reticence: "Extremely (and I am almost on the point of saying: deplorably) open to sympathy, I let my mind be held in check, during the war, on a natural slope that would have taken it very far and was unable to put up any resistance (I reproach myself with it sufficiently today) to the rash enthusiasms of the friends who surrounded me at that time. At the Van Rysselberghes',[50] in the constant company of Verhaeren, of Copeau, of Ghéon, of Schlumberger, of Vincent d'Indy, without exactly following their example, I did not have the force to protest. At least I considered it prudent to keep silent and gave all my time and almost all my thoughts to the work of the refugees with which I could busy myself without compromise." [51]

Some constructive signs did emerge from the Gide-Rolland acquaintance after the sequestration of the contents of the poet Rainer Maria Rilke's Paris apartment. Rilke had left Paris on a trip to Germany just before the outbreak of hostilities and, because of the war, was unable to return. With several interruptions he had lived in Paris from 1902 to 1914. During the early part of this period, he was secretary to Rodin, and lived at the Hôtel Biron, now the Musée Rodin. After 1907 Rilke began to take an active interest in the literary circles of the capital,[52] and both Gide and Rolland knew him. The correspondence between Gide and Rilke assembled by Renée Lang contains a substantial number of letters dated before the war. Rolland and Rilke were neighbors, Rolland residing at this time at 162 boulevard Montparnasse and Rilke in the rue Campagne-Première. Rolland lamented the fact that so many of the writing community who were neighbors and could have been friends never really became friends,[53] but this was not the case with himself and Rilke. The Viennese writer Stefan Zweig had introduced them,[54] and their correspondence beginning in the year 1913 consists of several letters and makes mention of several meetings. Rolland noted in his "Journal intime," in commenting on Rilke's death late in December, 1926, that Rilke had been very much involved in the circle of Gide, Valéry, and the "pure esthetes" in Paris. The social aspect of his own thinking, Rolland felt, was not adapted to Rilke's character.[55]

Be this as it may, it was to Romain Rolland that Stefan Zweig wrote from Vienna on December 30, 1915, of the misfortune that had befallen Rilke. Zweig had spent some time in Paris before the war and was a friend of Rolland's. Sequestered from Rilke's Paris apartment in addition to personal possessions were manuscripts on which he had worked and was working, and Zweig regarded their seizure as an irreparable loss for German art. "And all this because he wasn't able to send his rent." [56] Occurrences like this one, even more than the horrors of the battlefield, served to create hatred and bitterness between nations, Zweig added, because they became symbols of voluntary destruction; they were acts of hatred against defenseless persons.[57] Romain Rolland appreciated the tragedy of what had taken place two houses away from his own, and from Geneva he wrote Zweig that this was one of the cruelest pieces of news he had yet had. He promised to write to Copeau and Gide, who admired and liked Rilke,[58] and several days later, on January 7, 1916, notified Copeau of the affair.

> I have just learned a piece of news that rends my heart, and toward which neither you nor Gide can possibly be unfeeling. The good and inoffensive Rilke, who was living in Paris at 18 rue Campagne-Première, has been informed that all his furniture, all his manuscripts, and all his letters have been abruptly sold and dispersed. This is an irreparable loss for art, and a stroke of irrational cruelty against this quiet thinker and poet. I suffer not only for him but for the reputation of France. Will you see, as quickly as possible, if there is no way left to save something from the wreck? Do what you can for the honor of France.[59]

Gide indicated both to Renée Lang [60] and in his "Deux Rencontres avec Romain Rolland" that he had received direct word of the incident from Rolland himself. After describing his first meeting with Rolland in "Deux Rencontres," Gide added:

> I went for a long time without seeing Romain Rolland again. The war came. He wrote to me from Switzerland regarding the matter of Rilke's sequestration. I was informed too late and was unable, alas!, to halt the dispersion of our friend's library and furnishings or even to attend the sham sale that, almost in secret, allowed thieves and puppets to lay

their hands dirt cheap on precious objects, paintings and drawings of great value and a quantity of rare books—later on, I made vain attempts to get them back together again. Someday I will tell about it. I have kept all the documents relating to this tragic farce, to the complacent role of the sequestrator, and the correspondence I exchanged with Romain Rolland on the subject.[61]

Though Gide says Rolland informed him directly rather than through the offices of Copeau, there is no record of Rolland's letter to him. Yet Gide's letters to Rolland also indicate positively that Rolland had communicated with him directly from Switzerland. Rolland's "Journal intime," however, states that Gide's letter of January 11, 1916, was in response to his letter to Copeau.[62] In 1941, Rolland recalled that he had advised "André Gide et ses amis de Paris" of Rilke's misfortune.[63] Perhaps his recollection had faded; or if there was a letter informing Gide directly, it must be presumed lost or misplaced. At any rate, Gide's first letter to Rolland about the affair was dated January 11, 1916, and mailed in an envelope bearing the address of the Foyer Franco-Belge.

Dear Romain Rolland,
    Yes, I know full well that I was overburdened with work, I know full well that Rilke should have written us, that a simple note to his concierge would have prevented all this... No matter, I do not pardon myself for not having foreseen and acted accordingly while there was still time. To tell the truth, I did not think it possible and I doubt whether the sequestrator acted in this instance as he was supposed to...
    Upon receiving your note, I hastened with Copeau to the rue Campagne-Première: it is only too true that all was sold (dispersed?) about a year ago, the concierge said—a fine woman who cried as she told us this and who was able to put safely aside in trunks the letters and manuscripts—all the

papers, it appears, that were not "for sale." These trunks are, for the moment, in an atelier or shed that is unrented but could be occupied from one day to the next—the concierge would notify me in that case— I was not able to succeed in seeing the sequestrator today, but am not losing hope, if he is of good will—[that] with his directions I may manage to collect and bring together some of the books and objects to which Rilke was likely to be most attached. I shall write you again on the subject. —I would have—I have very real affection for Rilke; twice I passed by (about six months ago) to try to get some news; but the concierge's quarters were locked —No, I cannot console or pardon myself for not having been able to do in time for a friend what I would have been so deeply happy to do.

Be assured of my cordial regards,

André Gide [64]

Though Gide refused officially to endorse "Au-dessus de la mêlée," he was quite capable, in circumstances calling for a simple and personal act of humanity, of maintaining himself *au-dessus de la mêlée*.

On January 25, 1916, he again wrote to Rolland.

My dear Romain Rolland

Yes, I have indeed received your letter—your two letters. I was waiting to have a little more to tell you before writing you again: here is how far I have come:

I have been to see the sequestrator. No doubt I showed a bit too strongly my... astonishment at the hasty way in which this sale was conducted: he spoke to me with a most disturbing insolence and rage. But at least I was able to learn the name of the attorney who took care of the sale—an attorney who by a stroke of fortune happens to be a member of the board of the Foyer Franco-Belge of which I am vice-president —the attorney, too, of Mrs. Edith Wharton, who is also engaged in our work and knew Rilke personally. I informed her of the story and it roused her indignation as much as our own. Through the attorney I found out the name of the auctioneer and through the auctioneer the name of the three principal buyers of the books that had been portioned out by lots.

The total of the sale, books as well as furnishings, came to 538 francs, I believe. This is shameful pilfering... Just today (I have only had the names of the buyers since yesterday) I rushed to what I thought was their shop— But they are secondhand book dealers without a shop (?) [sic] and were not at home (rue de Seine or rue Guénégaud) and they can only be seen by appointment (so the concierge told me); and this is what I shall do.

I would so much like to be able to reassure Rilke about his manuscripts. Given the ill will of the sequestrator, it will be extremely difficult for me to get to look at his papers. For that, a word from Rilke himself would no doubt be necessary... as for this, wait until I have asked the attorney how to proceed. First I hoped to be able myself to take the trunks of papers to my home, and hold them in my custody—but perhaps it is better to leave them in the custody of the sequestrator, who, though insolent, is no doubt honest. I like to think that *all* his personal papers have been preserved.

I cannot understand—nor console myself—that Rilke has not written, either to you, or to me, or to his concierge, whom he knew to be so devoted. The slightest indication from him would so easily have avoided all this. He should have suspected, however, that if he remained over a year without paying his rent, he ran the risk of seizure... there has been nothing illegal here, strictly speaking—and the act seems monstrous to us only because we know what an inoffensive and distressed being Rilke was.

Can you reach Rilke only through Zweig? I deplore him— for I must tell you this here, as painful as it is for me to have to say it *to you* who will certainly think me blinded by hatred —that I hold Zweig for an out-and-out good-for-nothing and that I have my reasons for it.

Good-bye. Be assured of my devotion,

André Gide [65]

Gide had indeed taken the Rilke affair to heart, and
Romain Rolland made special note of it in his *Journal des
années de guerre*. Gide's remarks about Zweig irritated him
profoundly, however, for Rolland spoke of Zweig as "one
of my dearest Austrian friends" and went on to say that he
immediately took up Zweig's defense and demanded of Gide
precise reasons for his judgment.[66] (Hence there must have
existed yet another letter from Rolland to Gide, now lost
or misplaced.) Gide answered on February 17, 1916:

My dear Romain Rolland,
    I was waiting before writing you again to have something
new to tell you about Rilke.
    I have obtained information from the auctioneer about
the four principal buyers. The most important one is "en
voyage." Two others are unattainable: they are secondhand
book dealers without a shop, and can be seen at home only
by appointment. The fourth is a sorry little retail dealer who
remembers nothing, and if one speaks to him of "German
books," wants to hear no more.
    Fearing, if I wrote to the two others, to see them steal
away and escape from me definitively, fearing also, in case
they might not yet know the value of the books they had
bought, to open their eyes and enlighten them by my action
and the questions that this action would raise, I judged it
more prudent to resort to an intermediary, to F., a publisher
on the rue de Seine, who, if he also wanted German books,
would run less risk of awakening suspicion than would I as a
private individual. Not knowing him personally, I wanted
first to inform myself as to his character, to know if he could
be trusted, etc. My intention would have been, and still is,
to entrust to him the task of buying back, if possible, the best,
or at least what we would judge to be the most precious from
a sentimental point of view, and the most irreplaceable, of
Rilke's library; and to ask him kindly to store these books in
trust, in the hope of later being able to give them back to
Rilke. Visits, preliminaries, introduction, all this has taken

time, and only yesterday was I able to get in contact with F.—
The person who presented me to F., Pastor Wilfred Monod,[67]
whom I did not know formerly but with whom I was easily
able to communicate, seems to be taking this affair to heart
and wishes to assist me in investigating if this sale was cor-
rectly carried out and if everything was done according to the
rules, if there wasn't some sort of pilfering ("With a *boche*
it's not worth the trouble to put yourself out.") for the greater
profit of a few rogues. I want to take on a lawyer for this
affair—and if he discovers any irregularity—don't you think
we might talk to Mathias Morhardt, who, in the name of the
league of the rights of man, could take hold of the affair?—

Could I not have a catalog (as incomplete as it might be)
of Rilke's library—of the books to which he was most attached? As for papers, manuscripts, letters, etc., you will already have assured him, won't you? I am confident that
thanks to the concierge, at least this was preserved—and, in
any case, that is the most important.

But aside from the Rilke question, something in my last
letter has raised a Zweig question between us, and you ask
me for explanations. All that I shall be able to do today is to
stake out some lines:

Franz Blei, another German Jew, whom you perhaps know,
at least by name, and who is my principal translator in Germany (at least he is the one who signs the translations done
by his wife and other people), has always showed me the
greatest kindness, and if my name is a little known there,
I owe it first of all to him. In the (Revue) [*sic*] there appeared,
quite some time ago, a translation of my *Prométhée mal
enchaîné*—signed by his wife—which he proposed to me several years later to have brought out in a volume signed by
himself. Kippenberg [68] (was it indeed Kippenberg?) spoke of
illustrations. I accepted on the condition that I be allowed
to choose my artist, to whom a sum of about 100 francs a
drawing (there were five) was promised, with Blei acting as
an intermediary. I addressed myself to Bonnard [69] for this
work, which was forthcoming on the required date. —But
what was not forthcoming at all was the promised sum of

money—which I then paid out of my own pocket, letting
Bonnard think that it had been given to me for him, by the
publisher or by Blei, for I wished, at one and the same time,
to cover Blei and not to let Bonnard suffer on account of a
broken promise. —Besides I had nothing else against Blei who
I knew was not very well-to-do and was often reduced to
expedients. I proved to him some time later that I held no
bitterness by taking it upon myself to collect some drawings
for him that were supposed to be reproduced in a new review he was founding; I sent him a certain number of photo-
graphs of unpublished drawings, which Druet [70] kindly
placed at my disposition, and added a very beautiful original drawing by Van Rysselberghe—which it was clearly
agreed I was only lending him—but Blei took care to "mis-
lay" it rather than commit it to reproduction. The drawing had been entrusted to me by Van Rysselberghe, so that
I was extremely annoyed at this sneak thievery. —Soon after
there was new pilfering (?) [*sic*] of the proceeds from a production of my *Roi Candaule*... I have never completely been
able to get the straight of the matter—

But Zweig, in all of this?

Zweig has absolutely nothing to do with it. But the Zweig
affair is not mine, and I have promised not to speak of it.
Though of the same order exactly (and therefore having absolutely nothing to do with the war), it is much more serious—
serious even to the point of improbability, so that up till the
war one would still have preferred to doubt it; one did doubt
it. I still consent to doubt; but it is indeed certain that we
are not at this time going to be able to look for enlightenment
and straighten out the matter. In doubt, I shall remain silent;
but, in doubt, I prefer not to have any dealings with Zweig—
It would be exactly the same if we were not at war with
Germany, and today's situation does not in any way influence
my judgment.

So in lieu of the Zweig story I am telling you the Blei story
(in my turn I ask you to keep it to yourself, since I find it
hardly decent to add personal grievances to so many more
important ones).

Nonetheless I do not believe Zweig incapable of a certain friendly devotedness—very Jewish in this, very much the liaison agent, very attentive, very officious. I began dealing with him only shortly before the war. I cannot say to what point he displeased me. Naturally I do not offer my impression as a reason... but, all the same, when I learned of the story afterwards, I was able to explain my impression. And since I mistrust impressions, even though I was not the only one to have this one... a little more and I would say that this is what helps me doubt the story. Excuse me for not speaking more clearly. It costs me something not to speak, and particularly to you whom I esteem—but, once again, I am bound.

Excuse the length of this letter—and believe me to be

Cordially,

André Gide [71]

Rolland's reaction to the letter from Gide was decisive. He could not forget Gide's slight on the reputation of Stefan Zweig and wrote in his *Journal des années de guerre:*

He answers today, but evasively. He relates at length the petty villainies of another German writer, who made himself the showman of his works in Germany and who robbed him, he says. After which, passing on to my friend, he does a pirouette and is disengaged. He says it is an affair of the same order; but "it isn't his, and he has promised not to speak of it..." Then why did he speak of it, and in these outrageous terms? I reproach him rather severely.

(N.B.—He hasn't forgotten it.) [72]

What Zweig had done to merit Gide's bitter comments is difficult to ascertain. Gide is vague and deliberately so. Only a glimmer of light comes much later in Rolland's "Journal intime" for September, 1933, to June, 1934. Rolland spoke of a meeting he had had with Gide in which Gide clarified his long-standing accusations against Zweig; however, Rolland refused to divulge these accusations lest they incrim-

inate his old and intimate friend Stefan Zweig. But Rolland
went on to say that Gide's accusations were based on the
testimony of the Belgian poet Emile Verhaeren and especially
of his wife, both now dead, and that in the excitement of
the time, they may have been mistaken. Rolland lamented
that Zweig did not even know of the accusation so as to be
able to clear himself. Now it was too late, said Rolland, and
he himself could do nothing to rectify the matter, for to
advise Zweig of it would cause him a "bouleversement
inutile," especially since he had had a great liking for
Verhaeren.[73]

Verhaeren had been in close rapport with German thinking before the war. Rolland, in his "Journal intime" for
March 17, 1913, wrote of a dinner he had had in the company
of Zweig, Verhaeren, Rilke, and Bazalgette [74] at the Bœuf à
la mode near the Palais-Royal. Zweig expressed the wish that
Rolland should publish a journal designed to serve as a
guide for the thinking of all Europe. Rolland responded that
he was already doing this in his work and then outlined
another idea to which he had become attached: to found a
sort of "Correspondance littéraire" with three or four members like that of Grimm and Diderot which should bring
together the most significant thinking in the large Western
countries. "What is closest to my heart, what seems to me
to be our essential duty is the foundation, moral and intellectual, of European unity." [75] Better than Zweig and Rilke,
he said, Bazalgette and Verhaeren understood him.

So closely allied with German thinking was Verhaeren that
at the outbreak of hostilities German authorities voiced the
hope that he might associate himself with their war efforts.
After the violation of the neutrality of his native Belgium
and the horrors of Louvain, this was too much to ask of
Verhaeren; he felt that he had been cheated and duped.
Rolland himself wrote to Verhaeren from the Hôtel Beausé-
jour in Geneva on Saturday, October 17, 1914, that Zweig

was concerned for him. Zweig had written Rolland a letter "plein de cœur," but, said Rolland, simply did not realize the crimes of his race. "The best people are also the most taken in." Zweig himself had no doubt that the Germans actually *saved* Louvain at the peril of their own lives, for Louvain had been burning.[76] Several weeks later Rolland wrote again to the embittered Verhaeren: "No, do not hate. Hatred is not made for you—for us—let us preserve ourselves from hatred more than from our enemies." [77] Zweig in his own book on Romain Rolland recalled that after Rolland wrote to Gerhart Hauptmann, Rolland attempted to get Verhaeren to renounce his hatred, but without success.[78]

Can conclusions be drawn from these facts? In his fierce and sudden hatred for Germany, Verhaeren may have imparted to Gide information extremely damaging to the character of Zweig, information that may or may not have been true. Shortly before the war Zweig published with the Insel Verlag in Leipzig German translations of selected poems and plays by Verhaeren, as well as a study of Verhaeren, his life and his work, which was then translated into French. If, in the course of these publishing ventures, Zweig should have become involved, consciously or unconsciously, in any misunderstandings or in any transactions of a doubtful nature on the order of the "Blei affair," then this might serve as a basis to explain the "Zweig affair." The documentation available on the subject does not allow a more precise reconstruction. What is relevant here is that the charges brought against Zweig further alienated Romain Rolland from André Gide, this time on a personal level.

Passions heightened as the war progressed. A campaign of hatred bore down on Rolland from all sides and even from Gide. Rolland protested in vain that it was the combination of German power and idealism that had brought about this catastrophe and that he himself would suffocate under what he called Germany's intellectual militarism; for many French-

men he was now identified with the cause of the enemy. After
all, even the hero of his novel *Jean-Christophe* was a German.

However, if Christophe was a German, he was conceived
not in Germany but in Italy.[79] In a letter to Jean-Richard
Bloch written in December, 1914, Rolland explained:

> Do not believe that I have a weakness for the Germans. My
> situation is a paradoxical one. Love of music made me get
> into the skin of Jean-Christophe. Once there, I had to stay
> there until he was dead. But Christophe himself does not
> too much like the Germans; and I myself could not live six
> months in succession in Germany. . . .[80]

These were aspects of Rolland's thought that had been forgotten or deliberately ignored. Gide in the early part of 1916
joined in with the others to take up the axe. It is to his honor
that he did so privately by committing his thoughts to his
diary; secret, until it was released after the war.

> I pick up *Jean-Christophe* again from the beginning and
> make a great effort at sympathy without my consideration
> for Romain Rolland, or for his book at least, being increased.
> It breathes a sort of rough heartiness, vulgarity, and guileless-
> ness—which will please the reader to whom the artist always
> seems to be putting on airs. But that's that.
> What bothers me is the ease, the thoughtlessness, with
> which he makes a German of his hero—or, if you prefer, he
> makes his hero of a German. As far as I know, there is no
> other example of this, for even Stendhal takes care to point
> out that his Fabrice was born of a French father. What more
> are we expected to see in this? The Germanic quality of
> his tastes, tendencies, reactions, and impulses, which allows
> Romain Rolland, if not to paint Jean-Christophe precisely
> in his own image, at least to infuse life into him through
> sympathy? Or else the illusion of a generous but uncritical
> mind abstractly creating in Jean-Christophe a creature who
> is no more German than he is French, a musician, a vague

personality to whom he can attribute any sensations and
emotions he wants?

Oh, how Germanic is that very psychological inadequacy!
How inexpressive it is! [81]

Gide passed quickly over his own artistic criticism of the
novel in order to attack it purely on the grounds of its Ger-
manism. Yet some two and a half months later, on May 21,
he added a footnote correcting his original statement. What
he had said now no longer appeared just to him. In making
his hero a German, Romain Rolland had in reality been trying to obtain sufficient distance to judge clearly "la chose
française." [82] Indirectly Rolland had already answered Gide's
objection, and his statement in the *Parthenon* of November
5, 1913, not only contained the answer to Gide's objection
but clarified still further the background for Rolland's attitude toward the war and the peoples it involved.

The question of the Germanic origins of Jean-Christophe
demands a long answer. I had more than one reason for
choosing the Rhine region as the homeland of my hero. First
of all, its musical genius: this is a plant which up to the present time has not found conditions favorable for a vigorous
development in this country. Then, as you well express it,
my intention to observe France with the open eyes of a frank
and uncivilized Huron. But I had another secret and deeper
reason: this will be an answer to the harangues of the Pan-
Germanists who have just noisily celebrated the anniversary
of the "Battle of Nations."

. . . The country of Beethoven and Jean-Christophe will
never be a foreign land to me. I am not among those lamen-
table Frenchmen who, in their rage to impoverish France so
as to reduce her to their own size and that of their friends,
would not be past shrinking her boundaries to those of the
domain of their Philip Augustus, and who treat the Genevan
Jean-Jacques as a foreigner. I make no more allowance for
their narrow nationalism than for the arrogance of German

imperialism which spreads boldly, by right of conquest, into
lands it has stolen. In the face of both, I peacefully annex the
left bank of the Rhine, Wallonia, Geneva, and the French-
speaking areas of Switzerland. There I plant our flag.

. . . The Rhine is a flow of light that matures the hill
slopes and the souls of the Western world. It is no more yours,
Germans, than it is ours: it belongs to Europe. It does not
divide us, it unites us. May it be so, too, with my Christophe,
your son and ours.[83]

The Frenchman and the German were brothers, and it was
to the larger entity Europe, rather than to France or to Germany, that Rolland directed his gaze.

But Gide's criticism of *Jean-Christophe* was also rooted
in his own artistic principles. On March 28, 1916, he wrote
of Rolland's book in his *Journal:*

I am beginning the fourth book. I confess that, at moments,
the first ones had overcome my prejudices; a certain rather
crude grace, a use of the right key, made up for the lack of
style; but the third part of *L'Adolescence* (Ada) is excessively
unpleasant in its awkward frankness and painfully inadequate in its means of expression. Those tedious passages or
rather that willful spinning-out of the material, that heavy
rudimentary lyricism (Germanic, I dare say)—are all unbear-
able to me. And even the constant manifestation of the intention, which shocks me as an artistic immodesty, or lack
of tact.

But I can understand that such a book should make
friends, and many.

By January 30, 1917, though he still saw little artistic value
in the vast work of Rolland, Gide recognized it as an achievement of the highest importance. He wrote in his *Journal:*

I resume *Jean-Christophe.* I have reached *Le Buisson
ardent,* of which the beginning is certainly remarkable.[8] At

times it strikes me that this barbarous, rough-hewn book, without art, without grace, and possessing qualities apparently so un-French, remains the most important or at any rate the most typical thing produced in France by our generation.[84]

Gide ended his comments with the statement that he would write more on the subject, "if I did not have such a headache."

However, he later did write more on the subject. In a footnote to his *Réflexions sur l'Allemagne* in 1919: "of all our literature, it seems to me that the book one would most easily imagine to have been written in Germany is *Jean-Christophe,* and no doubt this accounts for its success beyond the Rhine." [85]

This was not all. What Gide had written in 1917 and chose to publish in his "Journal sans dates" in the July 1, 1919, issue of the *Nouvelle Revue Française* was of a most severe and unjust nature.

> Obviously what shocks me in the case of Romain Rolland is that he has nothing to lose as a result of the war: his book (*Jean-Christophe*) never seems better than when translated. I shall go further: he can only gain by the disaster of France, by the disappearance of the French language, and French art, and French taste, and all of those gifts which he denies and which are denied him. The final disaster of France would give his *Jean-Christophe* its greatest and most definitive importance.
>
> He is animated by such perfect good faith that at times he almost disarms you. He is an unsophisticated person, but an impassioned unsophisticated person. He early took his frankness for virtue and, since it is somewhat summary, he considered hypocrites those who were less rudimentary than he. I am sure that too often his attitude was permitted by a lack of sentiment and taste, even of comprehension that the mind brings to art, to style, and to that sort of Atticism that now

has no other home but France. Nothing is more amorphous
than his book; it is a Kugelhupf in which you sometimes encounter a good raisin. No affectation, no artifice; I am well
aware that this is why some like him.[86]

This is almost precisely the statement that Gide made in his
Feuillets, now incorporated into the *Journal* between the
years 1918 and 1919 in the Pléiade edition. Of all Gide said
in this passage, the harshest statement is perhaps the last
sentence of the first paragraph. Significantly this sentence
was omitted in the Pléiade edition (and in Justin O'Brien's
translation). Aside from his criticism of *Jean-Christophe,*
which he attacked on both patriotic and artistic grounds,
Gide had launched into a personal attack on the man Rolland.

When Roger Martin du Gard read Gide's article, he was
shocked and said so in no uncertain terms. In a letter written
in Paris and dated July 3, 1919, he told Gide that he had
opened the review with confident expectation, turned to
Gide's "Journal sans dates," read the first page, and closed
the review, "bouleversé."

How could you have passed this twenty-line judgment on
Romain Rolland and the ten volumes of his *Jean-Christophe,*
on Romain Rolland and the art of France, on Romain Rolland and the Great War, this judgment as brutal as a dagger's
slash? [87]

You wrote it nonetheless, Martin du Gard continued, and
one can almost imagine him shaking his finger at Gide as a
father would at a delinquent child—you reread it, recopied
it, and signed it, and then you published it in your review.
He called this gesture of Gide's "tendancieuse". He praised
Rolland for the "hidden vitality of his work but especially
for the purity of his belief," for a certain "integrity" which
their generation, approaching maturity, had sought in vain

in other novels of the time. How welcome would have been a study of Romain Rolland had it been worthy of him. "You did not want it so; and I ask myself in vain anguish what could have driven you to so rudimentary and definitive a gesture?" [88]

Gide's reply was prompt. On Sunday morning, July 6, he wrote:

> All that I can say in answer to your letter is that I am deeply obliged to you for having written me as you did.
>
> The *study* that you lament not seeing in place of this summary execution (and Jacques C.[opeau] will perhaps have told you that I was myself taken with the feeling you describe and wanted at the last moment to pull back)—the study I could have written would undoubtedly not have satisfied you very much, for I cannot manage to discover in *Jean-Christophe* all that you see in it—but at least the *tone* would have been there, and your own letter points out to me the tone that should have been taken. [89]

Gide recognized his lack of tact, and it is quite true that he attempted to stop the references to Romain Rolland from being printed. A telegram addressed to Jacques Rivière, then editor of the *Nouvelle Revue Française,* and which is presently in the keeping of his son Alain Rivière, was signed Gide and Copeau and postmarked June 27 at 5:50 in the afternoon:

> Do the impossible to suppress the passage from my Journal concerning Romain Rolland: even if you have to leave the page blank with a note censured would take on myself the cost of reprinting better to have slight delay

But it was too late. Rivière responded on June 29. When Gide's telegram arrived, the issue of July 1, 1919, was already printed. Despite the disagreeable aura that surrounded Gide

in this affair, there was a noble quality in his recognition of
the aptness of Martin du Gard's criticism and in his accept-
ance of it.

Further evidence that Gide harbored some regret over his
comments of 1917 can be gleaned from a letter to Martin
du Gard of April 2, 1924, in which he spelled out his reaction to Henri Massis's recently published *Jugements*. After
devoting considerable space to a generally unfavorable critique of Gide's work, Massis undertook a study of Romain
Rolland, opening with the words: "Dilettantism is not necessarily frivolous. Sometimes to throw us off the track, it
wraps itself up in solemnity and assumes an austere air." [90]
Massis proceeded to cite the first paragraph of Gide's criticism of 1917 in a footnote in order to lend support to his
own argument. As Gide told Martin du Gard, he deplored
and resented, among other things, the fact that Massis "has
used me against Rolland." [91] But Roger Martin du Gard
could not easily forget the grave slight to Rolland, for whom
his admiration was unbounded. When he was asked to write
in a golden book to be offered Romain Rolland on his six-
tieth birthday, he reminded Gide of the offense, then six
years old.

> Very perplexed. And even just about decided to compro-
> mise myself therein, out of integrity and, in short, out of
> gratitude. And then a little, too, with the idea that since I am
> so strongly rooted at the N.R.F. my gesture would repair
> many injustices, and notably yours! who passed judgment on
> Romain Rolland *without having read him! Yes!* [92]

The accusation was a strong one, and Gide himself rejected
it. Responding to Martin du Gard on June 9, 1925, he stated
plainly:

> Now allow me to protest when I hear you say that I pass
> judgment on Romain Rolland without having read him.

I lived for four months at Cuverville with *Jean-Christophe,* which I read in the *Cahiers de la Quinzaine,* if not all of it, at least up to four-fifths... after which I could no longer triumph over my inappetency. It has no doubt happened that I have praised a work on trust, without knowing it, or without knowing it sufficiently. But to criticize, no! [93]

Gide's protest is supported by an entry in his *Journal* for March 2, 1916, in which he said that he had been reading the second volume of *Jean-Christophe* on a train en route to his Norman estate at Cuverville.[94]

Gide terminated the discussion of *Jean-Christophe* in his letter of 1925 to Martin du Gard with the implication that a rereading of Rolland's novel would prove useless, since "most often rereadings only entrench me in my original opinion. . . ." [95]

In 1939, in the "Souvenirs de jeunesse" which have been incorporated into his *Mémoires,* Rolland avenged himself in a subtle but biting counterattack on Gide.

I read later in the *Journal* of a writer who thought he would come out in the lead, by attacking me in order to defend himself—(though I don't even think of attacking him, for, to tell the truth, I don't think about him, he holds no place in my thought)—that "Romain Rolland early took his frankness for virtue and, since it is somewhat summary, he considered (or considers) hypocrites those who were less rudimentary than he."

It is indeed possible that I am "rudimentary." The Apostle Paul was rudimentary too, he who could hardly stomach "those who say yes yes within themselves and then no no... For the Son of God, who is true, said not yes and no, but always yes within himself."

The young Christophe that I was, on my return from Rome, fiercely said "yes within himself"; and he hated amphibiousness of thought, that mixture of yes and no that infected the ages without faith and without vertebrae. Instead of seeing it for what it is, the malady of an emasculated soul that is powerless to keep its own faith and so is pleased to betray itself, I called it duplicity. . . .[96]

At no point was Gide's name mentioned. The attack is all the more poignant in that Rolland appears intent on communicating the impression that it would be beneath his dignity to permit someone like André Gide to disturb him. And yet Gide undoubtedly had disturbed him. Rolland would not have recalled so precisely an attack published twenty years earlier had this not been the case.

IV   Art and the Artist

The differences between Gide and Rolland were nowhere more strikingly apparent than in the attitudes the two men adopted toward the war. During this period Gide renounced any attempt to write what might be called a creative literary work, and what he did write in his *Journal* he refused to publish. Rolland not only wrote but published as well, and his writings revealed him to be a man profoundly concerned with and involved in the events of the time. Implicit in a number of Rolland's remarks was a criticism of Gide's refusal to play a more active part in ending the war. And Gide was not the only one he reproached.

To Rolland's way of thinking, the intellectuals had abdicated their mission to enlighten the people. Their duty it was to find the truth and extract it from the web of hatred and falsehood in which it was entangled, but they had renounced their task. This criticism applied in full measure to the artist, whom he ranked among the intellectuals. Ordinary citizens, deceived by their leaders, could be excused; but no excuse could be allowed those whose most basic responsibility was to investigate carefully all sides of the issue before casting their lot. Because of their attitude the peoples of Europe were being destroyed, and along with them the treasures of the human spirit. "Out of blind loyalty, out of a guilty sense of trust, they threw themselves with lowered heads into the nets that their imperialism set for them. They thought their primary duty was to defend, with their eyes closed, the honor of their State against any accusation. They did not see that the noblest means of defense was to reprove its errors and to wash their homeland of them." [1]

The attitude Rolland discerned among the intellectual community at the outset of the war in 1914 was not to change substantially by the war's end. In the concluding pages of the *Journal des années de guerre,* in 1919, he observed: "War has thrown confusion into our ranks. The majority of intellectuals have put their knowledge, their art, and their reason at the service of their governments. We do not wish to accuse anyone, to address any reproach. We know the weakness of individual souls and the elemental power of great collective currents. . . ." [2] But it was Rolland's hope that the experience of the war would at least have some value for the future. [3]

For Rolland the word "intellectual" did not designate a class apart, or at least he believed that it should not, in a harmoniously developed society. He viewed the social organism of his time as "incomplete and unhealthy" and saw the need for a group of intellectuals sufficiently informed and involved to provide an antidote. He saw the art of his time as poisoned. Artists had withdrawn in sterile pride from the community of men, and they had no regard for the humble pains and sufferings of the common people, their morals, or their consciences. They had withdrawn in order to form a separate élite dispensed from ordinary duties without thereby contracting any new ones. "No privileges among men! No man (whether an artist or not) has the right to live if he does not make of himself the servant of humanity; and the greatest of men has the greatest obligation." [4]

The primary obligation of the intellectuals lay in the scrupulous exercise of their own intelligence, in the loyal and valiant search for the truth, and finally in the free and sincere expression of that truth.[5] The truth had to be sought out and then expressed, and any subordination of this duty to another interest was a degradation. Though Gide's refusal to publish during the war might be regarded as a worthy gesture on the part of a great man, for Rolland it was not sufficient. As he had said some years earlier, art must not be lulled into passivity at this time in history.

> The art of our time . . . must not put us to sleep in sensuous enchantment (as does our contemporary Parisian art). *It must disturb us.* In an era of perfection like the Greece of Sophocles, art can be a serene light. In our society in shambles, wherein everyone is suffering and causing others to suffer, wherein everyone is victimized and at fault, art must be a severe director of conscience, showing us our faults and the means to repair them, and impelling us to action.[6]

The diverging attitudes that Gide and Rolland adopted with regard to art and the role of the artist had roots that were planted long before the war. Already then there had been clear indications that their thinking about the meaning and purpose of art was not the same. Rolland made this quite apparent in the letter of advice he wrote to Jean-Richard Bloch on February 3, 1911. His criticism of the Parisian literature of the time was bitingly harsh, and among those he criticized was André Gide, although he regarded Gide as one of the most intelligent of the Paris group. To Bloch:

> Nor do I believe that you will manage to get out of this state of *malaise* by reading Parisian literature. You tell me that the Blums, the Gourmonts, the Gides (I only mention

the most intelligent), "perceive the *malaise*." They not only perceive it, they are themselves the *malaise*.[7]

For Romain Rolland there could be no compromise. "One is either healthy or unhealthy." [8] Between the good man and the bad one, the difference is only one of degree; for evil, too, can be healthy. But between the corruption and the health of the mind there is death. "One does not compromise with the plague. . . ." [9]

It is true that Rolland admitted to a hasty judgment here, and wrote again to Bloch almost immediately, assuring him that he was right in trying to learn from all sources: "there is something to be learned everywhere." Nonetheless, Rolland would not reverse his decision: "Do not think that I look on Gide or Gourmont as mediocrities. Indeed not. But there is in them a principle of death." [10]

In thanking Gide in 1909 and again in 1913 for works received from him and in praising the beauty of these works, was Rolland simply trying to save appearances? The fact is that beauty did not have the same place and position in the writings of the two authors. For Rolland, less an artist in temperament than Gide, a work of art might be beautiful, but this did not suffice. Neither did it suffice for Gide, but for Gide it was enough to provide a justification, a *raison d'être.*

Rolland was quick to reject both symbolism and the theory of *l'art pour l'Art,* and with them the exalted status they reserved for the ideal of beauty. Yet even he, early in his career, showed some influence of these nineteenth-century modes of literary thought. The artist, he felt at that time, must close himself to the world about him to find his own world within himself. Art was not meant to reflect the life and thoughts of others; "the thoughts of others are pitiful, their life paltry." The role of genius was to construct an organically constituted world following one's own interior laws. And so the artist must live in this interior world and believe in it. It was the only true one.[11]

Whereas art for art's sake represented only an early and passing phase for Rolland, Gide never totally abandoned it. In a lecture from the summer of 1901 concerning "Les Limites de l'art" he said: "[A work of art] must be sufficient in itself; it must be its own end and its own perfect reason for being; forming a whole, it must be able to isolate itself and repose as though outside space and time, in satisfied and satisfying harmony." [12] Gide's quarrel with *l'art pour l'Art* was not so much that he did not regard art as an end sufficient in itself, as that this doctrine reduced art to that alone, making art an end in itself and nothing more.

I do not reproach Gautier for this doctrine of "art for art's sake," outside of which I am truly unable to find reason to live; but for having reduced art to expressing merely so little.

I do not reproach him for having proclaimed the poet king, but on the contrary for having so pitifully narrowed his domain.

I am grateful to him for having cast disgrace upon utilitarian art, but I cannot pardon him for having recognized thought as being only utilitarian, or for not having been acquainted with it at all.[13]

A work of art interested Gide fully only if he felt it to be in direct and sincere relation to the exterior world, and at the same time in intimate and secret relation with the author.[14] As for dramatic art, it was not and could not be an end sufficient in itself.[15]

Gide's rejection of symbolism was not immediate either, and came only after some hesitation and after he had tried his own hand at it in several earlier works. He was in fact a member of the circle that met every Tuesday at Mallarmé's home on the rue de Rome, and the symbolist master gave encouragement to the young, aspiring Gide. Gide recalled the wonderful atmosphere of the house on the rue de Rome where one could enter with Mallarmé into regions of hypersensitivity, where money, honors, and the applause of the world no longer had any value.[16] But he felt that he was losing contact with reality and soon renounced the symbolist school as being too ethereal. "The symbolist school. My great grievance against it is the little curiosity it showed in the face of life. . . . Poetry became for them a refuge; the only means of escape from hideous realities. . . ." [17]

Gide was too much absorbed in life, and especially in his own life. He wished to discover reality and especially his own reality, and then, through himself, to discover humanity. His trip to North Africa in 1894, as well as the writing of *Paludes* and *Les Nourritures terrestres* following that trip, were the beginnings of his lifelong search for self. As late as 1946, when *Thésée* appeared, the problem of the self was still a central one. "First of all one must understand well who one is . . . then one should take one's heritage to heart and in hand." [18] Through his works he attempted to clarify his own character to himself. He said in *Si le grain ne meurt* that he sought harmony for himself, and harmony became the purpose and end of his life.[19]

In his *Œdipe* of 1931, Gide portrayed the Greek hero addressing his two sons, Eteocles and Polynices, and stating very concisely the determining factors of Gide's own life and art.

> Each one of us as an adolescent, at the start of his run, meets a monster that sets up in front of him such a riddle as might impede his advance. And although this particular sphinx asks a different question of each one of us, my children, be assured that to each of these questions, the answer remains the same; yes, there is but one single and identical answer to such diverse questions; and that one and only answer is: Man; and that one and only man for each one of us is Oneself.[20]

The problem of the seeker is one that echoes and reechoes over the entire course of Gide's literary production. In a particularly beautiful passage from the *Retour de l'enfant prodigue* of 1907, in the interview between the prodigal son and his mother, the mother asks her son why he had left home.

> "I don't want to think about it anymore: Nothing—myself."
> "What were you looking for?"
> "I was looking for... who I was." [21]

For Romain Rolland art did not have as much personal significance. He resorted to art not so much to build and shape his own character as to build and shape the character of mankind. Arthur Levy in his *L'Idéalisme de Romain Rolland* is quite correct in stating that for Rolland "true art is that which tries to unite men among themselves, either directly through the power of love, or indirectly by combating all that opposes this union, this brotherhood." [22] "Union" should not be taken here in a purely ideological and humanitarian sense; this would be as applicable to Gide as it is to Rolland. Union and brotherhood were for Romain Rolland no vague terms; they had very serious political and social overtones. And just these preoccupations with the political and social order led Gide, among others, to question Rolland's credentials as an artist. Gide and Rolland might both place life on a level higher than art, but for Gide, art was much closer to life. If Gide could affirm with Oscar Wilde that nature, and therefore life, imitates art in fairly close succession, it is a bit more difficult to imagine such an affirmation on the lips of Rolland.

Neither saw art and life as being in opposition, since art could only be constructed from the elements of life. But for Gide, "only where life overabounds does art have the chance to begin. Art is born of excess, of the pressure of overabundance, it begins where living is no longer a sufficient expression of life." [23] The balance was reversed for Rolland, who confirmed the statement attributed to Richard Wagner that art begins where life ends, and that if we had a sufficiency of life we would have no need for art. The object of art is to compensate for what the artist himself has lacked.[24] When life can offer us no more, we cry out our want.

If we consider this to mean that through art the artist is able to experience all those forms of life denied him in his ordinary life, then there is a certain accord with Gide's view. The difference arises rather from the focus that the two men used in considering the question, and Rolland, contrary to Gide, chose to regard it from Wagner's standpoint. Art was born not from an excess of life but from an insufficiency of it. Gide recognized in himself numerous tendencies (each one sufficient to occupy the concerns of a lifetime), from the inclination to unrestraint to that of religious fervor and self-sacrifice. Never in the span of a lifetime could he have lived out each of these tendencies to the full. Some of them negated the others.

The solution he chose was to create a series of characters, each of whom might pursue one or several of these tendencies to the full. His *Nourritures terrestres,* for example, extols a philosophy of pleasure; Michel in the *Immoraliste* attempts to live this philosophy but finds that it, too, has its inconveniences; while Alissa and Jérôme in the *Porte étroite,* both endowed with a substantial amount of religious fervor, exhaust to the limit the possibility of self-abnegation. In the knowledge that he could not possibly experience all his tendencies to the full, Gide deliberately set out to limit the sphere of experiences through which he would pass during his lifetime; but through art he was able to live vicariously the experiences a lifetime would have been insufficient to test.

Romain Rolland, at least in theory, acknowledged that

man was composed not of one being but of thousands of beings, with very different and often opposing personalities. Some have stifled this interior world, and others have allowed anarchy to reign. Rolland maintained that the true artist tries to let live freely and completely all these beings of his interior world without ever losing mastery over them.[25] And he also warned against regarding *Jean-Christophe* as the expression of his whole self. "There are many other beings within me." [26] But if he did anything in his art, it was to extend rather than limit the sphere of experience through which he would live. He himself was not destined to die, as a result of the war, a death that would cry out in vengeance against war, and so he created in *Pierre et Luce* two characters whose deaths would so cry out in vengeance. In *Clerambault* the situation is similar, and Clerambault's change in attitude from one of unquestioning patriotism to bitter disillusionment was one Rolland wished the world to experience.

Even more frequently Rolland created characters from his own life, or from history, as is the case in many of his dramas, and sought neither to extend nor to limit the domain of conscious experience but simply to relate the actual. Gide, on the other hand, grasped for the possible. The problems of the thinker versus the man of action, for example, were the problems that Rolland encountered in himself. He was at times like Jean-Christophe, the man of action, and at other times like Olivier, the thinker. (Yet he was neither of them, just as Gide was not totally Jérôme or Michel, though both represented tendencies of his own nature. Gide would very likely have given a separate existence to Christoph and Olivier, allowing them to explore to the depths their own realms of conscious being. Rolland, however, did not separate the two, but rather compelled them to interact in the novel, just as the two forces interacted in his own being.) Like Annette, too, in the *Âme enchantée,* Rolland was torn between the passionate need for independence and the need for fraternity with other beings; and again he portrayed the actual. Perhaps it is somewhat unfair to compare *Jean-Christophe* with Gide's shorter and more narrowly focused novels or *récits,* as he referred to them. However, even in what Gide called his only novel, *Les Faux-Monnayeurs,* a book that assumes larger proportions similar to those of *Jean-Christophe,* he was very much the adventurer. Ever and again he sought to express the possible in order to experience it through his art and so test the overwhelming abundance of possibilities life had offered him. Jean Delay in his comprehensive study of Gide's youth cited from Thibaudet:

> The true novelist creates his characters out of the innumerable courses his possible life has to offer; the factitious novelist creates them out of the single line formed by his real life. The genius of the novel gives life to the possible, it does not give life to the real.[27]

The criticism weighs heavily on the shoulders of Romain Rolland.

Gide's ultimate rejection of art for art's sake and his rejection of the symbolist movement in no way lessened the role he assigned to beauty. In his preface to Baudelaire's *Fleurs du mal* he equated beauty with form, and called it "that harmony of contour and sound, wherein the poet's art is played out." [28] Elsewhere he wrote: "Beauty will never be naturally produced; it can only be obtained through artificial constraint." [29] This "artificial constraint" gives birth to form, and form is the "secret" of a work of art. Gide's concern for form was almost greater than his concern for content, and he described it as "cette raison de l'œuvre d'art." [30] But form and content should not be opposed, and Gide remarked in his *Traité du Narcisse* that "the arrogance of the word does not supersede the thought" in a work of art.[31] Yet the poet will seize a transitory form to give it an eternal one, and Narcisse, bent over the pool, knows that one gesture will suffice to destroy the time-bound image of himself reflected in the pool. And so, somewhat like the artist that Rolland idealized in his early years, Narcisse remains "grave et religieux" in contemplation.[32]

The eternal form which is beauty, obtained by the submission of the real to the idea of beauty preconceived,[33] this is what makes art eternal. In his *Journal,* Gide acknowledged this eternal quality of art as one of his own reasons for writing.

> The reasons that impel me to write are multiple, and the most important ones, it seems to me, are the most secret. Perhaps this one above all: to have something secure against death—and this is what makes me, in my writings, seek among all other qualities those upon which time has the least grasp and by which they escape all passing fads.[34]

Beauty and form were of less consequence to Romain Rolland. What mattered was the content, and if Gide might agree with Keats that beauty is truth, Rolland would agree with him that truth is beauty. What he wrote of his own conception of the theater is applicable also to other genres. "Strictly speaking, a people can do without beauty; it must not and cannot do without truth." [35]

In a letter addressed to the Académie des Sciences d'Art in Moscow on October 20, 1925, Rolland wrote: "Whatever my likes or dislikes for a political and social regime, they have nothing to do with my conception of Art. My art is free from all parties and against all parties: for its very function is to maintain a state of freedom against them all. Naked beauty. Truth in its entirety." [36] For Rolland beauty consists in the truth of whatever the author has attempted to convey; and the truth conveyed must be such as to edify the reader or spectator.

Gide wrote in his *Traité du Narcisse:* "For the artist the moral question is not that the Idea he presents be more or less moral and useful to the majority; the question is that he present it well." [37] Rolland would not have agreed, and his insistence on the edification of the reader has the unfortunate effect of lending a didactic air to certain passages of his work. When Jean-Christophe expounds his notions on music to his friend Olivier, engaging him to apply them to literature, his words seem almost directly leveled at Gide:

> Today's writers do all they can . . . to describe human rarities, or types that exist only in abnormal groups, on the margin of the great society of active and healthy men. Since of their own accord they have turned themselves out of the door of life, leave them and go where there are men. To everyday men, show everyday life: it is deeper and more vast than the sea. [38]

But perhaps more descriptive of Rolland's esthetics is Robert Dvorak's appraisal when he says that for Rolland the aim of art was neither "beauty" nor "instruction." The "spiritual substance," the "exaltation of the inner life," and the "strengthening of spiritual vitality," these alone were essential to him. [39]

For Gide it did not matter whether the truth was edifying. What mattered was for man to discover himself, to determine what he really was, whether the discovery proved edifying or not. "The novel has been concerned with misfortunes of fate, with chance, good or evil, with social relationships, with the conflict of the passions, with character and personality, but not with the very essence of man's being." [40]

Let there be no confusion: "l'essence même de l'être" of which Gide wrote in the *Faux-Monnayeurs* in 1925 does not have the same meaning for him as does the "inner life" of Romain Rolland. The "inner life" was for Rolland the combination of all those forces—the ideas and emotions—within man that are directed toward life and truth. The "inner life" is the combination of all those forces Rolland sought to enlist in the effort to spur man on to live, and, above all, to live a life of truth. Love is one of the ways to truth, by which the individual being tends toward Being itself and identifies with all the beings of the universe.[41]

"L'essence même de l'être," both in the *Faux-Monnayeurs* and throughout Gide's work, was directed first of all at the essence of a particular being, and in this he pointed the way to Sartre. Each being must look deep within himself, determine who and what he really is, and then live according to the discovery he has made. Gide's preoccupation was basically and primarily ethical; Romain Rolland's was first and foremost intellectual.

Literary form had always been an overriding concern for Gide, and it was essentially on the question of form that he took Tolstoy and Martin du Gard to task. Rolland had great admiration for Tolstoy both as a man and as an artist, and indicated this quite clearly in his *Vie de Tolstoy*. Gide much preferred Dostoevsky, and wrote and spoke about his work. To a degree the opposition between Rolland and Gide is similar to that between Tolstoy and Dostoevsky. What Gide disliked in Tolstoy's art he expressed in words he might equally have applied to Rolland. Reproaching both Tolstoy and Martin du Gard in the same context, he said: "They draw panoramas; art lies in creating a scene." There is no perspective and no shadow. First a point has to be determined from which the light will flow, and all the shadows will depend on it. In a footnote he added: "Dickens and Dostoevsky are great masters at that. The light that surrounds their characters is almost never diffuse. In Tolstoy the best-done scenes seem gray because they are equally lighted from all sides." [42]

In Dostoevsky Gide saw a tendency to group, concentrate, centralize, and create the greatest number of possible relationships among all the elements of the novel. Events do not follow a slow and even-paced course, as they do with Tolstoy

or with Stendhal, or, it might be added, with Rolland.
"There is always a moment in which they get entangled and
knotted up in a kind of vortex; these are whirlwinds in
which the elements of the story—moral, psychological, and
external—are lost and found again. We see no simplification,
no refining of lines, in his work. He delights in complexity;
he defends it. Never are feelings, thoughts, and passions
presented in a pure state. He does not clear the space around
them." [43]

As early as 1912 Rolland himself sensed a certain incompatibility between Tolstoy and Gide as he wrote to Jean-
Richard Bloch on January 14 of that year.

> I have just spent the afternoon with two old and intimate
> friends of Tolstoy, the one a Frenchman and the other a
> Russian. The Frenchman was telling me that one day he
> brought Tolstoy a work of Gide's he was enthusiastic about.
> Very partial to artistic novelties, Tolstoy began to listen [to
> the reading]. At the end of five minutes he was screaming in
> anger and his anger did not subside until the end of the
> reading. Then, out of respect for his friend's opinion, he
> took up the book again and reread it, alone; he came out of
> that second reading even more irritated. And while the
> Frenchman showed astonishment, in my presence, that Tol-
> stoy did not like this work, I was even more astounded that
> anyone could have thought for an instant that Tolstoy might
> like Gide, without ceasing to be Tolstoy.
>
> Once again, I am not criticizing Gide. If I mention him,
> it is rather for his talent. His art may be of the very first order.
> But it is contradictory to Tolstoy's. [44]

For Rolland form had far less importance than it did for
Gide. The order he referred to in speaking of a spiritual
and metaphysical illumination he had experienced on the
Janiculum one March evening in Rome in 1890 was not an
essentially artistic order, but rather a psychological order

which refused to allow the passions to dominate reason. "From that moment on, I learned to separate my mind from my heart." [45] The result of the illumination was not to be a suppression of his passions, for he could also say in referring to the evening on the Janiculum: "I made of my passions themselves the servants of my art." Passions might validly serve as a source of inspiration, but they must be harnessed. "I let them cast their first glow; and then I attached them to my plow." [46] In this the classically artistic mind of Gide would have concurred.

But order for Gide was primarily artistic order, the order achieved in a work of art. For Rolland, only the order that an uplifting and socially broad-based truth could create was of real importance. Art was the enemy of all that was inimical to life; love and unity were its ends.[47] When Gide talked about fraternity in art, he thought of this primarily on an individual basis from one person to another rather than in Rolland's larger social context. To some degree Gide resembled his own Philoctète, who, as he became from day to day less a Greek, became more a man, more human.[48]

The foreign attracted and stimulated Gide, and by foreign he meant not only that which was different by nationality but also that which was personally different in other individuals. "For want of being called forth by what is *different,* the rarest virtues can remain latent: unrevealed to the very being whose they are; or the cause for him only of vague uneasiness, the germ of anarchy." [49] Gide was convinced that by accepting and integrating the alien into his own personality he could attain greater humanity. This was the sole task of a great man "to become as human as possible." [50] Those who feared what was different only betrayed their own spiritual poverty. And to those who feared the loss of their own personality in accepting what was different, he replied strongly that of all fears, the fear of losing one's personality was the most "stupid." [51]

As for literature, his position requires further examination, since it presents a paradox.

> It is possible to imagine a people without literature . . . but how can one imagine a word that is not someone's expression? a literature that is not the expression of a people? . . . the most human works, those which retain the most general interest, are also the most particular, those in which the genius of a race is most especially made manifest through the genius of an individual.[52]

No work of art can have universal significance that does not first have national significance; and to have national significance, it must first of all have individual significance.[53] Greek art was the most individual and yet the most universal.[54] For Romain Rolland, a nationally oriented art need not necessarily lack universality.[55] But when he spoke of brotherhood and humanity in art, the overtones were definitely broadened to an international frame of reference,[56] and most especially, these overtones were social. Thus he had Olivier proclaim to Christophe: "Truth . . . truth is the fact that if there are frontiers in art, they are less barriers of nationality than of class. I do not know if there is a French art and a German art; but there is an art of the rich and an art of those who are not rich." [57]

When Romain Rolland spoke of internationalism, however, he was, in any case, not basically thinking in terms of art. His more fundamental concern was a social one, and it was in a social rather than an artistic context that his internationalism was nurtured.

Rolland's notions on the social mission of art are nowhere more plainly visible than in his essay *Le Théâtre du peuple,* in which he proposed doing away with the existing arrangement of the theater, which odiously fostered class distinction. Everyone, down to the humblest worker who has not had time to go home from work for a quick scrubdown, must be made to feel at ease in the theater, and to accomplish this the seating arrangement must be altered: "the brotherhood of men in art, which must be the purpose of the people's theater, will not be realized, nor will any truly universal art be realized until after the foolish supremacy of the orchestra and the loges has been broken, and the class antagonism provoked by the offensive inequality of the seating in our entertainment halls." [58] Rolland wanted a theater written for all, above all for the people and in their language. With this in mind he sought in his own plays to stage themes from French history capable of inspiring the people to grandeur.

Rolland had not always been fired with the sense of social mission. Early in his career in 1891 he wrote to Gabriel Monod from Rome: "art is too noble and too great to be shared with anything else. Wherever it exists, it is everything; where it does not exist, it is nothing." [59] And even if such a compromise were possible, he stated firmly, he himself could not achieve it.[60] The true artist has neither time nor energy sufficient for other preoccupations: an attitude much closer to Gide's.

On November 21, 1889, Rolland wrote to his mother from the Farnese Palace in Rome.

always the idea of future tranquillity, of dreaming, artistic indolence, sustains me when I work and act now. My goal is sweet isolation, later, with persons dear to me in God and in art. Today I fill myself with memories, observations, and thoughts in order to digest them during the remainder of my life, without any longer having need of the world, and without giving it any rights over me. So for several years I have been paying, and for some time to come shall pay, my due to life. Later I shall be free . . . ; as my character is not too much inclined to action but rather repelled by it—I want to rid myself as quickly as possible of this drudgery of an active life—I am immediately doubling the dosage, so that it will be finished sooner. . . . But I wish you to know how much I perpetually have to force myself, even to do what is agreeable to me: I do not like to *act!* [61]

Yet like his Christophe, whose story he began to write in 1903, Rolland also became a man of action, and this attitude of 1889 was short-lived. He insisted that he had adopted an active role in 1914 only with extreme reluctance,[62] but *agir* was in fact essential to Rolland; Gide preferred to *faire agir*. Rolland perceived in himself the artist, and in the man of action that he became, something else besides the artist. Like Christophe, "he had often mingled with his art preoccupations foreign to it: he assigned to his art a social mission." [63] André Gide seemed to be thinking of Rolland, René Arcos believes, when he wrote: "Bad literature is made with good intentions..." [64]

The differences that later separated Gide from Rolland in their reaction to communism were already sketched in clear outline in this controversy in esthetics. We cannot call Gide a pure esthete, he was a *moraliste*. "Il enseigne," says R.-M. Albérès in considering the question. But the word *enseignement* has two meanings: it can inculcate ready-made truths or it can teach one to find truth oneself, freely but lucidly, and only in the second sense is the word applicable to Gide.[65] Even if Gide was not a pure esthete, as he would have been had he remained faithful to his early attachment to symbolism, he was always very profoundly concerned with esthetics, whereas Romain Rolland, less exclusively devoted to art, was not.

V   Romain Rolland and the *N.R.F.*

Before the war Gide had been instrumental in the founding of the *Nouvelle Revue Française,* and unfortunately Rolland's relations with the new review were embittered from the very beginning. Though neither explicitly confirmed it, the disenchantment that arose between them was without doubt attributable in part to the cool reception given Rolland's work at the desks of the *N.R.F.,* or, as Rolland called it, the "groupe littéraire de Gide." [1]

The first issue appeared on February 1, 1909, and the beginnings are retold in detail by Jean Schlumberger:

> Before becoming the N.R.F. group, we were . . . a group of friends . . . of very diverse backgrounds, gifts, and tastes, but in agreement on a certain number of essential points. . . . This is what accounted for the team's original character and solidarity. Our understanding was not established around a program; our program was the expression of our understanding.
>
> We were not bringing a new formula along, since we had passed the age when one thinks one can find genius in magic

words; but we shared some great admirations that were sec-
onded by some very strong refusals to compromise, and some
principles that would have to be called moral just as much
as esthetic. Our bond consisted in a way of being, an ethic
rather than a way of writing; as a consequence our unity
never had anything uniform about it.[2]

The managing board was composed of six members: Gide,
his brother-in-law Marcel Drouin, who also used the name
Michel Arnauld, Henri Ghéon, André Ruyters, Jacques
Copeau, and Jean Schlumberger. To Schlumberger fell the
task of assembling some sort of manifesto or rather a statement of *orientation,* as he calls it, for the new review.[3] The
program that the review established for itself was a difficult
one at best, taking up a position on two fronts simultaneously:

> on one side, against so-called boulevard or magazine litera-
> ture, without root or continuation, on the other side, against
> traditionalist literature locked up in worn-out forms. . . .
>   What so much incensed the nationalists and reactionaries
> of all kinds against us . . . was that we accompanied such
> bizarre taste with perfectly reasonable critical judgments. In
> their eyes this mixture of common sense and nonconformity
> blurred the categories of good and evil and made them judge
> our influence as especially dangerous. They held against us
> our knowing how to speak with as much relevance as they
> themselves, if we had to, about Racine or about Florentine
> art; our respect for language seemed to them an infringement
> on their reserved domain, and the welcome we extended to
> foreign literatures put the final touch on convincing them
> that we were introducing a Trojan horse into the heart of a
> dismantled France.[4]

Schlumberger described Gide's influence in the *N.R.F.* as
"prépondérante." [5] This influence was felt not so much by
Gide's imposing his own tastes as by his setting an example

of humility in accepting the criticism of other members of the committee, and thereby establishing a certain cohesion essential to the proper functioning of the review. Gide, more than any of the others, took the undertaking to heart. He had the highest ambitions for the *N.R.F.*, and the gap between his dream and the reality caused him many a *nuit blanche*. Schlumberger recalled that Gide was prepared even to write addresses and paste stamps on the outgoing issues— "he would have gone himself to deliver the issues to our subscribers. . . ." [6] Schlumberger at one point mused over what the *N.R.F.* might have been, had Gide been given sole mastery:

> I have no doubt that if Gide had taken charge of managing the review all by himself, he would have made something more unusual of it. The rare and the refined would have appeared side by side with the bizarre; he would have created a laboratory for style and ideas, in which he would have made room for all that seemed curious and novel to him, but in which a common discipline, a literary movement, could not have been born. [7]

Originally the *N.R.F.* was associated with Eugène Montfort, who directed a small review called *Les Marges* which the founders of the *N.R.F.* generally held in esteem. [8] The name itself was suggested by Montfort and based on a *Revue Française* no longer in existence. [9] But Montfort's spirit was different from theirs; he was open to tendencies they wanted to combat, and the first issue, which appeared in November, 1908, was considered a "faux-départ." Independently they published another first issue in February, 1909. [10] During the war the *N.R.F.* suspended publication after the issue of August 1, 1914, because of the dispersion of its members, and reappeared only on June 1, 1919.

During the postwar period Romain Rolland also became involved in this type of work, when, together with a group of leftist writers, he founded the literary and political review *Europe*. The idea of bringing together into one magazine the highlights of European thought was an idea with which he had already been toying before and during the war, hoping "to found, with three or four people, a kind of literary Correspondence, like that of Grimm and Diderot, that would radiate its light over Europe, and that would group together the most significant thinking of the great Western countries." [11] In his study on Rolland René Arcos described the founding of *Europe*. *Europe* was a modest response to Rolland's idea for a great international review. Financial and other difficulties may have discouraged the founders from the outset, but Rolland never ceased to encourage and animate them afresh. They had to succeed, and Arcos called him "our everlasting oxygen balloon." [12]

When Arcos submitted a program for the review, Rolland responded on April 28, 1922, "Chauffez, chauffez!" "Do not fear to give it a personal flavor. And above all, *flavor*. Act as if you believe in it. Do better: believe in it. . . . Have nerve. And be assured that I am with you in what you are going to do." [13]

The possibilities for a title were numerous. *L'Arche, La Revue des Trois Mondes,* to take into account Europe, Asia, and America, *La Revue du Monde Nouveau, La Revue du Monde, La Revue d'Europe et d'Asie*. In the end *Europe,* the title proposed by Arcos with the agreement of Léon Bazalgette, won out. Romain Rolland approved wholeheartedly, but advised some form of initial commentary to indicate that the review did not intend to advocate a new European nationalism. "In the end, *Europe* had to win out," Arcos recalled. "And the review appeared—with his moral support and under the aegis of freedom of thought—to which we were all strongly attached." [14] The first issue appeared on February 15, 1923.

If most of Rolland's encouragement came from his "solitary refuge" in Switzerland, as Arcos noted,[15] Rolland himself explained this fact as well as his attitude toward the review in his "Journal intime" of October, 1925. Most of his young literary friends were grouped around *Europe,* and these included the writers Georges Duhamel, Charles Vildrac, René Arcos, Jean-Richard Bloch, Léon Bazalgette, and Panaït Istrati.

> But I remain completely independent of it. And if I have become established in Switzerland, this should clearly mark the fact that the center of my thought is not in France, but outside of all nations, in a "Weltbürgertum" that takes all free men of all nationalities and countries into its embrace.[16]

Despite the distance from Paris, Rolland was enthusiastic at first, but his enthusiasm soon waned. On August 12, 1924, he wrote: *"Europe* m'ennuie." *Europe* was composed entirely of men of good will whom he respected and even liked, but they bored him. "Paris (literarily) puts me to sleep." [17] A month later, in a letter to Bloch, he called *Europe* mediocre and spoke of his cooling relations with the review, reproaching it for treating Tagore, whom he considered a great artist, with *sans-gêne.* This determined his resolution, and on September 6 he wrote of *Europe,* "I am dissociating myself from it." [18] Elaborating on his complaints against *Europe* in December, he took the review to task especially for its lack of personality. Those who worked on it were all "nice people and good artists," but as a group they didn't really seem to know what they were aiming for. As time passed, Rolland's criticism became ever more severe. To his way of thinking *Europe* seemed to be departing from its original conceptions. On almost every subject of discussion, with art certainly not being the least important of these, *Europe* seemed to be drawing closer to the *N.R.F.,* to the point where he thought it was beginning to look like a satellite of the *N.R.F.*[19] The only subject on which *Europe's* contributors now could unite was the social question.[20] Unlike *Europe,* he felt, the *N.R.F.* knew what it wanted, and this fact alone must have been a thorn to Rolland. "A review that is not a 'moral person,' clearly individualized and distinct from all others, is for me only a *boîte aux lettres.*"

> How could *Europe* be anything more, when its most emi-
> nent contributors write today for the Bolshevik *Clarté,* to-
> morrow at the De Traz review [21] that denounced us during
> the war and has not yet laid down its arms, one day for the
> *Mercure,* another for *Marges,* and a third for the *N. Revue
> Française,* not to mention the *Revue Européenne?* [22]

Rolland now proceeded to denounce *Europe* for the same reasons that had inspired him to denounce the *N.R.F.* in 1911. "I cannot write where I cannot breathe," [23] he wrote in 1925. In 1927 he reproached *Europe* for its publication of pro-Jewish articles, for it seemed to be making a rule of conduct out of printing such articles, and it was this rather than the effort itself that he rejected.[24] Finally on November 15, 1930, he wrote that he had broken off with *Europe.* With the sole exception of Jean Guéhenno, and Rolland thought Guéhenno himself too weak, *Europe* had become a world foreign to him.[25] Jean Guéhenno was the editor of the review, and Rolland regarded him as a pure and sincere person, as an exception in the Parisian literary milieu.[26] But certain persons had slipped into the managing committee who were suspect to him. He would not, however, allow this to prevent him, he said, from communicating to *Europe* any documents that might be of help to the cause of free people menaced by oppression. It was only his personal collaboration he was withdrawing.[27]

But when the essayist Julien Benda wrote two articles that appeared as late as January and April, 1930, in the *Nouvelle Revue Française,* articles discussing the differences of approach that separated writers of the right from those of the left, and the contemplative from the man of action, Benda could still call *Europe*'s editors, at least in this basic area of their ideology, Romain Rolland's "moutons."

Schlumberger has described in some detail the depth and intensity of Gide's commitment to the *N.R.F.* Rolland's commitment to *Europe* was of another temper. Having returned to France from Switzerland on May 4, 1919, Rolland went back to Switzerland on April 30, 1921,[28] and was residing there when *Europe* was founded. His aid, as Arcos indicated, was rather of a moral nature. And so when he wrote that he would continue to submit to *Europe* any documents that might help the cause of free people menaced by oppression, and that it was only his personal collaboration that he was withdrawing, basically he must have been referring to the moral support he had thus far offered. In January of 1931 he wrote that his essential reasons for leaving *Europe* were linked to his withdrawal from the world of Paris. He had his own interior world which was sufficient to him.[29]

Despite his oft-voiced criticism, Rolland could still write in 1936 that though he suspected *Europe* of being perverted from its original intention, he deemed it unwise, and at any rate premature, to effect a complete break. His many years of association with *Europe* and the view that it was necessary as an instrument of action and so, better than nothing at all, seem to have dictated his decision.[30]

The *Nouvelle Revue Française* fast became the leading literary review of France, and Romain Rolland recognized this.[31] But his attitude toward it was one of hostility from the outset. In July, 1911, he wrote to J.-R. Bloch of "Gide's review": "always the same impression, when I read an issue of the *Nouvelle Revue Française*. I suffocate. Much talent, but no air." [32] But he considered this to be true also of Paris's other reviews, where there was less talent. Regardless of how stifling he found the *N.R.F.,* he continued to correspond with some of its editors. The results can only be described as unfortunate.

On April 3, 1912, Jacques Copeau wrote Rolland a letter of apology and explanation for not yet having published any of Rolland's works.

> I wish . . . to make my apologies to you for the fact that the *Nouvelle Revue Française* has not yet taken the opportunity to show the high esteem in which it holds your person and your writing. Here is the reason for that silence, for which we have been reproached more than once: for a very long time I have been asking one of our contributors, who seemed to me best qualified, to give us a study of the ensemble of your work. He has not yet had the spare time to carry out the project. And yet each time one of your books appeared, we put off speaking about it so as not to detract from the originality of the study in question. This is the completely banal explanation of a mystery which, if it were not cleared up, might pass for an impropriety in your eyes... While waiting for our contributor to fulfill his task (it cannot take much longer) may I ask you, Monsieur, if you would be pleased to honor the *Nouvelle Revue Française*—and to bring to an end this ambiguous situation, vexing to us alone, which our involuntary silence might support—by publishing a few pages therein? I am thinking very especially of a certain portion or the totality of a "Vie" of a great musician, great painter or great writer.[33]

Rolland responded to Copeau with a "thank you" from Rome on Easter Monday. Though he felt somewhat removed from the spirit infusing the *Nouvelle Revue Française,* he looked upon it as Paris' first literary review and said he would be happy at some time to write for it. It had never occurred to him to reproach Copeau's review for its silence regarding him. Rolland's impression was that the *N.R.F.* did not much like his writing, but here it was within its rights.[34]

On August 13, 1912, Copeau reminded Rolland of his expressed willingness to contribute, asking him to name a date by which he thought he might be able to "honor" the *N.R.F.,* and on October 13 Rolland promised him the first "œuvre d'imagination" with which he himself was satisfied. As for contributing any item of criticism, he preferred to abstain. The *N.R.F.* already had more than enough critics, and he himself would not have sufficient distance. He considered the critics at the *N.R.F.* remarkable and often of the first order, but found them all to be penetrated with the same "atmosphere." They formed a distinct group and represented a stage in the development of French art. This was what accounted for their historical importance, but it also marked their limits. And these limits hampered Rolland, who felt that he must remain outside, away from people and things in order to see them better.[35]

Some ten days later Copeau responded, thanking Rolland for his promise to cooperate and now identifying Michel Arnauld (Marcel Drouin), Gide's brother-in-law, as the person who had been assigned to do the study on Rolland.[36]

On two occasions before the middle of 1914, Rolland had recommended another writer for publication in the *N.R.F.,* one of them being René Morax.[37] Though his recommendation was not successful on either occasion, this did not deter him from a third attempt on behalf of Grazia Deledda on July 15, 1914.[38]

These rejections, together with what seemed to him the rejection of his own work, naturally contributed nothing to narrow the gap between Rolland and the *N.R.F.* Copeau's statements regarding Marcel Drouin, however, were quite truthful. Finally in the issue of February 1, 1913, the *N.R.F.* gave recognition to Rolland in a favorable review of *La Nouvelle Journée,* the concluding portion of *Jean-Christophe.* The critique was signed A.T., the initials referring to Albert Thibaudet.

Jean-Christophe is finished. Of this complete and substantial work, seen from the root to the summit, from the earth
that nourished it to the light that sings within it, another
will speak here. Another, and in the meantime, perhaps
Romain Rolland himself.[39]

Of Drouin, Schlumberger wrote: "What he was going to
accomplish the next day or the following year freed him
from the burden of what he did not accomplish that very
day." [40] Gide wrote of Drouin in a similar vein, and regardless
of the excuses he made for Drouin, has drawn a portrait of
him sufficient to help explain the confusion over the delinquent article on Rolland. In May, 1949:

I got to the point, at the end of the summer vacations,
of not daring to speak to him anymore of his abortive projects. . . . But each spring, his ardor is reborn; he used then
to speak about new projects with an eloquence so persuasive
that he thereby secured new credit from us all and even
from himself.[41]

"What troubles he caused us with so many authors,"
Schlumberger recalled. No one spoke of certain authors in
the *N.R.F.* because Drouin had reserved that right to himself,
claiming that he, better than anyone else, could render them
homage. Schlumberger footnoted his remarks:

Notably Romain Rolland, on whose work he was always
promising the great study that would have rectified everything—a study always promised for the next summer vaca-
tion and always put off under new pretexts—so that by its
incomprehensible silence, the *N.R.F.* seemed to be nourish-
ing a deep-seated hostility toward Romain Rolland. The
explanations we were able to give after the fact never di-
spelled the misunderstanding. The masterly work on Péguy,
received immediately after Rolland's death, made me feel,
and not without regret, how easy it would have been to find

points of understanding with a spirit so obviously loyal and concerned for fairness.[42]

The combined statements of Copeau, Gide, and Schlumberger go a long way toward clarifying the "misunderstanding" with Rolland, but what separated the *N.R.F.* from Romain Rolland was more than simple misunderstanding. His attitude toward art and theirs were not compatible. The misunderstanding was unfortunate, for had it not occurred, had Drouin published the long-awaited study of Rolland, that basic incompatibility might have diminished in importance, and professional differences might more easily have remained professional differences.

In 1915 relations between Copeau and Rolland degenerated sharply, and any degeneration in Rolland's relations with Copeau was bound to increase, subconsciously at least, his animosity toward the *N.R.F.* and all those associated with it, including Gide. Romain Rolland wrote to Copeau early in November, 1915, accusing him of disseminating false rumors that he, Rolland, had been spreading antiwar propaganda in the army. Rolland reminded Copeau of his work in Geneva with the Prisoner of War Agency, stating that the only public expression he had given to his thoughts had been in the *Journal de Genève*.[43] Copeau replied some two weeks later denying the charges, but stating emphatically that if he himself had kept silent, it was because in such difficult times the injuries inflicted by words could be among the most damaging.

And I firmly believe that we must forbid ourselves any movement—I was going to say any feeling—that might be capable of dividing us among ourselves. It is not a question of calling on our feelings, or even on our convictions, but only on all our strength and all our patience so that we shall win. Until victory is achieved, all Frenchmen can assume only one position, that of combat.[44]

At some time during this period Copeau had a meeting with Henri Guilbeau [45] at which they discussed the influence Romain Rolland's articles might have on morale at the front. Guilbeau then apparently told him that one of his own friends was going to the front in order to spread antiwar propaganda "sur place." In a bitter letter addressed to Guilbeau and dated the same day as his letter to Rolland, the 19th of November, Copeau denied ever having repeated a word spoken at their meeting regarding the influence of Rolland's articles on the front. But he admitted having repeated the story of Guilbeau's friend in a private conversation with the painter Gaston Thiesson. The story became garbled, and in the final version, friends of Romain Rolland's rather than one of Guilbeau's friends were leaving for the front to spread antiwar propaganda. "I simply remarked," Copeau retorted, "that it could be vexing for Romain Rolland if young men with whom he was known to have ties held such discussions." [46]

Who may actually have been responsible for the defamation of Romain Rolland has little significance for the present discussion. What is important is that the attitudes of the collaborators in the *N.R.F.* were not those of Rolland, either on the question of the war or on the question of art. What is important is that another misunderstanding had been created. Certainly this misunderstanding was not lessened when, as Rolland noted in the *Journal des années de guerre* on October 24, Thiesson reported that Copeau found him "un peu enfantin" and "un peu débile." [47] As Copeau himself recognized:

> You see, dear Romain Rolland, what is sad and distasteful in such misunderstandings is that one never manages to disentangle oneself completely from them, in a strict sense to rectify them. The more one argues the more confused one becomes, and a small stain can tarnish, despite all, those hearts that were best disposed to forgetting. [48]

Despite these misunderstandings, Rolland turned to Copeau in January, 1916, to tell him of the sequestration of the contents of Rilke's apartment. If Copeau ever answered him directly, Rolland did not record it; it was Gide who took charge of the affair in Paris.

Apparently some of Rolland's thought had filtered through to the front if only under the guise of Massis's pamphlet against him. In 1915 Roger Martin du Gard, then serving in arms, thanked Rolland for the only "breath of fresh air" he had been able to inhale for a year.[49] When the war was over, Martin du Gard, in spite of his friendship for Gide, informed Rolland of the attack Gide had just made against him in the *N.R.F.* of July, 1919. Martin du Gard assured Rolland that neither his attachment to friends at the *N.R.F.* nor his personal friendship for Gide could stop him from protesting against the attack, "as unworthy of him as it is of you." [50]

Rolland registered his reaction to Gide's "petite saleté," as he called it, ten days later in a letter to J.-R. Bloch.

> I am not surprised at this ill will of which I have more than once been the object in the past five years, on the part of one or another of these gentlemen of the *N.R.F.* And always in the form of a polite underhandedness. I prefer open enemies.[51]

Time and again Rolland's correspondence reveals bitterness toward the *N.R.F.* What was before the war a simple dislike based on ideological or, more especially, on esthetic differences became after the war a deep-rooted animosity based on personal injury. In September, 1919, Rolland wrote the American critic Waldo Frank that he had not the least sympathy for Copeau or for his review.[52] In November, 1920, Paul Zefferer, the Austrian ambassador to Paris and a friend of Stefan Zweig's, wanted to publish the works of a fellow Austrian, the writer Hugo von Hoffmannsthal, and expressed the wish that Rolland should facilitate his contact with the

N.R.F. Rolland, in turn, handed the affair over to J.-R. Bloch, saying that he himself had no relations with the *N.R.F.* and was only too delighted to have it so.[53] Some six weeks earlier he had written even more severely of the *N.R.F.* to Bloch:

> But what great aversion I have for that *N. Revue f.!* They are people for whom theory is the whole of life! Since they can create nothing (or so little) by themselves, they fabricate boxes, empty boxes—with the manic tenacity of confused wasps building up cells without ever putting anything into them. And how proud they are of their boxes! If at least they knew how to revitalize a little the form of the ornamentation with the ingenuity of the Eastern and Far Eastern artisans. But no indeed. They pride themselves in repeating stereotypes, in plagiarizing them. Nobly. Pompously. These are very distinguished minds. —France is well guarded. Oh! how glad I am to be outside it all! [54]

Delighted at having nothing to do with the *N.R.F.* in 1920, Rolland modified his tone in 1928 when he wrote to Jean Paulhan, the new editor who had succeeded Rivière on his death in 1925. Rolland looked upon Paulhan with some favor and said that in principle he had no objection to publishing in the *N.R.F.* If he had not yet done so, it was because the *N.R.F.* had not asked him.[55] This was not altogether true, of course, as Copeau's letters testify. And yet for Rolland, who questioned the sincerity of that offer, it may have been true. In 1932 he excused himself from writing an article on Goethe by saying that he was too busy, thus revealing at the same time his real attitude toward the *N.R.F.* Paulhan might speak of reconciliation, but had there been a quarrel? asked Rolland. He did say, however, that for the past fifteen years he had observed only two attitudes towards him on the part of the *N.R.F.:* ignorance and disparagement. What could he possibly have tried to do in their ranks? At present it was, at any rate, too late to change anything. Life had been played out.[56]

With the outbreak of a second world war in Europe, *Europe* suspended publication and Paulhan offered Rolland the hospitality of the *N.R.F.*, but Rolland was not eager to write at a time when the whole truth could no longer be expressed. In an attitude remarkably akin to Gide's during the first world war, he advocated unity in the face of Hitlerism.[57] Again in 1943, almost at the end of his life, Rolland referred to the *N.R.F.*, telling Paulhan of his willingness to discuss his contributing to it after peace had been made. But until that time he would abstain.[58] When the war finally ended, Romain Rolland was dead.

Rolland never forgave the *N.R.F.* for the injuries he felt he had suffered at its hands. But of all the grudges he held, the deepest seems still to have been the first one, for not publishing his work. A letter written in 1932, some twenty years after Copeau's apology, to Pierre Abraham on the editorial board of *Europe,* testifies that Rolland did not interpret the silence of the *N.R.F.* as anything but a slight against his work, a slight it was too late to repair. He had no illusions, he said, about the *N.R.F.* Through the years the successive editors of that review had been interchangeable, and he had known them too long to flatter himself into thinking that the ill will of twenty years, whether silent or expressed, was an "accidental silence." He was now too close to life's exit to be interested in belated regrets, sincere or otherwise, from a house that throughout his life had shown him underhanded hostility.[59]

VI God and Religion,
Christ and Christianity

In the preface to Rolland's correspondence with Louis Gillet,
published as the second of the *Cahiers Romain Rolland,*
Paul Claudel spoke of the generation of writers to which
Rolland and André Gide belonged. He alluded to some of
the problems that beset them and especially to the religious
crises that so many of them experienced. Most had reached
a stage in life where they no longer found the answer to
their needs in organized religion, whether these were needs
of the mind or of the heart. Some, such as Claudel himself
and Francis Jammes, returned to the church of their childhood; others, such as Rolland and Gide, rejected this solution, and Claudel's efforts to convert Gide to Roman Catholicism ended in failure.

Claudel looked on Rolland as one of the most typical of
their generation:

> I see in him the representative, the most typical hero, of
> this generation, or rather, let us say, that *levée* at the dawn
> of a new century. . . . A generation to which, more than to

any other, can be applied the words of Amos the prophet: I shall send you hunger, not hunger for bread, but hunger for the word of God. The generation of Péguy and Psichiari,[1] but also, and I list pell-mell, that of André Gide, Francis Jammes, André Suarès, Bourget, Barrès, Huysmans, and Brunetière. . . . One single common characteristic among them: none of them owed anything to the church of their birth, and those among them who at a late hour came back to the church found no encouragement, interior or exterior, from her.[2]

For Romain Rolland the *crise de la foi* occurred early. He recalled in his *Voyage intérieur* that between the ages of fifteen and seventeen, while still a *lycéen* at Louis-le-Grand, "I breathed in . . . the vapors of the abyss." [3] Before the colossal disorder of his interior life, all other problems faded, "God was dead." [4]

When he learned in 1888 that a fellow student at the Ecole Normale had passed away, he cried out against God for the death of this young man whose will was so great and whose life held so much promise in the world of action. "This is villainy on the part of God. All right for us who are artists, who can die for a minute of ecstasy, for ecstasy kills death!... But he, he who exists only as long as he has being—he, who will not even have been if he is not *completely*... this death that kills him totally is an atrocious thing." [5]

His first real act of self-affirmation during this period of adolescence, Rolland recalled, was to break with his religion out of a respect for himself and for the "hidden God," out of a refusal to play the role of a hypocrite. "This was my most religious act. . . . 'God! I am being frank with you! I no longer go to your Mass. . . . I do not believe in you.' " [6]

The break with Catholicism was a deep blow to his mother. His father was offended, for though a nonbeliever himself, he felt religion was a good thing for children.[7]

For Gide the problem was not quite the same, but this was owing in large part to his own temperament. He, too, was given a religious upbringing, and though his father died when he was still very young, his mother watched over the religious education of her child. Gide was brought up a Protestant, and in matters of religion and morals his mother was inflexible. Harshly puritan in her outlook, she attempted in every way to make her son conform to and adopt her own way of thinking.

Whereas Rolland's crisis, though tinged with some emotional overtones, was essentially a crisis of the intellect, Gide's crisis seems to have been first and foremost a physical one. The *Cahiers d'André Walter,* written in 1891, though obsessed with purity and the horror of sin, palpitates with sensuality. André Walter's own objective is to intensify life, all the while keeping the soul vigilant.[8] As time passed, the more Gide became aware of his physical makeup, the less homage he paid to the traditional morality of organized religion. Finally in 1897 in the *Nourritures terrestres* he advised Nathanaël not to see God as something different from happiness itself, and to place all his happiness in the present moment.[9] In the long run the purely hedonistic way of life that such a philosophy suggested was incompatible with Gide's character. The words Rolland used to describe himself were equally true of Gide: "I had to rebuild my entire being on new bases."[10]

Neither Gide nor Rolland was an atheist. Indeed both were deeply religious men. The solution to the enigma of God that Rolland had discovered at an early age was one that he retained throughout his life; but Gide's character was not fixed as was Rolland's, and his thoughts on God and religion wavered. At no point did he attempt to prove the existence of God, for he felt that all attempts either to prove or to disprove God's existence were equally absurd.[11] All of Gide's work implies God's existence and the problem for Gide, as

Germaine Brée discerned it accurately, is not the existence
of God but the paths by which men can find him.[12] Even
in the seemingly pagan *Nourritures terrestres,* Gide sought
to justify his newly found philosophy of pleasure in relation
to God. The book opens:

> Seek not, Nathanaël, to find God anywhere else than
> everywhere.
> Each creature points to God, none reveals him.
> As soon as our gaze is stopped by it, every creature diverts
> us from God.[13]

If each creature points the way to God, then man should be
able to turn to himself for that guidance, and this is precisely
what Gide made his Oedipus do in speaking to the priest
Tiresias. "What shall I look for in a God? Answers? I felt
myself an answer to I knew not yet what question." [14]

And so creator and creature exist in a relationship of
perfect dependence upon each other. One does not exist
without the other. Gide elaborated in the *Nouvelles Nourritures:* "God holds me; I hold him; we are. But in this
thought, I am simply one with all creation; I am dissolved
and absorbed in a diffuse humanity." [15]

Through nature and through other men who are a part
of nature we go to God. This is not to say that nature is
God, but rather that it indicates the way to God. "Beyond
phenomena to contingent pluralities, to contemplate ineffable
truths." [16] In his *Journal* for 1947 Gide said that much would
be accomplished by taking God off the altar and putting man
in his place.[17]

The problem has now become one of vocabulary. The
word "God" is empty of substance and will fit almost any
meaning man chooses to give it.[18] Gide refused belief in a
personal God, for to believe in a personal God and in his
Providence is to abdicate all that is reasonable in man.[19]
He preferred to say that from the moment something existed,

this was God. Any explanation was useless.[20] Rejecting reason in the search for God, Gide sought to rely exclusively on intuitive knowledge, and intuitive knowledge does not imply abdication of reason, nor belief in something contrary to reason, but rather a suspension of reason to permit belief in something which, though not contrary to it, is beyond its grasp. Even during a time of extreme religious fervor in his life that coincided with World War I, Gide rejected the attempts to prove or disprove God that philosophy, science, and textual criticism of the Scriptures had afforded. In *Numquid et tu?*, written as a result of his temporary crisis, he wrote, "In no way does my faith depend on that." [21]

In 1943 Gide published his *Deux Interviews imaginaires*. As it appeared rather late in his life, the thoughts expressed therein can be regarded as the conclusion he had reached.

> I find greater satisfaction in considering God as an invention, a creation of man, that man puts together little by little, and ever more tends to fashion by dint of his own intelligence and moral strength. Creation reaches toward and culminates in Him, rather than emanating from Him. And since time does not exist for the Eternal, this comes down to the same thing for Him.[22]

God is man's creation and the end point or, as Pierre Teilhard de Chardin [23] called it, the Omega point, toward which all of creation is striving. God is the end point and not the point of departure for all of creation, but this does not mean that creation in its entirety, from beginning to end, is not his work. It means only that the achieving of God will take place after us. "All evolution must lead to God." [24]

This God toward which creation tends can be regarded from two angles, designated respectively by Gide as the "côté Zeus" and the "côté Prométhée." The "côté Zeus" is the ensemble of the cosmos and the natural laws that rule it.

It is offset by the "côté Prométhée," the total of all human efforts directed toward the good and the beautiful and can be called the "côté Christ." But this God, the God represented by the "côté Christ," is nowhere to be found in nature. He exists only in and by man. Though Christ cried out in despair to one whom he called Father, asking why he had been abandoned, there was no real abandonment because there had never been an *entente*. The God of nature is deaf to human suffering, and the God represented by Christ, the "Dieu-vertu," must struggle not only against the natural forces but against the evil of man as well. "This last word of Christ would prevent me from confusing Christ with God if all else had not already given me warning." He whom Christ called Father never recognized a son. And yet it was only this son of man that Gide could and wanted to adore.[25]

Gide did not see harmony in all things; but he recognized that all things had need of man in order to be or in order to feel themselves as being. Without man they remained in suspension.[26] God does not inhabit the object itself, but inhabits rather the love man shows to all that with which he comes in contact.

When Gide first perceived that God did not yet truly exist but depended on man for his existence and that God was the end of man's existence, from that time on Gide saw his morality restored. In his *Journal* for 1942 he wrote:

As soon as I had realized that God was not yet but was becoming and that his becoming depended on each one of us, a moral sense was restored in me. No impiety or presumption in this thought, for I was convinced at one and the same time that God was achieved only by man and through man, but that if man led to God, creation, in order to lead to man, started from God; so that the divine had its place at both ends, at the start and at the point of arrival, and that the start had been solely in order to arrive at God. This bival-vular thought reassured me and I was unwilling to dissociate

one from the other: God creating man in order to be created by him; God the end of man; chaos raised up by God
to the level of man and then man raising himself up to the
level of God. To accept but one of them: what fear, what
obligation! To accept but the other: what self-satisfaction!
It ceased to be a matter of obeying God, but rather of in-
stilling life into him, of falling in love with him, of demand-
ing him of oneself through love and of achieving him
through virtue.[27]

Man must learn to surpass himself. First he imagined that
the sun traveled around the earth, and yet when he learned
that this was not so, nothing had changed except his own
knowledge. In the same way he must learn to see beyond
Providence. "We are not yet there. A good deal of moral
strength is required to reach this state of total atheism; and
more yet to stay there." [28]

Henceforth man had to exact from himself what he had
believed to be exacted by God. God exists only by virtue of
man, and to man's virtue and strength God must give way,
virtue being simply the best an individual can obtain from
himself.[29] "God is to come. I am convinced and tell myself
again and again: He depends on us. Through us God is
realized." [30]

Despite the oft-occurring hesitancy and change, this way
of thinking was the most characteristic of Gide and represented, at any rate, the culmination of his reflections on the
subject. The rigid and somewhat more traditional, if exaggerated, faith of the *Porte étroite* and, to a lesser degree, of
the *Numquid et tu?* were either correctives to tendencies
Gide saw in his own makeup or the profoundly human
responses he offered to himself and to the world. They did
not represent ideals, as he himself cautioned more than once.
Though Gide confessed in a late work, *Et nunc manet in te*,
that he could not partake of his deceased wife's belief in an
afterlife,[31] he let André Walter write much earlier for

Emmanuèle that although the world could separate our bodies, even death could not separate our souls.[32] The outline of Gide's whole career would suggest that his was a rejection of personal immortality rather than of immortality *per se*. The name atheist does not sit particularly well in the work of so religious a man. To prove that God is and to affirm that he is not, both were absurd.[33]

Changes in his approach to God, depending on the mood and the circumstance, account for the apparent complexity of Gide's thought on religion. In reality it is not so very complex, and in the final analysis not very different from that of Romain Rolland. Rolland found what he considered to be the truth early in life after the *crise de la foi* of his adolescence. Once he had found it, his position never faltered. Gide's attitude, wavering but constantly searching, and that of Rolland, steadfast and firm without any apparent need to reevaluate, were typical of the two men. A similar diversity of positions will be seen again in their attitudes toward communism, and it indicates something about the respective character of each.

Between his sixteenth and eighteenth years, in a cold room on a winter's night, Rolland came upon a text of Spinoza that brought liberation from the anguish of doubt. "But it must be noted that by the series of real causes and beings, I do not mean the series of particular and changing things, but only the series of fixed and eternal things." [34] "Les choses fixes et éternelles" were the most real of all beings, and all that was real was individual. There were no abstractions, only essences. "Des essences! Des êtres. Tout est être."

All the infinite ways of being partook of this single fundamental characteristic of being, and the dilemma was broken.

> Ecstasy!... Fiery wine!... My prison is opened. There then is the answer, obscurely conceived in sorrow and despair, called forth by cries of passion with broken wings, obsti-

nately looked for and desired in wounds and tears of blood,
there it is aglow, the answer to the riddle of the Sphinx that
has held me in its clasp since my childhood—the answer to
the overwhelming contradiction between the immensity of
my inner being and the character of my outer shell humiliating and suffocating me!... *"Naturizing nature"* and *"natu-
rized nature"*... It is the same thing. "All that is, is in God."
And I, too, I am in God! From my icy room, where the
winter night is falling, I escape into an abyss of *Substance,*
into the white sun of Being.[35]

All of creation was swimming, as it were, in this sea of Being,
and this was God. Rolland had found his equilibrium. "I can
only fall in Him. I am at peace." [36]

His own exaltation at the discovery of universal being and
universal Life, and the discovery that he was part of it, was
not different from Christophe's reaction to the same discovery.
Christophe here *is* Rolland.

Christophe, suffering from delusion, his whole being
strained, shuddered to his very depths... The veil was rent.
It was dazzling. With a flash of lightning he saw, in the deep
of night he saw—he was God. God was in him: He was break-
ing through the ceiling of his room and the walls of the
house; He was making being creak to its very limits; He was
filling the sky, the universe, space. The world was rushing
headlong within him like a cataract. In the horror and
ecstasy of that collapse, Christophe was falling too, carried
off by the vortex that was grinding up the laws of nature
like straw. He had lost his breath, he was enraptured by this
falling into God... the God of the abyss! the God of the
depths, the Forge of Being! Whirlwind of life! Madness of
living—without aim, without restraint, without reason—for
the rage of living! [37]

God is Life suffering with all who suffer, and fighting at the
side of all who must fight.[38]

As with Gide, the God of Rolland is one who evolves, and man must evolve with him, for he is up ahead, not behind.[39] Man must create him. " 'God has created man,' it is said. But man repays him well! He is far from having finished creating God!" [40] In this process of creation Rolland included the ever-evolving religious forms that must necessarily accompany it. "I am completely reassured of the permanence of the divine in human thought and of the slow birth of new religious forms for humanity." [41] As for the apparent contradictions in God, designated by Gide as the "côté Zeus" and the "côté Prométhée," Rolland also recognized these, but felt that man's aversion to the "côté Zeus" would have validity only if God were personal in nature. But he was not, for Rolland could not, anymore than Gide, believe in a personal God. Once in writing about death, Rolland protested against

> that abominable agony that would suffice to make one curse God if he existed—but fortunately, he does not exist—at least in the form of the all-powerful and all-knowing Master, offered to our childish imagination. Poor God, if he does exist— (he does certainly exist within us)—suffers and struggles with us; and the outcome of the struggle is no less than certain. This is why we must not abandon either the struggle or God himself (who has need of us)—even at times of the most bitter despair.[42]

The end result of Gide's discovery was not very different from Rolland's, though for Gide the accent was always of a more personal, though not necessarily more individual, nature. Gide's Oedipus finds in himself the answer to the riddle of the Sphinx; Rolland, too, found the answer in himself, but more especially in creation as the whole, of which he was a part.

Gide and Rolland both rejected the solution of organized religion as an answer to their questions. Gide classified

Catholicism as inadmissible, Protestantism as intolerable, and yet felt himself to be profoundly Christian.[43] Since their thinking along these lines was much alike, one is somewhat taken aback by one particular reference Gide made to Rolland, calling him an atheist. It occurred in a letter to Roger Martin du Gard dated September 11, 1948, concerning a possible deathbed conversion of Romain Rolland.

> Is it true that Romain Rolland, when he was dying, received a visit from Claudel; after which the unyielding atheist is supposed to have had a priest come and received the last sacraments, etc. This is what I read, not without amazement, in an Italian newspaper that lets me have it with a spicy sauce and hopes that Romain Rolland will serve as a good example to me.[44]

Romain Rolland was not an atheist in the proper sense of the term, just as Gide was not. He did not deny the existence of God, and, as with Gide, the problem is rather what he meant by the word "God." Like Gide, he stayed clear of organized religion, and this is what makes definition elusive.

> This is my only profession of faith:
> Since the age of fifteen, I have lived free from all established religions. But I respect the freedom of all those who believe—insofar as their belief is not intolerant or oppressive for others. My respect does not go out to one form of thinking—with or without God or Gods—but to men personally worthy of respect.[45]

Claudel, no doubt, would have liked to convert Rolland, just as he would have liked to convert Gide. He made mention of two instances in January and February, 1943, when Rolland was near death and underwent what might be called a religious experience.

He himself has written about it, and I have before my eyes at this moment the story of this amazing experience. He has three "visions," he uses the word himself, and one day or another I shall have to speak of them. "I was going to die," he said, "I knew myself to be at the very threshold of the abyss. At that moment I felt sustained and comforted by the prayers of all those friends, and especially my Catholic friends, who were lifting up their voices to God for me. I felt that burning communion of Christian souls, coming to the assistance of one among them in danger, and the bonds with which they surround God who himself aspires to that reciprocity of love. All this penetrated the arid solitude of fever; it was like the affectionate pressure of a friendly hand. Sublime idea of a God made man who at every moment sacrifices himself out of love for one and all, and of the communion of the faithful who associate themselves with this sacrifice, and participate in the measure of their ability. What consolation for the heart that in times of distress finds nothing for itself in an icy pantheism, which was sufficient in days of health! Moral poverty of pantheism! A Being in whom all beings are absorbed. What good if He and they are impersonal? This does not take into any account the real problem of the self—the selves (in the plural), this infinity of selves." [46]

Romain Rolland did not die in 1943; he "came back," as Claudel said. But even Claudel could not say that he came back to the faith. Belief in a personal God would certainly have been a powerful source of emotional and psychological stability and comfort to Rolland as he was approaching death, but his reason refused. In his biography of Rolland, Jacques Robichez noted that when Rolland agreed in his will to be given a religious funeral, he did so, not out of adhesion to Catholic dogma, but out of affection for those who loved him and believed. "Despite all, he holds himself on the threshold of belief without crossing it. . . . His heart, in a mighty surge, inclines him toward the faith. But

faith does not satisfy his religious exigence for truth." [47]
Claudel could say, quite truthfully, however, "Romain
Rolland's religious conceptions were not those of the Catholic
faith, but he was never an enemy of the Church that professes
them." [48]

Though Claudel's presentation is clear, his overzealous
terminology is apt to give rise to false impressions. Claudel
presented the description of the inner conflict Rolland experienced at the end of his life as Rolland himself supposedly
had given it. But in his enthusiasm Claudel exaggerated
somewhat when he called that description a "confession."

> "Strange duality of my nature! A reason, firm, composed,
> and inflexible, which does not believe, and on which no
> argument of faith takes hold. An instinct of the heart that
> abandons itself to flights of prayer—and perhaps especially
> to the mighty current of the invisible river that flows under-
> ground from centuries of believing souls who preceded me
> and gave me birth. Thus we go along on two parallel roads,
> without being able to do anything for each other, but with-
> out collision." "My reason refuses to believe," he says else-
> where, "but the word refuse is inexact, it cannot." [49]

For Romain Rolland, Christianity as a basically Western
experience did not suffice; for him religion must be world-
embracing. Though Christ remained a truly great figure for
Rolland, he was not the only one of his kind. There was
Buddha in the Orient, and the monism of the East was as
valid a way to truth as the dualism of the West.[50] Despite all,
Christ was still a man, and Rolland asked Tolstoy in a letter
of 1901 not to forget this. Both Christ and Christianity are
human, and no argument is valid simply because a great
man said so. Truth makes the greatness of a man, not the
man the greatness of the truth: "as religious as we may be,
and as convinced that every man carries divine light within
himself, we can only accept the viewpoint of reason—precisely

because reason seems to us to be the radiance of God within us." [51]

Christ united men in love, and this mission Rolland took it upon himself to advance. In *Pierre et Luce,* a short novel that appeared after the war, Rolland portrayed his two young heroes speaking of the coming Good Friday and the Passion of Christ. "Do you believe in Him?" asks Luce. And Pierre responds that he doesn't believe anymore. "But he will always remain a friend to those who have once received at his table." Pierre then asks her if she will go the next day "for his death" to Saint-Gervais, where there will be good music. Luce answers, "Yes, I would like to go to church with you on that day. Being close to him, we are closer to each other." [52]

For Gide, Christ did not fulfill precisely the same role. Gide had far greater need for Christ in his own personal life than did Rolland. Rolland lived two lives, and what he lacked in one was compensated for in the other. For a long time, the first of these lives obscured the second. Before maturity, and with it the achievement of direct communion with "la Vie universelle," Rolland had lived separated from that universal life.[53] But as he matured the imbalance was corrected. "I have always lived two lives in parallel—one, that of the person the combinations of hereditary elements have made me assume, in a particular location in space and at a moment in time—the other, that of Being without countenance, without name, or location, or century, which is the substance and breath of life." [54]

For Gide, however, the idea of a universal life provided inadequate consolation. His own needs were more immediate and too personal in nature. On a trip to North Africa with his friend Paul Laurens to find an ideal of *équilibre, plénitude,* and *santé,* Gide wrote: "I did not say good-bye to Christ without a kind of rupture, so that I doubt at present whether I really left him." [55] And still earlier he quoted in the *André*

Walter: "I do not know—I do not know anything. You called me, I have come. I do not know you; I do not know who you are nor even if you are; but I have come to you so that your divine heart will not sorrow because of me, if at times you did exist and you want me." [56]

Christ was both human and divine, but it might be argued that Gide conceived of humanity as divine, and then the distinction loses in importance. What Gide wanted, in any case, was not to believe Christ's word because he was the Son of God, but rather to recognize him as the Son of God because his word was divine.[57]

What disturbed Gide more than Christ's identity was the problem he himself called *"le Christianisme contre le Christ."* He was grieved and outraged by what the churches had done to Christ's teaching. There was so little in them of the Jesus portrayed in the Gospels. "Catholicism has linked to the figure of Christ and to his teaching a whole procession of ideas and a whole set of attitudes, so closely that it is today very difficult to reject the one without the other. . . ." [58] So tight had the bond become between Christ and the Catholic Church that any thought or attitude foreign to the Church appeared equally foreign to Christ. As a result, if one were not a Catholic, one could not be a Christian. "Yet as for these attacks against Christianity, Christ never deserved them, but the Church did; and everything I think against it today, I do so with Him." [59]

The interpretation of men had placed a mask of sadness and suffering over the Gospels.[60] The problem of Christ against the Church, or more accurately, of the Church against Christ, is broached allegorically by Gide's prodigal son, who tells his father that he left home because the House was too enclosing for him. "The House is not You, my Father." [61] The father replies that it is he himself who has created the House, and the son answers: "Ah! You did not say that, but rather my brother. You, You built the whole earth, both the

House and what is not the House. The House, others than
You have built it; in Your name, I know, but others than
You." [62]

The father then probes. Was it not out of love that you
returned? "Father, I told you, I never loved you more than
in the desert. But I was tired of having to go after my food
every morning. In the house, at least, we eat well." And the
father regrets having spoken harshly: the eldest brother, who
for Gide symbolized the Church, had wanted it so. It was he
who had said, no salvation outside the House.[63] "But listen:
I have fashioned you; I know what is in you. I know what
drove you out onto the roads; I was waiting for you at the
end of the trip. You would have called me... I was there.—
Come now; come home to the room I have had prepared for
you." [64]

The father is like Jesus. His words are the ones promised
by the Christ of the Scriptures to those who would be saved.
He is tender and human, the qualities Gide needed and that
his own temperament demanded of Christ. Romain Rolland,
perhaps somewhat more secure in his own skin, and therefore
probably also in his relations with others, could not feel this
need for the "côté Christ" to the same intensity. But it was
precisely this need that helped usher Gide into the path of
communism in the 1930's.

VII   The Morality of Individualism

Gide's preoccupation with the nature of God does not seem to have been born primarily of intellectual curiosity. Rather it stemmed from an emotional, physical, and moral necessity. Brought up in a religious atmosphere at home, Gide felt, when he was confronted with the riddle of the Sphinx, that he must first of all establish for himself what was man's relation to God before he could answer that riddle. Like Oedipus, he looked into his own being and found there the answers that men normally seek from a god. The God he recognized was a God within himself.[1] Like Oedipus, he was liberated from the doctrine and the morals preached and exacted by the established religions. Wisdom began, according to Gide, when the individual stopped fearing God and when he freed himself from all undue respect for any one or any thing: "all respect calls for a blindness from which one must be freed in order to progress toward the light."[2]

Liberation, though essential, was only a first step. "Free to what end?" Gide did not sanction anarchy; he held in horror a liberty that was not guided by a sense of duty.[3] One is not simply free, but free for a purpose, and that

102

purpose for Gide was to realize God in oneself. This was done first of all by being oneself. When Bernard in the *Faux-Monnayeurs* tells Edouard that he cannot accept a life *sans règle,* but that, by the same token, he could not accept the rule of life from another person, Edouard responds: "The answer seems simple to me: to find that rule in oneself; to have for an end the development of oneself." [4] One must be true to oneself, and if there is an opposition between being moral and being sincere, then option must be made for the latter. Man must derive his morals from within himself, he must not allow them to be superimposed from without. For such superimposed morals supplant the natural being, whom Gide calls "le vieil homme," with an artificial being who cannot be sincere. The old man was the sincere man.[5]

In Gide's estimation, Oedipus, with his heritage unknown, is in a privileged position. He has no past and consequently no model to which to conform, nothing on which to lean; he can create everything for himself, country and ancestors; he can invent and discover, for he has no one to resemble but himself. He can afford to be sincere. Oedipus asks how his brother-in-law Creon, submissive and conforming as he is, could possibly understand the beauty of such an existence. "It is a call to valor not to know one's parents." [6]

The problem of liberation was no simple one. Gide examined the faculty of reason and found it in perpetual opposition to the soul it sought to restrain and limit. "I have never known a happiness of which my reason does not disapprove." [7] In obeying one's passions, one appears to be a slave, but when one escapes these passions and lives according to what is acknowledged by the majority as a standard, one is considered free. One form of slavery has merely been exchanged for another, the slavery of the passions for a moral servitude. One now listens to reason and has the illusion of being free. But the difficulty experienced in welding one's nature to the dictates of reason should serve as a gauge of the error.[8] Gide proposed to man an escape from the oppression of reason, and in the *Nourritures terrestres* he, or the narrator, condemned himself for the spiritual blindness of a life that had been too empty. "In default of logic I become conscious of myself. O my dearest and happiest thought! What business have I to seek any longer to legitimize your birth." [9]

Gide's purpose was not to discard reason but to limit its influence, allowing it to intervene only in those areas that concerned it exclusively. At the call of emotion, reason must be cast aside. [10] A new rule of life is adopted as the only valid one: "to act in accord with the greatest sincerity."

In the case of one who can act without prior reflection, the smallest efforts take on a greater significance. Since they are no longer reasoned, they are truer to oneself. [11] Man must live without laws that he may hear the new law, [12] and so heed only that law which the heart dictates. "Nathanaël, ah! satisfy your joy while your soul yet smiles—and your desire for love while your lips are yet beautiful to kiss, and while your embrace is glad." [13]

Intuitive knowledge is sufficient in the search for the self, for the unformulated is the most precious part of oneself, [14] and religion, now freed from the shackles of reason, will be based solely on love. [15]

> I soon no longer felt my soul but as a will to love . . . throbbing, open to all comers, like unto all things, impersonal, a simple incohesiveness of gluttonous appetites and desires. . . . So I abandoned myself to this more sincere and natural disorder that would organize, all by itself, I thought, considering furthermore that even disorder was not so dangerous to my soul as an arbitrary order that had to be factitious since I had not invented it. [16]

Although Gide once again temporarily consented to acknowledge the law and the sin that would follow, it is evident that he did so with regret: "I was once without law, and I lived." [17]

Gide affirmed his true self when he wrote in his *Journal:* "everything must be questioned anew . . ." [18] Adoration of the past must not be allowed to prevail over the future, and if Bossuet could say that there was nothing more opposed to the life of grace than a life according to nature, Gide replied, *tant pis.*[19] "Nathanaël, I shall teach you that all things are divinely natural." [20]

> Commandments of God, you have saddened my soul. . . .
> Will you always teach that there are always more things forbidden?
> New punishments promised for thirsting after everything that I shall have found beautiful on the earth?
> Commandments of God, you have made my soul ill.[21]

The narrator tells Nathanaël of the anxiety that had plagued his youth. The only way he could be sure of not sinning was by not acting at all, and the salvation of his flesh was bought at the expense of the imprisonment of his soul. "Nathanaël, I no longer believe in sin." [22]

One must dare to act, and Gide's approval went to the soul that found happiness in the experience of its own turbulent activity. "To live with intensity—this is the most wonderful thing." [23] *"Being* became exceedingly sensuous to me." [24] Gide wanted to taste all forms of life; for to do good, one must be capable of doing evil, and, only then, refrain from performing it. Virtue performed in blindness did not deserve the name, and here Gide could speak from the experience of his own youth.[25] If man was to cast his blindness aside, he must first know life, living it to the full, and not think of sin and death.[26] "Let the dead bury their dead," Gide wrote, quoting from the New Testament and reproaching Christianity for not heeding the words of Christ.[27] Death would not be particularly difficult for those who had loved life the most,[28] and his own great regret was not to have taken greater advantage of his younger days.[29]

Already in 1890, in a note inserted in the *Traité du Narcisse,* Gide had spelled out some thoughts on how man should live: "Every phenomenon is the Symbol of a Truth. Its only duty is to manifest it. Its only sin: to prefer itself. . . . Every man who does not manifest is useless and bad." [30]

What man is to manifest he learns by listening to the silence of the universe. He learns to be himself, and throughout the range of Gide's career, this theme of sincerity was the dominant one. Seek not to resemble others, to fit yourself into the mold they have cast for you, even though they resist what is new and oppose what is different. Thus the older brother reprimands the prodigal son returned home: "You will never know how long it has taken for man to elaborate man. Now that the model has been found, let us stick by it." [31] But man must not remain attached to the model, and in his autobiographical *Si le grain ne meurt,* Gide protested against those who tried to teach him how to live:

> In the name of what God, of what ideal, do you forbid me to live according to my nature?... Until now I had accepted the morality of Christ, or at least a certain puritanism that I had been taught as being Christ's morality. By forcing myself to submit to it, I had achieved only the deep disarray of my whole being. . . . But I am coming to the point of doubting whether God himself exacted such constraint? [32]

Gide found it unprofitable and uninstructive to judge human actions or to appraise their value from the standpoint of good and evil. The reassuring bourgeois idea of the good was a sedative lulling humanity into stagnation, whereas what society called evil could have greater instructive value and so might serve as a guide to progress.[33] Narrow were the

minds that thought theirs the only truth. For things to become true it was sufficient for us to think them true.[34] The
youngest brother, he who had idealized the prodigal, later
approaches him disappointedly, "So you have ended up by
renouncing what you wanted to be." [35] The boy decides,
nevertheless, that he must leave the house just as his brother
had once done, and though the prodigal is resigned to his
own submission, he embraces his younger brother: "you
take with you all my hopes. Be strong; forget us; and forget
me. May you not come back." [36]

Man must have the courage to burst the model fashioned
for him, for if he would not show himself as he was, he was
worthless. *To be* was essential and not to seem, Philoctète
discovered in the loneliness of his island.[37] In like fashion,
Ménalque advised Michel in the *Immoraliste:*

> We are afraid of finding ourselves alone: and we do not
> find ourselves at all. . . . What we experience as different
> in ourselves is precisely what is extraordinary in us, what
> gives each one of us value; and this is what we try to sup-
> press. We imitate, and then we say we love life.[38]

As if the common were more natural than the rare.[39] The
average man was of little consequence for he could be found
everywhere and replaced.[40] God himself must look in horror
at the uniformity imposed by the Christian ideal in its campaign to silence nature.[41]

> I was convinced that every being, or at least the elect, had
> a role to play on earth, his very own, which resembled no
> other; so that every effort of submission to a common rule
> became a betrayal in my eyes; yes, a betrayal, and I likened
> it to that great sin against the Spirit—that would not be
> pardoned—by which a particular being lost his significance,
> special and irreplaceable, his—flavor—that could not be given
> back to him.[42]

André Gide's highly individualistic morality was shared to some degree by Romain Rolland. But for Rolland the problem of morality did not assume the dimensions it did for Gide. In fact, there was no real problem at all, and those thoughts on morality that he did record showed as little tendency to waver as did his thoughts on God.

Life was as important to Rolland as to Gide, and a notation he made at the Ecole Normale on June 17, 1888, is a veritable hymn to life. "Life! the foundation of my nature, that which defines it and makes it inexplicable to others around me, that which fulfills me. It is my faith, my art, and my will. Beauty and goodness are for me equal to life." [43]

Like Gide, Rolland recognized that the "moi" was not "haïssable." Each man's obligation was to be himself and the task could not be a simple one, for opposition was bound to come from the majority who fell into the mold that society had created. Just how stormy this opposition could be Rolland himself knew from the old days of World War I when hatred and contempt were heaped upon him from every corner. His hero Christophe, forced to cast aside his illusions about life in Paris, experiences the same bitter lesson: "all men were everywhere the same; one had to make up one's mind about that and not become obstinate in a childish struggle against the world; one had to be oneself, with composure." [44] This was the secret.

To abdicate one's own being to espouse another was only to destroy oneself, and it brought gain for none. "One's primary duty is to be what one is. To have the courage to say: 'This is good, this is bad.' One does more good for the weak in being strong than in becoming weak like them." [45] Rolland saw the world suffering not so much from the evil of the bad as from the weakness of the good, a weakness rooted in laziness and in the fear of making personal judgments, in moral timidity.[46]

Rolland advocated indulgence toward weaknesses committed, but never compromise with a weakness one might have the tendency to commit.[47] Gide might have preferred first to investigate the tendency, and again there is divergence.

When he and Rolland spoke of being true to the self, the term did not have the same significance for them. When Olivier's son George visits Christophe, who is now no longer a young man, he expresses the need of the human mind to think in a group. The mind needs certitude, it needs to think along with others, to adhere to certain principles admitted by all men of a certain time. The still independent-minded Christophe exclaims in surprise, "Find your own laws. Look into yourself." [48] These were not the laws Gide had in mind when he directed the gaze of Oedipus down into the depths of his own being.

When Rolland told man to be himself, he was addressing not the moral but the intellectual side of man. Even more than moral entities, good and bad were intellectual entities. It was not so much to man under the cover of his own house that Rolland spoke as to the man of action, the man who had to think for himself in the crowd. One cannot in the full sense of the word speak of individualism in the case of Rolland. For him it was not the individual but society that deserved prime consideration. The difference between Rolland and Gide in questions of ethics was a difference between a public and a private morality; the difference between the man of action and the artist; the difference between a man who, though an extreme individualist, regarded humanity as more important than the individual, and a man who regarded the individual as more important than humanity. In Gide's eyes it was only when each individual had become what he was that humanity and society could be what they should be.

VIII Gide, Rolland, and Communism

Some of the beliefs and concerns that had held Gide's attention and sparked his imagination during youth and middle age he found wanting as he grew older. Chief among these was his overriding commitment to the individual, and by the 1930's this commitment had begun to waver. The postwar world gave birth to a social conscience that had existed only in an embryo state before 1914, and in this new world Gide hesitated and faltered.

> For a long time I was convinced that the moral question was more important than the social question. I said and I wrote: "Man is more important than men." . . . I believed that for forty years: today I am no longer so sure.[1]

Virtually going against his own way of thinking, Gide made a choice. His choice was to support the experiment in communism undertaken by Soviet Russia. On May 13, 1931, he wrote in his *Journal:*

110

But above all I should like to live long enough to see Russia's plan succeed and the states of Europe obliged to accept what they insisted on ignoring.[2]

This first open avowal of support for the communist venture was published in the *Nouvelle Revue Française* of July, 1932, with the undramatic heading, "Pages du Journal," and was to be followed in September by another statement in favor of Soviet Russia that Gide had written in his *Journal* more than one year earlier on July 27, 1931: [3]

I should like to cry aloud my affection for Russia; and that my cry should be heard, should have importance. I should like to live long enough to see the success of that tremendous effort; its realization, which I wish with all my soul and for which I should like to work. To see what can be produced by a state without religion,* a society without the family.[4] Religion and the family are the two worst enemies of progress.[5]

* Without religion? Perhaps not. But a religion without mythology. [Gide's footnote]

Though he had always sought to remain open and alive to all possibilities, and not to limit these possibilities by making a choice, Gide saw in the choice he made no radical departure from his basic tenets. In his eyes, just as in the eyes of Romain Rolland, Christianity had failed, and he recognized that there was no Christian society in existence worthy of the name.

When one thinks of the teaching of Christ and when one sees what the modern world has made of it, one is deeply distressed. . . . I consider Christianity to have gone bankrupt. I have written and profoundly believe that if Christianity had been able to impose itself, if the teaching of

Christ had been accepted such as it was, there would be no
question of communism today. There would not even be a
social question.[6]

Even though he was at variance with the teachings of the
Christian churches, Gide never ceased to regard himself as
a true Christian, and he could find no contradiction between
his own conception of Christianity and the ideals of communism. Indeed he felt that Christianity had led him to
communism. His mind was not that of a politician, an econ-
omist, or a sociologist; his mind was that of an artist, and
his temperament a very human one. These two factors are
essential to an understanding of Gide's "conversion" to communism. As an artist, he needed his independence; as a
Christian and as a humanitarian, he had a conscience alive
to the social evils of the world, and this especially after what
he had observed on a voyage to the Congo in 1925. Born into
a family of relative ease, his own favored position in the
world seemed intolerable to him. He spoke of refusing to
learn the property limits of the Norman estate at La Roque
that he had inherited from his mother. He did not want to
think that all that he loved at La Roque was personally and
exclusively his, and he decided that his soul was that of a
communist, and not that of a proprietor.[7]

The belief that there is an afterlife that will compensate
the oppressed for the evils suffered in the present mollifies
those who might otherwise cry out in revenge. It makes them
the playthings of their oppressors, who find it to their advantage to proclaim themselves Christians, all the while ignoring the precepts of Christ.[8] Confronted with the attitudes
of certain rich people, Gide asked in his *Journal* in 1918:
"how can one fail to feel communistically inclined?"[9]

At one point Gide said that he had become a communist
so as not to disappoint certain friends whom he admired.[10]
This may be true, and it reflects a rather unfortunate side

of Gide's character; but whatever the case may have been, when Gide "converted" to communism, he did not see it as a break with the past, but as the continuation and fructification of the principles to which he had always adhered.

> in heart as well as mind I have always been a communist; even while remaining a Christian; and this is why I had such trouble separating them from each other, and even more trouble opposing them to each other. I should never have reached this point all alone. It required people and events to educate me. Do not speak of "conversion" in this case; I have not changed direction; I have always walked forward; I am continuing to do so; the great difference is that for a long time I saw nothing in front of me but space and the projection of my own fervor; at present I am going forward while orienting myself toward something; I know that somewhere my vague desires are being organized and that my dream is on the way to becoming reality.
>
> Howbeit, utterly unfit for politics. Do not therefore ask me to belong to a Party.[11]

Romain Rolland's relationship to communism was of a somewhat different nature, and its roots went back much further in time. Though it was not Christianity that drew him to communism, he would have seen no contradiction between communism and a Christianity that lived up to the teachings of Christ. His "Souvenirs de Jeunesse," forming the first part of his *Mémoires,* show that already in 1889, on the evening of the opening of the Exposition du Centenaire, he felt himself more drawn to the idea of the Republic than to France; believing in a Republic of the future that would embrace the whole world, he would sacrifice his fatherland to the Republic as he would sacrifice his life to God.

> My social ideas went no further. The socialist thinking of Jaurès had not yet made an impression on France's young

bourgeoisie. Our education left a lot to be desired. My socialism was one born only of instinct. But in a few years
everything was going to change.[12]

As Rolland grew older his ideas on government and social
structure began to take form. Having lived through World
War I and its aftermath, he became convinced that the only
practical way to abolish war was to abolish the present system of government and the present structure of society,
which he saw as the cause of war.[13]

In January, 1933, Léon Pierre-Quint published a comprehensive study of Gide's work in which he explored the beginning of Gide's struggle with the communist "temptation."
Pierre-Quint drew a parallel between the thought of Gide
and Rolland, saying that it was remarkable that another
great mind, whom Gide at times had slighted on literary
grounds, should arrive at almost the same moment at such
similar conclusions. Rolland was outraged and responded
quickly, protesting that Pierre-Quint had simply chosen to
ignore the efforts he had made in behalf of communism ever
since the war. He resented the comparison between himself
and this "nouveau venu."

> I thank you for your kind words—both on (?) and in your
> book. I have just paged through it with interest and I will
> read it attentively. But I cannot wait to protest against an
> improbable error concerning me.
>   On p. 323 you write:
>   "Is it not striking *that at the same moment*" (in 1932 then!)
> "Romain Rolland" (I skip all the epithets) "comes *almost
> at the same time* as Gide to conclusions analogous to his
> own? *In terms very close to those used by Gide* R.R. has
> declared himself in favor of Russia's great experiment."
>   These lines denote such a disregard (ignorance) of my un-
> interrupted action for the last *fifteen years* on behalf of the
> Russian Revolution that I find them revolting. I know what

casualness postwar French writers uniformly display in regard to history. But this goes beyond all limit.

Need I remind you that less than three months after the Russian Revolution, on May 1, 1917, I sent from Geneva a Salut "à la Russie libre et libératrice" (see "Les Précurseurs")—that in August and September, 1918, I was affirming my feeling of *"international solidarity with Russian Bolshevism"*—that in August, 1919, in my "Déclaration d'indépendance de l'esprit," I declared that *"Russian thinking is the avant-garde of world thinking"*—that ever since then, untiringly, for twelve years, I have written and published to extol or defend the Russian Revolution—. . . . If I have retained my freedom of discussion with my friends, the Russian communists, and if in their newspapers, and in Russia itself, I have engaged in more than one free debate with Bolshevik theorists, on this or that point of doctrine, I have always fought for the Russian Revolution and for the heroic work of Lenin and Stalin.

Rolland added that in reviews such as *Comoedia* and the *Nouvelles Littéraires,* not to mention the *N.R.F.,*

there is little chance of one's being aware of what I think and what I write. But there isn't a communist in the U.S.S.R. who is not aware. . . .

I am accustomed to many inaccuracies about myself from French writers; and I do not waste my time answering them. But from you, whom I hold in esteem, I will indeed not let pass in silence an assertion that so distorts or suppresses fifteen years of my life. It is an atrocity to represent me, vis-à-vis the Russian Revolution, as a follower of your eleventh-hour man—whose rallying to the cause I do appreciate moreover.[14]

Romain Rolland's contention was, of course, quite true. He dated the beginning of his own political activity from August, 1914.

Only in August, 1914, and very much in spite of myself, did I become concerned with politics. Until then I had been imbued with the ideology of my time and class, which I denounce . . . the ideology of *the abstract man,* detached they said then, freed from the contingencies of political and social life. It would not have seemed worthy of a writer's concern.[15]

Rolland recalled in 1927, ten years after the revolution in Russia, that he was among the first in Europe to acclaim that revolution.[16] On May 1, 1917, he had published from Geneva a statement of support for the revolutionaries in an article entitled "À la Russie libre et libératrice."

Brothers in Russia, you who have just accomplished your great Revolution, we have not only to congratulate you; we thank you. Not for yourselves alone have you labored in winning your liberty, but for us all, your brothers of the old Western world.[17]

He called on the Russian revolutionaries to complete the work of the French revolution; and his faith did not diminish with the passage of time. That the revolution in Russia was not free from certain wrongs, stupidities, and even crimes, he recognized full well, but he did not allow that fact to obscure his basic confidence. He looked upon this revolution as the greatest, most powerful, and most fruitful social effort undertaken in modern Europe.[18]

By the 1930's even Gide was impressed. Though his primary interests had always resided elsewhere, he noted in his *Journal* on July 19, 1932, his growing obsession with social problems.

When I had begun this new notebook, I had promised myself, however, not to deal with such questions here. The result of this was simply that I spent several weeks without writing anything. These questions preoccupy me almost exclusively; I constantly return to them and cannot turn my thought away from them. Yes, really, I think of almost nothing else.[19]

From 1932 on until Gide's final break with communism, accomplished unequivocally with the publication of the *Retouches à mon Retour de l'U.R.S.S.* in 1937, the ties between Gide and Romain Rolland were renewed and strengthened. During this period they met again, this time in Switzerland, and their names appeared together in association with a number of congresses and organizations.

In 1932 some attention was aroused by a poem that Louis Aragon published in the review *Littérature de la Révolution Mondiale*. The poem was entitled "Front rouge," and was a glorification of communism, a satire on the aristocracy, and an incitement to disorder. When Aragon faced a court charge and a sentence of five years in prison, his fellow surrealist, André Breton, took up his defense, protesting against the right of the court to interpret a poetic text for judicial ends.

> The charge against Aragon for his poem "Front Rouge," which appeared in the review *Littérature de la Révolution Mondiale,* a charge that carries with it a penalty of five years' imprisonment, constitutes an action without precedent in France.
> We rise against any attempt to interpret a poetic text for judicial ends and demand the immediate cessation of the proceedings.[20]

In their campaign to lift the charges against Aragon, the surrealists attempted to engage the support of Gide and Rolland. But neither would consent to sign the petition, Gide assuring the surrealists that for the time being there was a question only of inquest and not of indictment.

In his *Misère de la poésie* Breton spoke of this attempt to enlist Gide's and Rolland's support. He related a scene in the Café de la Légion d'Honneur, where Gide spoke with a surrealist delegate about the "affaire Aragon," convinced that nothing would come of the charges. Gide said that he himself had gone to the Ministry of Justice and that the ministry did not wish to follow up on the charges. He hinted that a change of cabinet might alter Aragon's situation, but presumed that a new cabinet would, if anything, be further to the left. And then, quite suddenly enlarging the scope of the conversation, he asked:

> why demand impunity for literature? . . . Thought is as dangerous as action. We are dangerous people. It is an honor to be condemned under such a regime.[21]

Rolland's response to the surrealists came in the form of a letter from Villeneuve on February 4, 1932. He disagreed with Breton that a poetic text could not be interpreted for judicial purposes and refused to approve the terms of the protest, "for the very honor of Aragon and the Surrealists." In Rolland's estimation a writer was responsible for what he had written, and if what he had written was revolutionary in nature, he could not, on poetic grounds, escape responsibility for the consequences.

> We are combatants. Our writings are our arms. We are responsible for our arms just as are our worker comrades or soldiers. Instead of denying them, we are obliged to accept responsibility for them. Let each one of us be judged individually for the arms he uses.[22]

Postwar Europe was as divided as ever and the efforts at disarmament that characterized the twenties seemed doomed to failure, as nationalist forces came to power. The thought of another war was ghastly to Rolland, and this time Gide joined him in his work for pacifism. On May 28, 1932, the weekly *Monde* announced the meeting of a world congress against war, and Rolland among others, such as Mme Sun Yat Sen, Theodore Dreiser, Albert Einstein, Maxim Gorki, and Upton Sinclair, was on the *comité d'initiative*. After his *Appel* of June 17 addressing all men of good will to unite against war, even Gide asked to have his name added to the rosters. On July 7, Gide wrote to Félicien Challaye: [23]

> I beg you to add my name to the signatures of those who, without distinction of homeland, faction, or religion, are declaring themselves ready to oppose war with all their might; in whatever form it might take, in whatever form it might skillfully be displayed for us by those who direct public opinion.[24]

The congress was held in Amsterdam from August 27 to 29, and Rolland's efforts even before the actual date of assembly were not negligible. On June 10 he addressed an *Appel* to the Ligue des Combattants de la Paix, warning them that war was hanging over Europe and blaming the Versailles treaties of 1919 for the uneasy peace. War had to be opposed, and the most practical method of opposing it, he felt, was to refuse to bear arms, to insist on the right of conscientious objection.[25]

Addressing the congress in Amsterdam, Rolland reminded the delegates that "the purpose of thought is action." [26] Gide did not go to Amsterdam, and his association with the congress remained theoretical.[27] But even this theoretical support did not escape Rolland's approving notice.

> let us remember the statement of adherence addressed to the Congress by an élite of French intellectuals in whose first rank . . . André Gide, whose recent declarations have stirred the anxiety of the bourgeoisie of all countries. . . .[28]

Also in 1932, there was formed in France an Association des Ecrivains et Artistes Révolutionnaires, the A.E.A.R., based on a Soviet counterpart. Its guiding principles were relatively simple: first, there was no such thing as a neutral art or neutral literature; and second, the revolutionary art and literature already in existence in France and the proletarian art and literature now coming into being, and needing development, must be made to come together in common purpose and so mirror the rapprochement of the intellectuals and the workers.[29] The A.E.A.R. was decidedly antifascist, and both Rolland and Gide became allied with it in protest against events in Germany. Hitler had become chancellor on January 30, 1933, and when the Reichstag was burned on the night of February 26–27, he used this as a pretext to arrest thousands considered subversive to the government. On February 28, the guarantee of individual liberties that had been part of the Weimar constitution was suspended. A meeting of the A.E.A.R. held in Paris on March 21, 1933, reflected this state of affairs.[30] Romain Rolland did not attend the meeting, but from Valmont on March 20 he addressed a letter of support.

> Though I am ill, I do not want my voice to be absent from your meeting of protest against the butchers of Germany. Let these murderers, these torturers, be dealt a blow in the face by the giant fist of the revolutionary masses of the world! In the space of a few weeks these madmen have made the Western world slip back several centuries.[31]

As for Gide, he was not only present but addressed the meeting in words that could easily have been spoken years earlier by Rolland.

> The social struggle is the same for all countries, and the peoples who are sent out to fight, for reasons which escape them and of which they would often disapprove if they really knew what they were, these peoples all have the same deep interest and they are beginning to be aware of it.

The soldiers who died during the course of the Great War, and were told that they were making war against war, had been wronged. The only way to wage war against war, Gide affirmed, was to wage war on imperialism, each in his own country, "for all imperialism necessarily engenders war." [32]

Germany had deprived some of her citizens of their political voice. This had also happened in Russia, but for Gide the purpose there was different. There an abuse of force was perhaps necessary to establish a new society: "in German terrorism, I see a return to and a revival of a most deplorable past. In the establishment of Soviet society, an unlimited promise of the future." [33] What he condoned in Russia he would not condone in Germany.

Gide and Rolland reacted to the Germany of the thirties in a more united fashion than they had to the Germany of 1914. Both men were enemies of Nazism, and both spoke out against it. The *ordre du jour* adopted unanimously by the A.E.A.R. at its meeting of March 21 roundly condemned fascism, at the same time, however, assigning a large share of the blame for the situation in Germany to French imperialism, which the association held responsible for the advent of Hitler. The German people had been reduced to a state of despair.[34] Romain Rolland himself wrote on May 14, 1933, to the *Kölnische Zeitung:*

> The future will enlighten you—too late—on your deadly error, whose only excuse is the delirium of despair into which the blindness and harshness of your conquerors at Versailles cast your people for fifteen years.
>
> For myself, I shall maintain in spite of you, and against you, my attachment to Germany—to the true Germany—dishonored by the crimes and aberrations of Hitler's fascism.[35]

Rolland condemned the Germany of the thirties perhaps even more severely than he had condemned the Germany of

World War I, but again he refused to lose sight of that "other" Germany, *la vraie Allemagne,* as he called it.

From September 22 to 24, 1933, a Congrès Mondial de la Jeunesse contre la Guerre et le Fascisme was convened in Paris, under the honorary chairmanship of Gide, Rolland, and Henri Barbusse, among others.[36] On September 1, Gide noted in his *Journal* the response that he had sent in August to a questionnaire circulated by the *comité d'initiative:*

In this autumn of 1933, before the arrogant resurgence of nationalisms, before the glorification of ancient idols in whose name nations are being led to combat, the anniversary of the Russian Revolution takes on a particular importance. We must take advantage of it to consolidate our union.

Today people claim to see Moscow propaganda in every popular uprising in any country whatever; that there is propaganda goes without saying, but perhaps not in the way people think. The event whose sixteenth anniversary we are celebrating today has, in itself and in its example, a sufficient force of persuasion, far more stimulating than subsidies and speeches; no repression can do anything against it. The chief force of that propaganda is that it favors a legitimate aspiration. The example of the October days aroused peoples from the despondency in which capitalistic oppression maintained them. The great cry uttered by the U.S.S.R. aroused all hopes, but would not have found an echo if it had not replied, for so many hearts, to so many muffled moans; for so many minds, to so many obvious failures.

There was a time when it was toward France, after 1789, that all eyes turned. But the cause we cherish today is no longer that of a single country. The enemy remains the same, in France as well as everywhere; it is against him that we must unite our efforts. That the U.S.S.R. still has to overcome very great difficulties of all sorts, it may be; but those who shout failure are rejoicing a bit too soon; it is important to prove this to them.[37]

On August 14 Gide had remarked in his *Journal* that the question of conscientious objection was one the congress should consider, and, like Romain Rolland, he went on record as approving it.

> It seems to me that the World Congress in preparation must pay quite special attention to honoring the young people who refuse to take part in the game of war, English or American students, French school-teachers, "objectors" of all countries; to clearing them of that perfidious accusation of cowardice by which people try to discredit them and disqualify their conduct. It is important to let them know, in reply to such calumnies, that we give them our esteem, often even our admiration, knowing full well that it requires more real courage to be opposed individually to a collective enthusiasm than to follow the example, even if it were in order to face death; knowing all the initiative that this personal courage involves, and that it leads, not only to material sanctions, but also to those, even more dreadful for some, of opinion.
>
> It behooves this congress to propose this new form of heroism to youth.[38]

Gide approved of conscientious objection as a means to oppose war, and yet by September 1, the day on which he recorded in his *Journal* the declaration of support for the Russian revolution that he had sent to the *comité d'initiative* the preceding August, he still had not sent a statement on the question of conscientious objection to the congress.

> My reply to the "conscientious objectors" has been lying on my table for a fortnight; I have not been able to make up my mind to send it. Not that my thought (I was about to say: my conviction) is uncertain on this point; but I am held back by the fear that it might be used to force me to play a political role for which I feel utterly unqualified.[39]

Already on June 31, however, Barbusse, in the weekly *Monde* of which he was the editor, had mentioned Gide's name among the members of the *comité d'initiative* of the congress. But by August 31, Gide had begun to withdraw, and he wrote to Barbusse from Cuverville:

> Be assured that I very much appreciate the cordiality of your letter. But... no! Do not announce my name, I beg you. If afterwards I did not make an appearance at this meeting, it would only cause disappointment. But if I did make an appearance, it would be even more disappointing; and more yet if I spoke. I am not cut out for public meetings.[40]

There is clear indication even at this early date that Gide did not feel entirely at ease in adopting the activist role he was now playing, and this uneasiness was not to diminish. To the office of the Congrès Mondial de la Jeunesse he sent the following message:

> I have already declared my *sympathie* (and the word does not seem at all weak to me) for the ideas that inspire you. I shall find yet other occasions to declare it. But be assured that I am worthless at meetings, that I do not have the voice that is needed for speaking in public and am very poorly qualified to preside over anything whatever. This role is not made for me, does not suit me, and I would only disappoint. Kindly then do not let my name appear on the program of the congress, if it has not already been printed, and be assured that I am, nonetheless, very cordially by your side. Let me write in peace what I still have to write; this is how I shall best and in the most lasting way be able to assist you.[41]

Romain Rolland's involvement with the question of conscientious objection was much greater than Gide's, and his position on the subject passed through several phases of development. Influenced by Tolstoy and Gandhi, he accepted and, in fact, embraced it from the outset. In the early twen-

ties Rolland engaged in a controversy over the issue with
Barbusse who was convinced that revolution could legiti-
mately resort to violence, if necessary, to accomplish its ends.
Rolland refused to agree to the compromise. If violence was
wrong, then it was wrong under all circumstances. In a letter to Barbusse written in Paris and dated February 2, 1922,
Rolland said: "Our enemy, Barbusse, is the oppressive violence of human society such as it presently exists. But against
that violence, you are arming an opposing violence. To my
way of thinking, . . . this method leads only to mutual destruction." [42]

Barbusse had no right to banish from the revolution those
who did not think as he did. "The revolution is the home of
all those who want a happier and better humanity. It is,
therefore, also mine." [43] Rolland went on to defend the no-
tion of conscientious objection, or *non-acceptation*, as he
often referred to it.

> I do not say: nonresistance: for, make no mistake, this is
> the highest resistance. To refuse one's consent and coopera-
> tion to a criminal State is the most heroic act that can be
> accomplished by a man of our times; it exacts from him—
> from him an individual, alone, in face of the giant State able
> to strangle him coldly within four walls—it exacts an energy
> and a spirit of sacrifice incomparably greater than those re-
> quired to confront death, to mingle one's breath and death
> sweat with those of the herd. Such moral vigor is possible
> only if there is awakened in the heart of men—of each man,
> individually—the flame of conscience, the almost mystical
> sense of the divine that inhabits each spirit, and that has
> exalted great peoples to the stars in the decisive hours of
> history.[44]

Later years and more reflection caused his attitude to
change, and, though he would never condemn conscientious
objection as a way of thought, he regretted that conscientious

objectors, himself among them, had separated from those who sought to spread the revolution by physical force. In an excerpt from his "Journal intime" of December, 1932, to September, 1933, Rolland said that both violence and nonviolence must serve the revolution. "All can and must serve in the common struggle. . . . He who would be unable to use all the resources for varied action at his disposal would be a poor leader of men and might." [45] He warned the Congrès Mondial against the illusion of thinking that war could immediately be stopped solely by adopting a position of nonviolence.

> I find seriously guilty certain of your leaders who leave you with illusions on this point and lure you on with the hope that war will be stopped in the face of people standing with their arms crossed. It will be stopped—yes!—but after passing over the bodies of those who bar the way. It will be stopped by the swell of world opinion aroused by the sacrifice of those who subscribe to passive Resistance. This sacrifice alone can herald—or prepare—humanity's coming victory, the salvation of future generations. But this sacrifice cannot be avoided. [46]

Rolland then turned to those who were willing to resort to physical force in the pursuit of their ideals, believing that unity rather than discord would better serve the revolution. Cooperation was a must between those who sought peace in conscientious objection and those willing to use violence to achieve it. Their goals were the same, to put an end to war through social revolution.

Late in 1933 three Bulgarian communists, Dimitrov, Tanev, and Popov, and the German communist Torgler were tried in Leipzig. All were accused of instigating the Reichstag fire in Berlin. Both Rolland and Gide sought to arouse support for the accused, Gide stating in a declaration reproduced in *l'Humanité* on October 15, 1933:

I associate myself wholeheartedly with the sympathy and admiration of Romain Rolland for the courage of Dimitrov, his Bulgarian companions, and Torgler.[47]

The accused were finally released, but the head of the German Communist party, Ernst Thaelemann, remained in prison, and two years after the Leipzig trials Gide spoke on his behalf at a meeting organized by the Comité Thaelemann in Paris. The Comité International pour la Libération de Thaelemann and other victims of Nazism had been formed almost a year earlier in January, 1934, under the presidency of Gide and André Malraux. Rolland and Henri Barbusse also pledged their support.[48]

In 1935 Gide and Rolland were among the first to call for a congress to discuss means of safeguarding culture in those countries where it was threatened. The congress itself took place in Paris from June 21 to 25; before adjourning, the members decided to form the Association International des Ecrivains pour la Défense de la Culture to be directed by a permanent Bureau International composed of one hundred twelve members. These one hundred twelve were headed by a presidium of twelve, among whom were Rolland and Gide.[49]

Rolland's and Gide's opinions did indeed seem in those days to be following similar patterns, and when the novelist André Suarès wrote to Rolland on February 19, 1933, delivering a ferocious attack on Gide, Rolland chose to ignore it. Suarès accused Gide of being false in everything, charging that if Gide had now gone over to Stalin and the Soviets it was because they were at present the "mensonge triomphant." [50] Rolland's response, written four days later, undertook to defend Stalin, but made no mention of Gide. Rolland was at this time, of course, seeking a rapprochement with Gide.

The Archives Romain Rolland contain evidence of a letter

written by Rolland to André Gide regarding Carl von Ossietzky,[51] who, as the editor of *Weltbühne,* a weekly devoted to
political, economic, and artistic discussion, was one of the
more prominent victims of Nazism. On a small fragment of
note paper is the draft of a letter in Rolland's own hand-
writing, and listed in the Archives as having probably been
written prior to September 17, 1933.[52] The exact date is very
likely somewhat later than the one supposed at the Archives,
for a copy of the actual letter sent to Gide is in the Bibliothèque Doucet, and this letter was assuredly based on the
fragment since it followed the fragment almost word for
word. The letter was dated April 8, 1934, and written from
Villeneuve in Switzerland. Rolland began somewhat timidly.
Gide's name, he was aware, was all too often solicited for
appeals. But here was one appeal worthy of Gide's attention,
an appeal on behalf of Carl von Ossietzky. No one had led
a more fearless struggle against German reaction, and no one
had drawn fiercer hatred upon himself. But Ossietzky wrote
independently of all parties, with the result that no party
would undertake to fight for him. Rolland thought it would
be beneficial if the *N.R.F.* and *Europe,* which he described
as their two friendly reviews, would undertake to defend
Ossietzky. They might at the same time recall public attention to other independent, international, and pacifist writers
who had been imprisoned. Such as Kurt Hiller,[53] on whom
a deadly silence had fallen for a year already. Rolland closed
with cordial greetings, adding in a postscript that he was enclosing a letter from *Die neue Weltbühne* in exile in Prague.[54]

One might expect that Rolland and Gide, through their
common and relatively frequent association with various
congresses and organizations, had numerous occasions to become more personally acquainted. But this was not so;
throughout this period they met only once. In his "Journal
intime" for September, 1933, to June, 1934, Romain Rolland
stated that on Tuesday morning, May 1, 1934, while still in

bed, he received a note from Gide. The note was delivered by a "lady," Elizabeth Van Rysselberghe, the daughter of Théo and Mme Van Rysselberghe (whom Rolland did not identify at this point). Gide wanted to take advantage of a stay in Switzerland to see Romain Rolland. Rolland said that he would expect Gide, and received him quite simply in his room in a "robe de chambre." The meeting lasted one hour. Upon Gide's departure, Rolland again encountered Elizabeth Van Rysselberghe, who had come to get Gide, and this time he identified her by name.[55] Gide's letter has been preserved. It is without date except for the day of the week, Tuesday, and bears the heading "Bex—Hôtel des Alpes."

My dear Romain Rolland,

Shall I take advantage of my passage through Bex to chat with you? But I shall certainly respect your privacy, and desire this meeting only if I know that you desire it equally.

Heartily,

André Gide [56]

Gide spoke of the meeting with Romain Rolland in a passage he wrote for *Vendredi* when it devoted its issue of January 24, 1936, to Romain Rolland in observance of his seventieth birthday. What Gide wrote was a eulogy without tarnish for Rolland's record. He simply drew a line canceling out their differences during the war, and even blaming himself indirectly for the criticism he had leveled at Rolland during that time. But the occasion for which Gide's eulogy was written must be borne in mind. Perhaps its cordiality can be attributed, too, to the rapprochement that developed between himself and Rolland in the thirties.

Gide recalled their first encounter at the Sorbonne, where Rolland was giving a course on music, and then spoke of their common effort on behalf of Rilke during the war, finally directing his attention to the meeting of 1934.

Time passed. Two years ago, finding myself in Switzerland, called to X——, not far from Villeneuve, where I knew Romain Rolland to be living, I had the keen desire to see him again. I wanted to show him a mark of my high esteem. He informed me that he would gladly receive me, and I think he understood with what emotion I responded to his welcoming embrace when I saw him again. Of the conversation we then had, I find nothing to relate. In what he said to me I felt a great unity of heart with him. The consistency and resolution of his thought had stamped the hollow features of his face with nobility. Emerson says in one of his *Essays* that a man's moral greatness is made manifest in his smallest gestures and that the radiance of his personality is felt immediately, from the first approach. I do not know whether this is indeed always true; but at least I thought on that day that Romain Rolland did not make a liar of Emerson.

The attitude that Romain Rolland adopted at the time of the war and preserved throughout his whole life with admirable consistency, is a source of great instruction for us. He was at first all alone or almost so; for a long time he had to bear blame, derision, and insult. Those who held him in scorn, and, because of their patriotism, hated him most, must recognize today that the figure of Romain Rolland is among those in whom is incarnate the honor and glory of France and of all humanity.[57]

Rolland's version of the meeting was not nearly so flattering for Gide, but far more searching and far more revealing. His version, however, was confided to the secrecy of his "Journal intime," and even at this date Mme Rolland did not wish me to transcribe the entry verbatim, but has allowed me to paraphrase it. The fact that Rolland was writing in his diary is not necessarily significant, however. He simply could not forget; the wounds of the past still bled. He had seen Gide before 1910, he said, when Gide had come with Verhaeren to hear one of his courses at the Sorbonne. With glacial brevity and finality Rolland remarked that he and

Gide were divided both in thought and in nature. Gide's nerves betrayed him, perhaps in order to veil their "éloignement." Gide was searching for an equilibrium that escaped him: "too much repression and release." With Gide, everything, including his own nervous reaction, was complicated. Both wanted a rapprochement after the misunderstandings that had plagued their lives, and Rolland admitted this as his real reason for writing to Gide about a joint action on behalf of Ossietzky, who had served only as a pretext. The meeting was "friendly and without constraint." They spoke of their own personal revolution bringing them together. Hyper-individualists both, they had to experience a moral crisis before they could recognize that their individualism and independence of mind did not provide sufficient reason for living. But his Protestantism was an important factor with Gide, Rolland observed, and already Gide was uncertain in his commitment to communism. Nonetheless, Rolland did not foresee retreat; Gide would not renounce the commitment he had made. He could not very easily do so, though for a Gide the debate would never be closed. The problem was that of freedom: to renounce it was to renounce one of the main reasons for living. Gide placed great stock in art, in his art, for which there would not be much room in the new world to come. As Gide had no contact at all with Gorki and no liking for Gorki's latest books, Rolland asked his wife (whom he called "Macha") to send Gide translations of some of Gorki's articles.

Gide was contemplating a trip to Moscow and was quite disturbed at the prospect. He could not envision himself among the Russian communists, and the thought of finding himself in a *tête à tête* with Stalin turned him to ice. What could they possibly say to each other?

In political and economic matters Rolland judged his visitor "unbelievably ignorant," a man who made no effort, moreover, to inform himself. Rolland diagnosed the élan that brought Gide to communism as a psychological one, and said that Gide was the product of "nervous irritations" against certain moral and social entities that had weighed upon him, such as family and religion. Rolland found him extremely generous, however, generous to the point of sacrificing intellectual and artistic values for the welfare of the proletariat. Rolland himself was convinced that these values would undergo regeneration and not destruction, but for Gide there was no such consolation; and his sacrifice was, therefore, a very beautiful one. His friends perhaps did not realize this; he did not often speak of it, fearing that it might be harmful to the communist cause.

Gide's health was another disquieting factor in his consideration of a trip to Russia, but Rolland assured him that he would be given the services of the Kremlin doctor. Thereupon Gide exclaimed that he did not want to be obliged to engage the doctor who would be assigned to him. He wanted to be able to say: I don't want bread, I want biscuits. Rolland attributed such an attitude to Gide's "finicky puritanism" that made even the simple things in life difficult. Not even the Russian communists would forbid him to eat biscuits if he had a sick stomach!

Few had such instinctive repulsion for the masses as Gide. It was difficult enough for him to converse with several people at once, a crowd became a nightmare to him, and after being among crowds he was unable to sleep for several nights. The experience was too violent for his sensitivity. These incompatibilities gave all the more value to his decision to support communism, a decision made "contre sa chair." The question now was would he be able to maintain his position?

Gide spoke of the difficulty of being an old man, and Rolland countered that it could be very wonderful to be old if one continued to progress. Avidly Gide agreed, hoping even now that he might one day yet achieve harmony. Rolland said that he wished this for Gide because he deserved it.

Rolland then proceeded to draw the conversation back to the misunderstandings that had plagued a part, if not all, of their lives, saying that they both had their share in the responsibility. Gide assigned the principal cause of their misunderstanding to a circumstance Rolland claimed almost to have forgotten. Gide recalled that during the war he had made some accusations against a German friend of Rolland's and said that on account of these accusations Rolland had taxed him with nationalism. Rolland's friend was, of course, Stefan Zweig. To himself Romain Rolland exclaimed, "If I had had only that reason." Rolland saw this as an attempt on Gide's part to divert their attention from what he called the true reasons, that of a man of letters and that simply of a man.

When after twenty years Gide finally outlined his accusations against Zweig, Rolland did not record them, fearing they might incriminate his old and intimate friend. Apparently Gide asked Rolland to make contact with Zweig so that he might clear himself of the charges made against him by Verhaeren and his wife, but Rolland refused to do so, saying that this would cause even greater and useless damage, since Zweig had had deep affection for Verhaeren. Rolland saw this as the reverse side of Protestant virtue, so quick to condemn, and said he would not have expected Gide to be willing to commit a greater crime than the one he wished to erase.

They then spoke of Ramon Fernandez,[58] Martin du Gard and Barbusse; Gide had apparently never met Barbusse. Gide felt that the communists were trying to use him and hoped that he had made it clear to Vaillant-Couturier [59] that he would not allow himself to be used by his new communist friends. For two years he had been so "bouleversé" that he could do nothing in the way of pursuing his own art. This proved for Rolland the seriousness of the crisis through which Gide had come.

Rolland concluded by saying that the meeting was simple and cordial to the end. Gide was seated in Rolland's swivel chair in front of his work table, while Rolland himself sat in a half-reclining position on a sofa. Gide smoked almost continuously until he noticed that the smoke was making Rolland cough. Rolland described Gide's conversation as simple and frank, or rather it was an attempt to be frank. There was no trace of vanity, and both authors were silent in regard to their own works. Mme Rolland took part in the conversation for several minutes when it turned toward the U.S.S.R., and Rolland's sister appeared for a moment, without recognizing Gide. On going through the parlor to accompany Gide back to his car, Rolland greeted his "compagne d'auto," Elizabeth Van Rysselberghe. The guests were shown some lacquer pieces from Palekh,[60] Rolland adding that neither of them knew anything about Palekh.

The same afternoon Rolland received the visit of a young Austrian painter named "Aliosha" who talked to him about Engelbert Dollfuss, chancellor of Austria, who had recently been murdered by the Nazis in Vienna. During their conversation Rolland alluded to a story Gide had told him that morning about a lady in Geneva. The lady was shocked by the menace of socialism and communism, which amounted to the same thing for her, and was perplexed at the prospect of no longer having a maid, for she would then no longer have time to knit for the poor. For both Rolland and Gide the story illustrated the "hypocritical naïveté of these circles." [61]

And so the second and final meeting between Romain Rolland and André Gide had ended. It was a long meeting and an important one, for in it lay the seeds of the approaching storm that was to break Gide's already troubled relations with communism and, in turn, tear to shreds the understanding that had been built between himself and Rolland since 1932.

On January 29, 1936, Romain Rolland celebrated his

seventieth birthday. Gide's eulogy was written for the January 24 issue of *Vendredi,* and on the last day of the same month he presided at a *soirée d'hommage* for Romain Rolland held at the Salle de la Mutualité in Paris. The fact that Gide participated in these festivities brought Rolland unexpected happiness. He noted in his "Journal intime" for the end of January to early February, 1936, that there had been an avalanche of letters and messages.

> *Vendredi* of January 24 and *l'Humanité* of the 26th are publishing pages of testimonials from my brother writers; I have the happy surprise to see André Gide in the first row. . . .[62]

On February 5 Rolland wrote to Gide from Villeneuve thanking him for his part in the commemoration. He was touched by the part Gide had taken in these birthday festivities and by the words of affection Gide had had for him. It was a joy to him that toward the end of their lives he and Gide were able to come together. This joy had been refused to so many of their predecessors who, though made to be allies, died estranged. This rapprochement with André Gide was simply one more reason for him to show gratitude toward communism, to which he referred as "mankind's great cause," whose servants both he and Gide had become.[63]

On June 17, 1936, Gide left France on a trip to the Soviet Union. Romain Rolland had visited Russia almost exactly one year before at the invitation of Maxim Gorki. Upon return the two writers reacted quite differently to their visits.

On a train bound for Moscow on Sunday morning, June 23, 1935, Rolland wrote his first words on Russian soil in a letter to Gorki. While in Russia he spent a considerable amount of time with Gorki, and was made to feel at home with him. After the visit had ended, Rolland wrote again, saying that if his body had returned home, his spirit had remained in

Russia. He went on to express contempt for the Western press, which he accused of not appreciating the greatness of what was happening inside Russia; and as for his own visit to the Soviet Union, he resented what he called the "silence" of the French press. Aside from people to whom he had written, hardly anyone who knew him in France or in Switzerland knew, or appeared to know, of his trip to the U.S.S.R. With the exception of *l'Humanité,* the newspapers had maintained a complete blackout. Rolland mentioned having been impressed by the "abyss of silence" that separated the West from the U.S.S.R., beginning at the Polish border, and even more so at the Austrian border. It was as though all that was going on in that mighty world of 160 or 170 million people did not exist. Rolland launched into an attack on the French newspapers for carrying all sorts of nonsense in their pages, with an occasional cry of horror from some of them over the famine and executions in the U.S.S.R. As if the Red Army no longer had anything to eat! A pack of old idiots he called the members of the news industry, but their efforts would not convince the people and petty bourgeoisie who knew full well that there was no unemployment in the U.S.S.R., even as their own situation worsened and hope waned.[64]

Though his correspondence and his published works reveal very little about his visit to Russia, Rolland seemed generally satisfied with the trip. Writing to his biographer Christian Sénéchal from Moscow on July 9, 1935, he spoke of a *fête populaire* where one hundred twenty thousand young people paraded in Red Square: "a stream of joy." The economic situation, too, was showing improvement and in the well-ordered capital of Moscow the crowds were healthy and well nourished.[65] Several weeks later from Villeneuve he again wrote to Sénéchal, delighted at the success his books were having in Russia. *Jean-Christophe, Colas Breugnon,* and the *Âme enchantée* were known not only in the cities but among the workers and peasants as well.[66] The questions of individual, personal, and artistic liberty, questions of such crucial importance to Gide, Rolland did not discuss.

On September 25, 1935, he wrote a letter which he sent to *l'Humanité* on October 23, extolling the joy of Soviet youth in accomplishing social reconstruction. He believed this social faith to be greater than the religious faith of the churches. In a letter of September 21, 1934, he had undertaken to answer and defend the "combat contre Dieu," when he stated positively that there were those in Moscow who had never stopped going to religious services, and that they had never been mistreated because of it. He cited his wife's first mother-in-law as an example.[67]

It is absurd to speak of persecution of the Christian faith in the U.S.S.R. The freedom of worship is assured. . . . There is only strong antireligious propaganda, but it is obliged by law to respect places of worship. Whoever would perpetrate scandal in a church would be condemned. If many churches have been closed, this is because of an established principle (and I approve of it) that places of worship and their ministers must be supported by the believers. If these are not sufficiently numerous or generous to meet the expenses, the State does not have to bear the burden.[68]

Rolland added that antireligious propaganda in Russia was no worse than the anticlericalism that had existed in France in the 1880's and that he himself had witnessed as an adolescent. In the anxiety they manifested, the various religions betrayed only their own weakness.[69]

Gide arrived in Moscow by plane on June 17, 1936, and the beginning of his visit was somewhat less auspicious than Rolland's. Gorki died the following day. On the 20th Gide took his place in the funeral cortège beside various Russian writers and members of the government, and before Stalin, delivered a eulogy of Gorki and the Russian revolution in

Red Square. The revolution was bringing culture to the masses, and for the first time in history it enabled writers to swim with rather than against the current: "by being a revolutionary the writer is no longer an adversary." [70] Mme Marie Romain Rolland recalled that her husband rejoiced when he heard Gide's pronouncement on the radio: "Now he can no longer pull back."

The November after his return, Gide published his *Retour de l'U.R.S.S.*, and it was apparent from the outset that some of the fears he had entertained in his conversation with Rolland in 1934 had proved only too real. The opening passages of the *avant-propos* set the tone for the book:

> Three years ago I declared my admiration and my love for the U.S.S.R. . . .[71]
>
> If I was mistaken at first, the best thing is to recognize my error as soon as possible; for I am responsible here for those the error leads on. No conceit is valid in this case; and besides I have very little. There are more important things than the U.S.S.R.: humanity, its destiny, its culture.[72]

But even now Gide hoped that Russia would triumph over what he considered to be its errors, and he lauded many aspects of Soviet society, joy among the workers, "joyous fervor" among the young. And yet: "What I admire in Leningrad is Saint Petersburg." [73] Gide was above all an artist.

The individual at first seemed to fuse with the masses, Gide wrote, and it was as though one could say "man" rather than "men." He was impressed. "I am taking a plunge; I plunge into that crowd; I am taking a bath in humanity." [74] But he was soon disappointed. Visiting the collective farms, he found each one totally independent and there was no question of mutual help among them. From each one of the houses he visited there issued forth an atmosphere of complete depersonalization, the same portrait of Stalin, and nothing else, not the slightest personal memento. "The happiness of all is obtained only at the expense of each one. To be happy, conform." [75] Conformity, the ultimate of horrors for one who throughout his life had preached the glorification of the individual, for one who believed that what was most precious in each man was precisely that which distinguished him from others! Gide could not bring himself to look upon depersonalization as a step toward progress. Each morning *Pravda* told the people what it deemed fitting for them to know, think, and believe; and the citizen did well to remain within these limits. "The result is that every time one converses with a Russian, it is as if one were conversing with them all." [76] Stalin was everywhere and on all lips, and Gide feared that the dictatorship of the proletariat had given way to a one-man dictatorship.[77] He feared, too, that there would soon arise in Russia a bourgeoisie of satisfied workers too much like the bourgeoisie he himself knew in France.[78] And now he reconsidered the statement he had made just a few months ago in his eulogy at Gorki's funeral. What would happen, he asked, if the social State eliminated all reason for protest from the artist? Could the artist simply allow himself to be carried by the current? While there was still struggle the artist could depict that struggle and assist it in the march to victory. But then what? In Soviet Russia conformity was demanded even of art, and the artist who did not conform was refused all honor.

> In the U.S.S.R., however beautiful a work might be, if it does not follow the party line, it is put in disgrace. Beauty is considered a bourgeois value. Whatever genius an artist might have, if he does not work within the party line, attention turns away from him, or is turned away from him: what is demanded of the artist or of the writer is conformity; all else will be given him in the bargain.[79]

With the triumph of the revolution, art ran as great a risk as under the oppression of fascism, the risk of becoming orthodox; and from the moment art allowed itself to be subjugated it was lost.[80]

If, as Rolland complained to Gorki, the French press had passed over his Moscow visit in silence, press comments were certainly not lacking in the case of Gide. Ever since Gide had publicly announced his support for the Soviet experiment in 1932, the comments were there, ranging from attempts to understand his reasons for turning to communism to simple and ferocious attacks on the man and the artist. Still others foresaw the fact that the marriage with communism was fated to end in divorce. In March, 1933, *Candide* had asked, "André Gide is a communist. For how long?" [81] On September 10, 1932, François Mauriac in the *Echo de Paris* had reflected that it would prove vain to try to show Gide that the Bolshevik dictatorship was one of the most oppressive ever known to humanity.[82] And on the day before Christmas of the same year *Nouvelles Littéraires* smiled knowingly at the enthusiasm of the Soviet press.

> We would be distressed at destroying such beautiful enthusiasm, but the Soviet press is making a mistake if it takes André Gide for an interpreter of bourgeois values, and if it imagines that in this recent incarnation he is betraying them for the first time.
>
> And besides, M. André Gide will never belong to any but his own party.[83]

The essayist Thierry Maulnier in the *Revue Universelle* of April 15, 1934, had attempted to show that the best known supporters of communism in France, Rolland and Gide, were not true Marxists, and asserted that for French intellectuals Marxism was nothing more than economic equality and popular government: the will of the people reigning in the economic order.[84]

Still others had spoken of Gide's individualism and saw a contradiction in his adherence to communism. Gide himself was repelled by reading Karl Marx.[85]

In his message to the first Congress of Soviet Writers held in Moscow from August 17 to September 1, 1934, Gide had stressed the need to develop a "communist individualism" in art and literature.

> Communism will be able to impose itself only by taking into account the particularities of each individual. A society in which each person resembles the whole is not desirable; I will even go so far as to say it is impossible; and for a literature, even more so. Every artist is necessarily an individualist, however strong his communistic convictions and his attachment to the party may be.[86]

As early as February 21, 1932, Gide had called for the coexistence of communism and individualism.

> A well-understood communism needs to favor worth-while individuals, to take advantage of all the individual's values, to get the best output from everyone. And well-understood individualism has no reason to be opposed to what would put everything in its place and bring out its value.[87]

On August 12, 1933, he elaborated on this position:

> when I write that I am unwilling to recognize as essentially irreconcilable a "properly understood" communism and a "properly understood" individualism, I mean: such as I understood them myself. I must therefore explain how I understand them. It is certain that I do not see an equalitarian communism, or at least that I see equality of conditions only at the outset; that for each person it would imply merely equal chances, but in no wise a uniformity of qualities, a standardization that I consider at one and the same time impossible and hardly desirable, for the individual as well as

for the mass. And, likewise, an internationalization of economic interests would in no wise imply the suppression and
ignoring of racial or geographical peculiarities, the happily
irreducible differences among cultures and traditions. The
very diversity of the players makes the wealth and beauty of
the symphony, and wishing that all the instruments, brasses,
violins, oboes, or clarinets, produced the same sound would
be as absurd as to think that each instrument would play
better if it broke away from the ensemble of the orchestra
and ceased following the measure.[88]

In a speech given in Paris on October 23, 1934 before the
A.E.A.R., Gide discussed the role of literature in relation
to the communist revolution. The revolution could free
men, but man himself it could not change. The only way
literature could serve the revolution was by being true.

That literature and art can serve the revolution goes without saying; but it need not be concerned with serving it. It
serves never so well as when it is concerned solely with truth.
Literature need not put itself at the service of the revolution.
A servile literature is a debased literature, however noble
and legitimate the cause it serves. But since the cause of truth
is identified in my mind, or rather in our mind, with that
of the Revolution, art, in being concerned solely with truth,
is of necessity serving the Revolution. It does not follow
along with the Revolution; it does not submit to it; it does
not reflect it. It enlightens it.[89]

In these last lines Gide underscored an essential point. For
him as well as for Romain Rolland, truth and the revolution
were inseparable. Though Rolland's notions of equality may
have been broader and somewhat more chimerical than
Gide's, both believed that the communist revolution would
necessarily achieve harmony and the general well-being of
humanity, for this was mankind's destiny and its truth. Both
recognized the value and necessity of liberty in a well-

developed society, and both knew before going to Russia that
Soviet society would not in all respects live up to their own
personal aspirations. Rolland, however, returned convinced,
just as he was before his departure, that despite all, Soviet
Russia was on the right track; André Gide returned with the
impression that the Soviet experiment had derailed some-
where along the line.

On August 25, 1936, the night after his return from Russia,
Gide spoke to his friend and colleague Jean Schlumberger,
asking him whether he had been following the trials of
certain Trotskyists who had been indicted in Russia. Bent
on purging the Soviet system of all ideological deviation, the
Stalin government had accused the Trotskyists of reaction and
indicted sixteen persons. The testimonies forthcoming were
incredible, with the accused testifying against themselves and
their accomplices. Schlumberger suggested that probably their
wives or children were being held hostage or that they
themselves had been threatened with torture. Gide replied
that this was like Hitler's coup against his S.A. leader, Ernst
Röhm, and Schlumberger remarked, "Now I know all I need
to know." [90] Gide and Schlumberger knew each other well,
and already in 1933 Gide had confided his hesitations to him,
saying that he was being led further than he wanted to go,
and that this was not his *métier*.[91] Nevertheless, Schlumberger
was a bit taken by surprise.

> What was astonishing was the abruptness with which his
> faith had vanished. One felt none of the regret, hurt, or anger
> that great disappointments cause. No upheaval. A belief
> without roots. The utopian mirage had been dissipated with-
> out leaving any traces.[92]

Gide's mind was changing. On September 5, 1936, he
pondered in his *Journal* what the significance of the Moscow
trials would be. Three months later he wrote to Martin du
Gard:

Communism at present is on the wrong track; it can save itself only by ceasing to remain under Moscow's lead. Faith in the U.S.S.R. is shaken; following the trial of the 16 there were many expulsions from the party. You can well imagine that I am following the affair closely.[93]

The thought that there might be unjust persecution in Russia had been troubling Gide for some time. When this question was raised in June, 1935, at the congress that created that Association International des Ecrivains pour la Défense de la Culture, certain pro-Stalinist elements in attendance at the congress aggressively sought to stifle debate over the issue. Though Rolland subsequently continued steadfast in his support of the Stalin regime, Gide, according to the anti-Stalinist writer Victor Serge, was appalled by what he had witnessed at the meeting, and went to see the Soviet ambassador for some explanations on what had taken place—to no avail! [94]

As the Moscow trials continued on into 1938, they became a "torment" for Rolland too, and he saw that the consequences could only be disastrous.[95]

Rolland knew of the existence of the *Retour de l'U.R.S.S.* before it actually appeared. In his "Journal intime" for August 1, 1936, to April 15, 1937, he noted that Gide was preparing a work that seemed to be a disavowal of communism. He regretted that Gide had not had the "courage" to express his convictions while still in Russia, saying that he would have risked nothing had he done so. Rolland regretted, furthermore, that Gide chose to execute his work at this critical moment when "fascists and Trotskyists" were gaining strength in Spain. The course Gide was pursuing could only serve to help divide the revolutionary forces in that country and endanger the Republican effort.

Trotsky had become a defiant opponent and even rival of Stalin, and for some years already, found himself in exile from the Soviet Union. He rejected Stalin's concept of building socialism in one country at a time and envisioned rather the use of the Russian Soviet model as a springboard for the world communist revolution. In Spain and elsewhere his followers were seeking to lure support away from the Stalin regime, and this became a source of profound concern to the Stalin government.

Rolland was aware that the *avant-propos* of Gide's book was to appear in *Vendredi* on November 6, and the pacifist Francis Jourdain had assured Rolland that he and the writer Georges Friedmann had insisted on Gide's introducing into his book some acknowledgments of the great accomplishments realized in the Soviet Union.

Rolland maintained that Stalin could not incarnate the multiple personality of the U.S.S.R. and now accused Gide of being weak and of having succumbed to the influence of the French Trotskyists. The U.S.S.R. was no longer "à la mode," she had become vulgar, and if Gide remained attached to her, he would no longer be considered the "arbiter elegantium [*sic*]."

Rolland charged that Gide's turnabout had already been six months or more in the making and referred for confirmation to Gide's "Pages du Journal" of October, 1935, which the *N.R.F.* had published in March, 1936. By way of conclusion Rolland added that he did not want to judge in advance, but that by being faithful to nothing, Gide was being faithful to himself.[96]

Gide's *Journal* entry for October 30, 1935, was in fact rather mild in tone, and Rolland might have found more critical indications of the coming change in Gide's conversation at their meeting in 1934. Gide's *Journal* of October 30, 1935, reads:

> No, it would be false to say that my opinions, my thoughts, have not changed, and it would be dishonest of me to claim

it. But the great, the very important change is this: I had thought, until quite recently, that it was important first to change man, men, each man; and that this was where one had to begin. This is why I used to write that the ethical question was more important to me than the social question.

Today I let myself be convinced that man himself cannot change unless social conditions first urge him and help him to do so—so that attention must first be paid to them.

But attention must be paid to both.

It is also, it is in great part, the stupidity and dishonesty of the attacks against the U.S.S.R. that today make us defend her with a certain obstinacy. They, the fault-finders, will begin to approve her just when we shall cease to do so; for they will approve her compromises and concessions, which will make the others say: "You see!" but by which she will wander from the end she originally pursued. May our eyes, while continuing to focus on that end, not be led, thereby, to turn away from the U.S.S.R.[97]

Rolland wrote to J.-R. Bloch on March 19, 1936, that Gide had been showing "singular and very disturbing uncertainty. . . . I have no great confidence in the duration of his Soviet sentiments." [98] And so his astonishment at the tone of the *avant-propos* to the *Retour de l'U.R.S.S.* when he read it in *Vendredi* in November, just before the book was published, could not have been very great. On November 8 he wrote to Bloch that he did not suppose it had caused him much surprise either. Rolland said that he himself had been more surprised by Gide's speech before the Kremlin the day of Gorki's death. The article from the *N.R.F.* of "April last" that Gide was now using to explain his change had prepared Rolland for it. But "le plus beau" was that Gide was now accusing the U.S.S.R. of having changed. Gide said that when he spoke of the U.S.S.R. he meant "the one who directs it." The anti-Stalinists in Paris were many, both masked and unmasked, continued Rolland, and they, he

countered, had no trouble at all directing Gide, whom he
called a weak man. Rolland did not wish to say that one
could not be sure of Gide; Gide himself was never sure,
never. Rolland still hoped that the book would not merit the
anxiety with which Francis Jourdain had recently written
him. But it could be expected that one day or another Gide's
anxieties would be realized. He was not cut out to forget
himself, as were those millions now preparing the "trim-
mings" of a world to come.[99]

The article from the April issue of the *N.R.F.* that Rolland
referred to was, no doubt, the passage from Gide's diary that
had appeared in March. Gide himself published nothing in
the April issue, and the only article touching on communism
was Jean Grenier's *L'Âge des orthodoxies*. Grenier sharply
criticized the communists for exempting Karl Marx from
the historical and dialectical process.[100] He cautioned against
substituting a "mutilated" peasant culture for the actual
"vitiated" bourgeois culture, and continued:

> Instead of narrowing the mind, socialism should broaden
> it. . . .
> Today, nevertheless, an effort at intellectual abasement is
> being worked out, on the pretext of spreading a new culture
> that would be the true one. . . . Spread culture, yes, but do
> not create a situation in which an elementary mentality will
> triumph over the working class after it has won over the
> bourgeoisie.[101]

On the whole, Rolland's criticism of the *avant-propos* to
Retour de l'U.R.S.S. was somewhat unjustified, and it betrayed a misunderstanding of Gide's position. Clearly Gide
believed that however important the individual was, true
fulfillment lay only in the renunciation of his individuality.
In his *Conférences sur Dostoïevsky* Gide spoke of "that
happiness that can only be obtained by renouncing what is
individual in us; for self-attachment prevents us from plung-

ing into Eternity, from entering the kingdom of God and from participating in the confusedly vague feeling of universal life." [102] And earlier in the *Conférences:* "The individual triumphs in the renunciation of his individuality. He who loves his life, who seeks to guard his personality, will lose it. . . . Resurrection in total life, the forgetting of personal happiness." [103]

In 1933 he wrote in his *Journal:* "And since I believe, furthermore, that the personality never asserts itself more than by renouncing itself, it seems to me that . . . the only ones who can worry about communism are the indecisive personalities, or those who think they can assert themselves only at the expense of others." [104]

Even though the individual must be prepared to renounce his individuality, he must never renounce his belief in the individual. First he must be given the opportunity to know what he is and to develop freely, and only then did renunciation make sense—a self-imposed renunciation, one not exacted from without, as Gide saw it in Soviet Russia.

Just after the *Retour* appeared, Romain Rolland wrote to René Arcos, November 27, 1936, from Villeneuve, asking him to be kind enough to send a copy of the book. Rolland had only read excerpts published in several newspapers and wished to judge for himself.[105] On the following day Rolland again wrote to Arcos, rescinding his request, saying that he had just received a copy. His reaction to the book was one of contempt. Some days later on December 10 he wrote to another correspondent that Paris was in ferment with wild opposition to the U.S.S.R. and the Communist party. But he was not taken by surprise. Gide's book, which he called a ridiculous little pamphlet that was more superficial and childish than spiteful, had just created an unbelievable din. Unveiled and revealed were the pent-up hostilities of three quarters of the French bourgeoisie. And those who had thought themselves favorably disposed to new ideas and to

the new Russia were not exempt. Such elements could be
organized rapidly, and their advisors, who Rolland claimed
were four or five leaders of the Trotskyist opposition, were
masters at the game.[106]

Rolland did not specifically call Gide a Trotskyist, but
here and elsewhere there lurked the hint of such an accusation. Certain elements of the French press did make the
accusation, and Mme Marie Romain Rolland recalled from
a passage of the "Journal intime" which she did not make
available to me that Rolland himself mentioned Gide's having
seen Trotsky's son before going to Russia. She seemed to
imply that this would cast an interesting light on the purpose
of Gide's Russian trip and his published reactions to it.
Trotsky himself lived in France from July, 1933, to June,
1935, but there is presently no evidence of Gide's ever having
met him.

One section of the Trotsky papers at Harvard University
may possibly contain more information on the question; however, this section will not be opened to scholars until 1980.
In a letter addressed to me just prior to the publication of
this book, Jean van Heijenoort, for many years Trotsky's secretary, and presently professor of philosophy at Brandeis
University, wrote me that Trotsky's son Leon Sedov and Gide
did not meet before Gide's Moscow trip. He thought it unlikely that they met later, after the first and second Moscow
trials, but did not entirely rule out the possibility. Joseph
Hansen, Trotsky's personal secretary in Mexico and presently
the editor of the Intercontinental Press in New York, wrote
me that Leon Sedov might possibly have corresponded with
Gide or attempted to see him in an appeal to him and other
intellectuals and artists to join in efforts to investigate charges
brought against the accused at the Moscow trials, or to enlist
Gide's support in the efforts of Trotsky's wife, Natalia Sedova,
to ascertain the fate of another son, Sergei, who had fallen
into the hands of Stalin's police. Mr. Hansen believes, how-

ever, that any overtures made to Gide would have had no connection whatever with Gide's plans to visit Moscow.

In July 29, 1932, Gide had spoken in his *Journal* of a

> Dreadful confusion after reading the Trotskyite manifestoes that Pierre Naville [107] lent me. But, however well founded certain criticisms may seem to me, it strikes me that nothing can be more prejudicial than divisions within the party.[108]

In 1933 he expressed a certain "consternation" on literary and intellectual grounds at an article against Trotsky that had been published by the *N.R.F.* At the outset he specified, however:

> You know that I am not a Trotskyist and what I reproach here is not the fact of displeasing the Trotskyists but of giving them such good reason to be incensed at the *N.R.F.* (and this for no one's satisfaction... that I know of).[109]

Before the trip to Russia, in any case, Gide had been forewarned, Pierre Naville stated in the preface to his brother Claude's posthumous book of 1936, *André Gide et le communisme.* Stalin's Russia, with all the petty social and national differences it had accepted within Russia itself, was no longer on the true path of the communist revolution. "We opened before him the dossier of anti-marxist, anti-proletarian repression in the U.S.S.R. he was preparing to visit." [110]

Romain Rolland later accused Gide of collaborating with Victor Serge, a writer and activist who had a definitely anti-Stalin, pro-Trotsky orientation. The son of Russian émigrés, Victor Serge was born in Brussels. He became a member of the Russian Communist party and the editor of the *Communist International,* but by 1923 had joined the opposition against Stalin. After 1925 he devoted himself to internal struggles of the party in Moscow, and found himself expelled from the party in 1928. He was virtually a prisoner in his own country, when Romain Rolland, on his visit to Moscow in 1935, personally intervened with Stalin on Serge's behalf. Stalin gave his promise to authorize Serge to leave the Soviet Union,[111] and in 1936 Serge was banished. He translated into French and published Trotsky's *Révolution trahie*, which it is clear that Gide read,[112] and wrote several books denouncing the Stalin regime, which he believed to have dashed the hopes of the revolution. He maintained that what was needed was more personal well-being and more liberty, more dignity and more respect for humanity,[113] and with these objectives Gide undoubtedly concurred. When Gide wrote in the summer of 1937: "what is the status of the U.S.S.R.? Dreadful bureaucracy, administrative mechanism has never been stronger," [114] his agreement with Victor Serge was complete. Gide met Serge several times, and Serge had been able to observe him well, noting his fears and hesitations, and the integrity that was essential to his communist commitment and that was becoming increasingly difficult to maintain. Just prior to Gide's departure for Moscow, Serge had addressed to him in the *Bulletin Oppozitsii* an "open letter" reminding him that the U.S.S.R. and the working class could be served only with complete lucidity, and begging him to have the courage to remain lucid.

Upon Gide's return from Moscow, Victor Serge was able to observe him again. Filled with doubt, Gide weighed every word of the notes he had made on the U.S.S.R. But his doubt centered not on what he had written but rather on the decision to publish. In condemning, he still held fast to his hopes for what he thought true communism in Russia should be. He did not want his book to appear pessimistic, especially with the critical situation in Spain, but it was becoming difficult not to be pessimistic.

I was hoping to be able to do much in Moscow for many victims... I saw immediately that there was absolutely noth-

ing to be done... I was overwhelmed with banquets—as if I
went there to go banqueting!...[115]

That Victor Serge enjoyed a fairly good acquaintance and
even a certain concurrence with Gide does not offer any
proof, however, of any secret collaboration between them.
    Nevertheless, on February 17, 1937, Gide wrote in a letter
to Guéhenno that the Soviet Union had made compromises
of principle and so was jeopardizing the cause of the revolution, whereas Trotsky had remained faithful to it.

> For having denounced these compromises, Trotsky is
> treated as a public enemy (whereas he is an enemy only of
> Stalin's compromises) and by the same fell swoop made to
> look like a fascist, which is really far too simple. He is much
> more an enemy of fascism than Stalin himself, and it is as a
> revolutionary and antifascist that he denounces the compro-
> mises of the latter. But try to make a deluded public under-
> stand that! [116]

Trotsky himself was familiar with Gide's *Retour de
l'U.R.S.S.*, and, according to Trotsky's biographer Isaac
Deutscher, "filled . . . with shame and anger" against the
Stalin regime because of what Gide and others had reported.[117]
Trotsky admired Gide's perspicacity and said so in a speech
written late in 1936 and scheduled for delivery in New York
via radio from Mexico in 1937: "Gide is a friend of the
Soviet Union, but not a lackey of the bureaucracy. Moreover,
this artist has eyes." Trotsky proceeded to narrate a little
incident that had occurred toward the end of Gide's Russian
trip, and that Gide himself had recounted in his *Retour de
l'U.R.S.S.* As an act of courtesy to thank Stalin for the warm
reception he had received in Russia, Gide had wanted to

> send a telegram to Stalin, but not having received the inquisi-
> torial education, he referred to Stalin with the simple demo-

cratic word "you." They refused to accept the telegram! The representatives of authority explained to Gide: "When writing to Stalin one must say: 'leader of the workers' or 'chieftain of the people,' not the simple democratic word 'you.' " Gide tried to argue: "Isn't Stalin above such flattery?" It was no use. They still refused to accept his telegram without the Byzantine flattery. At the very end Gide declared: "I submit in this wearisome battle, but disclaim all responsibility. . . ." [118]

The telegram Gide was obliged to sign was not the telegram he wanted to send but one that was dictated to him.

Despite this statement and to the surprise of Pierre Naville, who had for some time been trying to caution Gide against Stalin, Trotsky had little to say about Gide's book. Naville, in his *Trotsky vivant,* believes that Gide may have been somewhat disappointed at Trotsky's silence. Nonetheless, Gide even entertained for a time the thought of going to meet Trotsky in Mexico, the place of his final exile. But this was not to be! Naville adds that in truth Trotsky did not like Gide, that he was completely put off by the art and thought of the man who had written *Paludes,* and that this in turn led him to underestimate the author of the *Retour de l'U.R.S.S.* as an esthete.[119]

Jean van Heijenoort wrote me that there was never any direct communication between Gide and Trotsky. Joseph Hansen, on the other hand, in his letters to me, recalled that Trotsky invited Gide to visit him in Mexico and that Gide responded cordially. But Mr. Hansen himself had not seen the correspondence and could speak only from what he had heard in the Trotsky household. The now closed section of the Trotsky papers at Harvard, or another as yet unused source, may possibly contain relevant documentation.

Clearly, Gide and Trotsky were aware of each other, and on occasion Gide's sympathetic understanding of Trotsky's position was apparent. To conclude from this, however, that

Gide entertained any ulterior motives during his trip to Moscow, or that the trip was dictated by such motives, would be to go beyond the evidence presently available. As Gide himself wrote, furthermore, to Jean Guéhenno on February 17, 1937: "I maintain that one can disapprove of Stalin without thereby immediately becoming a Trotskyist." [120]

Rolland's definitive and public response to *Retour de l'U.R.S.S.* was written in the form of a letter dated in Villeneuve January 5, 1937, and published in the January 18 edition of *l'Humanité* under the title "L'U.R.S.S. en a vu bien d'autres."

Dear comrades,

I understand your indignation in regard to André Gide's book. This bad book is, besides, a mediocre book, astonishingly poor, superficial, childish, and contradictory. If it has created such a din, it certainly does not owe this to its value; it has none. It is due to the clamor that surrounds the name Gide and to the exploitation of his celebrity by the enemies of the U.S.S.R., always on the watch and ready to use against her all the arms offered to their spite.

I react like Ostrovsky.[121] I hold a grudge against Gide, less for his criticism, which could have been made openly when he was in the U.S.S.R., if he had been straightforward, than for the double game he has been playing, lavishing declarations of love and admiration while in the U.S.S.R., and, no sooner home in France, striking the U.S.S.R. in the back, all the while declaring his "sincerity"!

I hear it said here that Gide claims he did not want to wrong the U.S.S.R. and the Revolution, and that he is complaining that the press that is hostile to the U.S.S.R. is using his book against her! Not that he lacked forewarning! I know that friends had cautioned him about the evil he would be doing, and begged him insistently to think it over. He paid no attention and hastened to publish his book, in a large first printing and at a low price. That he should now be protesting against the congratulations and the humiliating panegyrics of members of the reaction and even of the *Völkischer Beobachter* [122]—I imagine he is embarrassed! These are so many accusations against him. But it is a bit late to find that out! The evil is done. Will he have the strength to undo it? I doubt it... If only he had the will! The coming months will tell us.

But once again, like Ostrovsky, "I don't want to speak of him anymore." Neither he nor anyone nor anything whatsoever can ever halt the march of history and the development of the U.S.S.R. The U.S.S.R. has seen others like him!

But, dear comrades, each one who works and fights for the Revolution must . . . see to it to the best of his ability that the work for which he is responsible is accomplished as well as possible.

. . . Life is a continuous struggle for progress and advance. So let us all struggle, let us never consider ourselves satisfied with the ends attained, let us pursue ever higher ones! . . .

And Stalin himself—I need not say "the master of peoples," as Gide claims he was obliged to say, maintaining that in the U.S.S.R. one cannot call Stalin "comrade," or simply say "you" to him! though I readily called him "you" during our conversations in the Kremlin, at Gorki's house, and in *Pravda* of July 23, 1935—Stalin himself once upon a time wrote in his *Problems of Leninism* that *"modesty is the ornament of the true Bolshevik."*

Let us then be true and modest but unshakable in our battles and in our continuous efforts to enrich and embellish the great universal workers' fatherland, which was founded by the October Revolution!

And let us not be affected by the snarling hatred of our enemies, or by the failure of friends who are too weak and who cannot follow us! Let us rejoice in the fertile pains (they are joys) of our present glorious and difficult work, and in the happy future they are building.

I greet you all fraternally,

Romain Rolland [123]

The question of Gide's dealings with Stalin is an intriguing one. Rolland had been able to converse with Stalin in person during his trip to Russia. Gide was never given that opportunity, for certainly the two men could have said little, if anything, to each other on the day of Gorki's funeral. The author Louis Guilloux indicated in the *N.R.F.*'s *Hommage à André Gide* in 1951 that Stalin may have deliberately avoided Gide. Guilloux had accompanied Gide on his trip to Russia, and could therefore speak from his own recollections. Gide was hurt by the apparent snub, and if it had any influence at all on the tone of his book, that influence would certainly have been pejorative to the cause of the U.S.S.R. In "D'un voyage en U.R.S.S.," the contribution Guilloux wrote for the *N.R.F.*'s *hommage,* May 4 and 5, 1951, he recalled that from the beginning of the trip everyone had talked of Gide's expected visit to Stalin.

> we were expecting great news. We dined without Gide— whom we did not see again until the next day. He had, in effect, gone to the Kremlin, but he had not seen Stalin. His guide had taken him to a concert. This is what I am able to tell you on this point, and I have until now forbidden myself to tell it out of fear that ill-intentioned use might be made of such facts. This is so easy to do! But finally I am telling it today because one owes the truth to one's contemporaries. It was said later, during the trip (but when?), that Gide had the intention of speaking to Stalin about some new laws promulgated in the U.S.S.R., and very severe, it was said, against homosexuality, and that this was why Stalin did not wish to see Gide. Perhaps, after all, it was only idle gossip. Gide never spoke, at least I never heard him speak in my presence, about this abortive visit.[124]

During January, 1937, Rolland referred to Gide on several occasions, the first being on the 3rd of the month, when he wrote about the visit of "X" and his young wife, just returned from the Tyrol.[125] "X" had been on assignment with *Europe* to write an article on Gide's book, and he and his wife had met Gide in the Crimea. Rolland characterized "X" as a difficult person to define, unstable, and, in the complexity of his nature, unable to make a choice. On the one hand "X" was indulgent toward the "nasty little piece of libel" that was Gide's book on Russia; on the other hand, he revealed terrible information about Gide. Rolland had raised the point that Gide must have been influenced by others, but "X" dismissed this as though it could not have a real bearing. Nonetheless, he said that to write his book Gide had locked himself up with his "petits amis" in a château near Paris. These friends, he said, were the leaders of the Trotskyist organization in Paris, La Vérité. Since "X" was favorably disposed to Gide, Rolland contended that the information could not be doubted. "X" maintained that Gide's homosexuality had to be taken into account to understand properly his book against the U.S.S.R., while Rolland tacitly observed that it would be difficult to find sterner arguments against Gide than had this "benevolent advocate." "X" confirmed what Rolland called the enormous and disastrous success of Gide's book: one hundred thousand copies sold in two months. *Vendredi* itself had distributed free of charge two hundred fifty thousand copies of the issue in which it had published Gide's *avant-propos*.

Rolland regretted that many French writers, hypnotized by Gide's art and esthetics—which counted more for them than the revolution—did not want to talk about Gide or his book. "X" himself had agreed to write the article for "Z" in *Europe* only to "repêcher" Gide. "X" and "Z" both hoped for his return to the support of the Communist party and knew he had to be handled delicately.

Rolland ended by saying that "X" 's "book" was excellent from a technical standpoint, and that it irrefutably revealed

Gide's errors. But "X," instead of condemning Gide, practically embraced him with an admission of agreement.[126]

The author Rolland designated by the letter "X" must have been Georges Friedmann. Friedmann's article, "André Gide et l'U.R.S.S.," which was dated December 10, 1936, and published in the January, 1937, edition of *Europe,* fits Rolland's description perfectly. The following year it was incorporated in his book *De la Sainte Russie à l'U.R.S.S.,* and published by Gallimard.

Rolland's next relevant entry in his "Journal intime" concerned a visit one day later on January 4, of the pacifist Gabrielle Duchêne, who was also a champion of women's rights, and active in the struggle to obtain better working conditions for them. Mme Duchêne, just returned from Bex, where she had met Gide, found him "très vieux Monsieur," "unbelievably colorless, superficial," ignorant of the best-known persons and things, "a tear in his eye ready to flow at the slightest provocation." She proceeded to tell Rolland how Gide had brought out all the reviews of his *Retour* and exhibited them to the people in the hotel, meanwhile continuing to protest his affection for the U.S.S.R. He refused to listen to reason and had no understanding of economics or politics; for him all was an affair of "sensibilité," or more exactly of "émotivité." To Mme Duchêne's question as to whether he would go to see Rolland, Gide reacted with a "fearful recoil." She found him weak, inconsistent, and pretending to be more naïve than he actually was.[127]

Rolland's January, 1937, "Journal intime" also acknowledges a plea from the foreign workers of Magnitogorsk asking him to publish in the French papers a "Message" they had sent him. "I refused to do it, for their Message was insulting to Gide, and I did not want to appear to be hiding behind them to attack Gide." [128] Having refused to publish their letter, Rolland had it returned to them by his wife

"Macha," and told them to publish it themselves. He then sent them his own letter dated January 5 and left them free to publish it in the Russian papers. This letter is essentially the same one that was published by *l'Humanité* on January 18.

In June, 1937, Gide wrote his *Retouches à mon Retour de l'U.R.S.S.* as an answer to those "critics of good faith" who had protested against the *Retour*. Alas, there were also those, he felt, whose only wish was to insult him, and among these was Romain Rolland.

> The publication of my *Retour de l'U.R.S.S.* has brought me many insults. Those of Romain Rolland have grieved me. I never liked his writings; but at least I hold his moral person in high esteem. My sorrow is due to this: how rare are those who reach the end of their life before having shown any limitation on their greatness. I believe the author of *Au-dessus de la mêlée* would severely judge Rolland grown old. That eagle has made its nest, and reposes there.[129]

Rolland had gotten wind of this statement even before the *Retouches* appeared. In an excerpt from the "Journal intime" dated June 29, 1937, he made mention of a meeting with Aragon in which Aragon had spoken to him about Gide, whose new book on the U.S.S.R. was to come out in two days. André Malraux had read the advance proofs, and Aragon assured Rolland that it was a violent pamphlet against the U.S.S.R., sparing nothing. Rolland listed the source of the lengthy documentation furnished Gide for his book as V.S., the initials referring to Victor Serge. From what had been told Rolland in advance, he concluded that Gide had treated him abusively.[130]

The conversation with Aragon turned eventually to the Spanish revolution. Rolland had indicated earlier that he thought the appearance of the *Retour de l'U.R.S.S.* in 1936

ill-timed because of the effect it might have on the outcome
of the revolution in Spain. Now his comments were more
precise.

Aragon had poured out all his pent-up bitterness and scorn
for Gide and had every reason to be put out by him. In the
year gone by, the *N.R.F.,* Gide's review Rolland called it,
had sued Aragon for failing to keep a written agreement to
submit five or six works, and won damages of over 60,000
francs. In the acute state of financial difficulty the Aragons
were in, such a sentence was cause for despair. But when
Gide had proclaimed his rallying to the Communist party,
Aragon had decided to forget all his grievances against Gide
and had asked him, too, to forget the fact that they had been
enemies. As they were now fighting for the same cause, as
long as Gide remained faithful to that cause, they would lay
bitterness aside. But Aragon now felt freed of his promise
and was taking it back. Rolland remarked that Aragon, and
indeed all French writers of the left, had been excessively
kind in their treatment of Gide, even after the appearance
of the *Retour de l'U.R.S.S.* Aragon had begged Gide not to
allow this book to come out at a time when the destiny of
Republican Spain was at stake. He had brought and read
to Gide letters that would have moved anyone who had a
heart. But he also had had advance warning of Gide's be-
trayal. Aragon returned from Spain on the eve of Franco's
drive on Madrid. Everyone thought Madrid would be taken,
and Aragon hastily sought to form an international committee composed, not of extreme leftists, but of moderates, lib-
erals, and Catholics, to appoint a delegation to go to Madrid.
The members of this delegation were to serve as witnesses
and thus as a guarantee against the horrible excesses that
were anticipated and feared. Gide got hold of the idea and
forestalled its execution. Because of him no delegation at all
had been sent to Madrid. Victor Basch,[131] indignant but ill
and alone as he was, had flown down to Spain to save face.

People like Paul Langevin,[132] Albert Bayet,[133] and Andrée Viollis [134] were revolted by the explanations Gide tried to give of his conduct. Gide had shown greater concern for serving the interests of Franco's partisans in Madrid than for helping those fighting for the Republic. Viollis attacked him, and Bayet refused to shake his hand. When Gide left them, Langevin could only exclaim, The wretched man! [135]

The revolution failed in Spain; and with the assistance and support, both material and moral, of fascist Italy and Germany, Franco's power was established.

Gide had disapproved of the handling of the Spanish revolution by the U.S.S.R. and the communists. On December 17, 1936, *Pravda* spoke of "cleaning up" the Trotskyist elements in Spain; the support of Stalin's Russia for the Spanish revolution could be purchased only at the price of a decided hostility toward all elements tarred with Trotskyist influence. In February, 1936, the two principal Marxist factions in Catalonia had united to form the Partido Obrero de Unificación Marxista. The P.O.U.M. was criticized by Trotsky himself. Nevertheless, the communists and those associated with them persisted in denouncing it as "Trotskyist." An uprising broke out in Barcelona in May, 1937, and the severe action taken against the P.O.U.M. at this time was, as one historian states, "wholly in accordance with Soviet wishes." [136]

Claude Mauriac noted in his *Conversations avec André Gide* that on October 21, 1937, Gide willingly accepted his services in trying to obtain his father's signature on a protest against the "scandalous imprisonment" of the members of the P.O.U.M. The name of François Mauriac would be so useful, Gide had said.[137] And then:

> Suddenly he [Gide] has another face; his teeth clenched in a strange and hard smile, his eyes glowing, he says: "I prefer Hitler's method. The assassination of Röhm was a monstrous thing, but accomplished before the world. Hitler denounced

justice directly. He had no shame of the shameful law he was invoking. Whereas nothing is more abominable than the pretenses of the Stalinists. They judge those they have condemned in advance. An absurd show, a masquerade. . . .[138]

The protest itself was recorded by Claude Mauriac on October 24, 1937, in the form in which it appeared in the press:

> Five French intellectuals have sent the following telegram to the Negrín-Prieto government: Let us urgently ask the Spanish government to assure to all those politically accused, guarantees of justice and especially rights to asylum and due legal process. With great attentiveness. André Gide, Georges Duhamel, of the French Academy; Roger Martin du Gard, François Mauriac, of the French Academy; Paul Rivet.[139]

Gide's position during the war in Spain was also at the root of a dispute with Jean Guéhenno and *Vendredi*. On December 17, 1937, Guéhenno published in *Vendredi* a "Lettre ouverte à André Gide."

> Recall that conversation we had the other night. You decided that *Vendredi* was not free because of its refusal to become enlisted among your followers in a quarrel between you and *Isvestia* over the communists and the Spanish anarchists. I explained to you that all I write and publish myself in *Vendredi* is far from being all that I would like to write and publish therein. This is because I do not prefer myself over *Vendredi*.

The intent of *Vendredi,* Guéhenno reminded Gide, was not to divide but to unite all the left-wing factions. "Must we espouse all your quarrels?"[140]

Gide's response was published one week later in the issue of December 24. There was one subject on which he refused to compromise: his "fidelity to the Republican cause."

To hear myself treated as a "new ally of the Moroccans and Black Shirts" [141] is intolerable to me; and since Guéhenno prides himself on being especially sensitive to what he calls "the commitment of friendship," allow me to tell you that in the face of such an accusation I find that it was up to *Vendredi,* above all, to protest; *Vendredi* which recently published my declaration of indefectible association with the Spanish Government (useless to add: Republican; that would be to recognize another).[142]

In the same issue of *Vendredi,* Guéhenno answered by serving notice that he would not support Gide in his quarrel with the Soviet Union and the communists, and stated further:

We did not have to ask the difficult question, which is still very obscure to us, of the relations between the different Spanish republican parties in your regard, and even less did we have to appear to decide them once and for all, as you yourself appear to be doing.[143]

Gide's views on Russia were not what they had been earlier in the thirties. In his *Retouches à mon Retour de l'U.R.S.S.* he said that since he was by nature inclined to believe in praise, he was instinctively repelled by the vicious tone of so much that had been written in detriment of Soviet Russia. "I more willingly believe love than hate." [144] The Russian people, miserable as they were, appeared to be happy. But this was only because misery, being "mal vue" in Russia, had to hide. If all that he had seen in Russia seemed joyful, it was because all that was not joyful became suspect. Not Russia but Siberia was the place for unhappiness and complaint. But truth was above all parties, and no party could prevent Gide from choosing the truth.[145]

The U.S.S.R. is not what we were hoping she would be, what she promised to be, and what she is still trying to pre-

tend to be; she has betrayed our hopes. . . . But we shall
not turn our gaze away from you, glorious and sorrowful
Russia. If at first you were an example to us, at present alas!
you are showing us into what sands a revolution can sink.[146]

André Gide's "communist temptation" was over. What he
rejected was not so much communism as he thought it might
and should be, but rather what Russia had made of it. If he
still entertained any hope of a change in the social order, it
was for him no longer a vital force, and he scarcely spoke of
it anymore.

On Wednesday, August 16, 1939, Claude Mauriac wrote
of Gide in his *Conversations:* "This morning he was dying
to accompany us to Vézelay, it was apparent; but in the same
instant he denied himself this pleasure for obscure reasons
typical of his character." [147] One of these reasons might have
been the fact that Romain Rolland had purchased a house in
Vézelay in 1937, and had been living there since 1938. Mme
Rolland assured me that Claude Mauriac did not visit Romain Rolland that day in Vézelay, but Gide may possibly
have felt a certain uneasiness at the thought of finding himself in Rolland's proximity. They had drifted too far apart.
One more meeting would undoubtedly have been painful
and useless for both.

So ends the relationship between Gide and Romain Rolland. Two years later, when another war engulfed Europe,
Rolland's attitude closely resembled Gide's during World
War I. It was more difficult in 1939 to remain "above the
battle" than it had been in 1914. With France largely occupied by the enemy, and divided territorially, it was not easy
to maintain a solid front of resistance. Rolland was now living in France, and his thinking was more obviously allied
with France's interests than it had been during World War
I. He was convinced that Nazism must be destroyed, and, as
he wrote to President Edouard Daladier on September 3,

1939, his allegiance to the democracies that undertook this task was total.[148] Whereas Gide, thankful in 1938 that war had been averted, gave lukewarm welcome to the Munich accords that recognized Hitler's claims to the Sudetenland,[149] Rolland denounced these accords as a "degrading capitulation." [150] Gide, recognizing better than ever before, after his communist adventure, that his strength did not lie in politics, refrained from speaking out in public on the issues. Even in the Midi, where he spent the first years of the war, and then in Tunis and Algiers, where he hoped to collect his physical strength and creative energy, he preferred to keep silent and maintain his independence of mind, avoiding the conformity that inevitably arises from thinking in a group.[151] As the war dragged on, Romain Rolland, too, fell silent on the questions at hand. He was old and ill; his thoughts turned inward rather than out to the world. Both Gide and Rolland, however, had faith that France would emerge from the struggle revitalized and rejuvenated. Before the war was over Rolland was dead. Except for a brief reference in a letter to Roger Martin du Gard regarding a possible deathbed conversion, Gide wrote of him no more.

IX Conclusion

In his last letter to Gide, Romain Rolland expressed regret that they had remained too much apart for most of their lives. They were different kinds of people, however, and even in speaking of the same thing their meanings were often very different. Both spoke of truth, but Rolland sought truth in his relationship to the exterior world, whereas Gide sought it within himself.

Rolland was generally consistent, Gide was not. Although Rolland's attitude toward violence and war underwent some modification in the course of his lifetime, these modifications alone do not warrant the label of inconsistency. On the whole, his attitudes were inflexible, and once defined and elaborated, they were no longer subject to change.

Gide, on the other hand, was the epitome of inconsistency. All his life he had been seeking an inner harmony that seemed to escape him; and, as he told Rolland at their meeting in Switzerland in 1934, he had not yet found it. He had written *Les Nourritures terrestres* and the *Immoraliste*, but needed the rigidity of *La Porte étroite* as a corrective to the freedom and even license of the earlier works. Since *La Porte étroite* was no more of a solution than the others, it, too, needed a corrective. His "conversion" to and renunciation of Russian communism constituted but another indication of the inconsistency that had become a characteristic part of his search. But as he said in *Retour de l'U.R.S.S.*,

> I have always professed that the desire to remain constant with oneself too often implies a risk of insincerity; and I believe sincerity is important, especially when the trust of a great number of people is involved with our own.[1]

Both men were fiercely independent. For Romain Rolland the duty to truth was greater than any other. Perhaps the most graphic symbol of his stubborn independence was Annette, the heroine of his *Âme enchantée*. "We cannot give what is not ours—my free soul." [2] Like Rolland himself in the domain of political and social thought, Annette in the domain of human affection tries to remain "au-dessus de la mêlée." But this is no simple task. "How ill-arranged life is! We cannot do without mutual affection any more than we can do without independence. One is as sacred as the other." [3] But Annette recognized that almost always it was the most passionately independent who were the most capable of love.[4]

If Rolland, starkly individualistic as he was, could accept communism, it was because he did not consider communism and individualism to be necessarily opposed. Whereas Gide hoped that a synthesis could be created out of the apparent antagonism, Rolland was confident that such a synthesis would be created.[5]

As to their sense of humanity, Gide and Rolland were at the same time similar and different. Rolland could sketch a picture of friendship between Christophe and Olivier that was a masterpiece of mutual understanding and even warmth, whereas Gide subscribed to, and even used as an example to confirm his own view, Ibsen's statement to the Danish literary critic Georg Brandes that friends were an expensive luxury. If one had a mission in life, one could not afford to maintain friendships, the danger arising not so much from what one did in their behalf, as from all one neglected to do out of concern for them.[6] Clearly these were not the characteristic attitudes of Rolland and Gide.

Rolland was intrigued more by ideas than he was by people, and he made this quite obvious in a letter written to his mother during the period 1890–1891:

> Ah! dear, beloved Mamma, it isn't this love or that friendship that might cause you jealousy; on the contrary, by attaching me to everyday life, they could serve your purpose; but your greatest enemy is God, art, the impersonal ideal, and my all too beloved solitude. . . . I cannot love like everyone else, for I love through God, in whom I see everything that is. God *is* first of all, *then* you and I. What can I do? I can scarcely manage to forget God in my moments of passion, anger, or violent attachment to my own personality and to others. (When I was in pain some time ago, I had forgotten him.) You will think I would do better not to tell you what I am telling you; for it distresses you. No matter, I am what I am; I prefer Ideas to beings; and prefer eternal Truth, Beauty, and Good to myself and to those I love. Ah! I do not love them less, as much, or more than ordinary young men because of this. But I love the ideal before all else, and I lose my idealism only in my crises of offended egoism or passion over which I have no control.
>
> I embrace you... in God.[7]

This contrasts markedly with Gide:

> Before the slightest act of self-giving, of self-sacrifice for another, for an abstract duty, or for an idea, I go down on my knees. If all must end here, then the rest of the world is not *de trop:* all the immense misery of man.[8]

This is true friendship to Gide, "un sentiment désintéressé," more incomprehensible than the world's elaboration and evolution from nothingness.[9] Describing his own childhood in *Si le grain ne meurt,* Gide told of a Russian boy he had liked. One day the boy stopped coming to school without Gide's knowing why. Gide kept the matter to himself but described it as one of the greatest sadnesses of his life.[10]

The feelings friendship arouses can also bring joy. In the *Faux-Monnayeurs* Bernard speaks to Edouard of a conversation he had with Olivier regarding suicide. Olivier had said that he could understand suicide only after one had climbed to such a summit of joy that nothing remained but to descend.[11] And, having attained that summit in his friendship with Edouard, Olivier attempted to commit suicide. Or again, there is the beautiful description of the beginnings of a friendship from the *André Walter:*

> This is the embarrassment and the anguish; the soul trembling and wanting the other to know—but it cannot and feels itself imprisoned. . . . Yet this is nothing: the worst suffering is that of two souls unable to draw near to each other.[12]

Gide's man cannot remain alone, and the renunciation of love and friendship, even for noble motives, leads to destruction and unhappiness, as *La Porte étroite* well illustrates.

Pierre Herbart in his *À la recherche d'André Gide* drew a very unflattering portrait of Gide as a calculating egoist. But the German essayist Ernst Robert Curtius, in preparing Thomas Mann's young son Klaus for his first interview with Gide, warned him that if Gide spoke only of himself in his books, he spoke only of others in his conversation.[13] Egoism? Altruism? Undoubtedly both have their place in the makeup of an individual. At any rate, people were necessary to André Gide, and if Romain Rolland could live for an idea alone,

Gide could not. In this, their temperaments were simply not alike.

Of all the differences that separated them, perhaps the most important of all was the difference in their conceptions of art. Here the first and deepest wounds were cut, for both seem to have regarded their art as the most vital factor in their lives. These wounds never really healed. And so, if the two men should have walked the same path, as Rolland suggested, they did not. Instead they went their separate ways, isolated from each other and estranged.

NOTES

CHAPTER I: The Two Men

1. Letter from Jean Paulhan to Frederick J. Harris, March 19, 1968.

2. Letter from Rolland to Gide, February 5, 1936, Archives Romain Rolland.

CHAPTER II: First Contacts

1. Carlo Bronne, *Rilke, Gide et Verhaeren* (Messein: Imprimerie Centrale de l'Ouest, 1955), pp. 65–66.

2. Rolland, "Journal intime," September, 1933–June, 1934, Archives Romain Rolland.

3. Gide, *Littérature engagée* (Paris: Gallimard, 1950), p. 124.

4. Gide, "Réponse à l'enquête: Pourquoi écrivez-vous?," *Littérature,* X (December 1919).

5. Letter from Rolland to Gide, July 8, 1909, Bibliothèque Doucet.

6. Jean-Richard Bloch (1884–1947) was a student of history before he became a writer. For quite some time he looked to Romain Rolland for guidance and inspiration.

7. Rolland, *Deux Hommes se rencontrent* (Paris: Albin Michel, 1964), p. 41.

8. *Ibid.,* p. 41.

9. *Ibid.,* p. 100.

10. *Ibid.,* p. 99.

11. February 25, 1913, was not a Tuesday. February 29 fell on a Tuesday, but the manuscript appears to read February 25.

12. Letter from Rolland to Gide, February 25(?), 1913, Bibliothèque Doucet.

13. Gide, *Dostoïevsky* (Paris: Plon-Nourrit, 1923), p. 73.

14. Letter from Rolland to Clara E. Collet, December 29, 1913, Archives Romain Rolland.

CHAPTER III: War

1. Rolland, *Journal des années de guerre* (Paris: Albin Michel, 1952), pp. 32–33.

2. Gide, *Journal*, Pléiade ed. (Paris: Gallimard, 1951–1954), I, 450. Justin O'Brien trans., *The Journals of André Gide* (New York: Alfred A. Knopf, 1949–1951), II, 50.

3. Rolland, "Au-dessus de la mêlée," *L'Esprit libre* (Paris: Albin Michel, 1953), p. 83.

4. Rolland, *Clerambault* (Paris: Albin Michel, 1920), p. 26.

5. Letter from Rolland to Maxim Gorki, January 8, 1931, Archives Romain Rolland.

6. Rolland, *Quinze Ans de combat* (Paris: Rieder, 1935), p. 114.

7. Rolland, "Pour la 'Fête de la Paix' à Lyon," November 10, 1928, Archives Romain Rolland.

8. Rolland, "La Volonté de la paix," *La Volonté de la Paix*, V (October–November, 1928).

9. Gide, *Si le grain ne meurt* (Paris: Gallimard, 1945), p. 272. Orig. ed. 1920–1921.

10. Gide, "Réflexions sur quelques points de littérature et de morale," *Œuvres complètes* (Paris: Gallimard, 1932–1939), II (1936), 433. Orig. ed. 1897.

11. Henri Massis, *Romain Rolland contre la France* (Paris: H. Floury, 1915), pp. 11–12.

12. René Arcos, "Souvenirs," Archives Romain Rolland.

13. Rolland, *L'Esprit libre*, pp. 112–113.

14. Rolland, excerpt from the "Journal intime," December, 1924–December, 1925, Archives Romain Rolland.

15. Rolland, *Journal des années de guerre*, p. 1695.

16. *Ibid.*, p. 443.

17. René Gillouin, philosopher and publicist born in 1881, brought out studies of Emmanuel Kant and Henri Bergson. He was also interested in religious questions and in the possible alliance of Catholicism and Protestantism. He accompanied Gide on his trip to Russia in 1936.

18. The Union pour la Vérité was a group founded by Paul Desjardins and directed by Georges Guy-Grand as a "Foyer de libre esprit."

19. *André Gide et notre temps* (Paris: Gallimard, 1935), p. 55.

20. Gide, *Si le grain ne meurt*, p. 32.

21. Malwida von Meysenbug (1816–1903) was a memoir and story writer and advocate of women's rights. Banished from Berlin in 1852, she went to London where she lived in the house of the Russian philosopher Alexander Herzen. After 1897 she lived in Rome, counting

among her friends Romain Rolland, Garibaldi, Liszt, Wagner, and Nietzsche.

22. Réne Cheval, *Romain Rolland, l'Allemagne et la guerre* (Paris: Presses Universitaires de France, 1963), p. 74.

23. Letter from Rolland to Clara Collet, April 25, 1906, Archives Romain Rolland.

24. Rolland, *L'Esprit libre,* pp. 63–64.

25. *Ibid.,* p. 66.

26. Rolland, *Journal des années de guerre,* p. 687.

27. Gustav Ador (1845–1928) was a member of the Geneva government after 1874 and presided over it in 1892 and 1906. He was president of the International Committee of the Red Cross after 1910 and at the start of the war founded an association to improve conditions for the prisoners of war and to facilitate communications with their families.

28. Henri Bachelin, who was serving in arms during World War I, wrote studies of Gerard de Nerval, J.-K. Huysmans, Charles Louis-Philippe, etc.

29. Letter from Gide to Rolland, October 20, 1914, Archives Romain Rolland. A considerable portion of this letter has been published in Rolland's *Journal des années de guerre,* pp. 92–93.

30. Letter from Rolland to Gide, October 26, 1914, Archives Romain Rolland. Published in large part in the *Journal des années de guerre,* pp. 93–94. Permission to reprint the unpublished portions was not granted by Mme Rolland.

31. As a writer, Jean Richepin (1849–1926) continued the romantic tradition and attracted attention by his scorn for convention.

32. Letter from Rolland to Alphonse de Châteaubriant, September 19, 1914, Archives Romain Rolland.

33. Rolland, *L'Esprit libre,* pp. 197–198.

34. *Ibid.,* p. 198.

35. Rolland, *Journal des années de guerre,* p. 940.

36. *Ibid.,* p. 476.

37. *Ibid.,* p. 1483.

38. Gide, *Journal,* I, 500.

39. Henri Ghéon (1875–1944) was one of the founders of the *N.R.F.* and one of the promoters of the Vieux-Colombier Theater.

40. Gide, *Journal,* I, 525.

41. Gide, "Deux Interviews," *Attendu que* (Algiers: Charlot, 1943), p. 40.

42. Letter from Gide to Rolland, November 10, 1914, Archives Romain Rolland.

43. Rolland, *Journal des années de guerre*, p. 213.

44. *Ibid.*, p. 123.

45. Rolland, *L'Esprit libre*, p. 85.

46. *Ibid.*, p. 78.

47. Rolland, *Journal des années de guerre*, p. 78.

48. Rolland, *L'Esprit libre*, pp. 91–95.

49. Rolland, *Journal des années de guerre*, p. 296.

50. Van Rysselberghe: family of the Belgian artist Theo Van Rysselberghe, with whose daughter Gide became intimately acquainted.

51. Gide, *Journal*, I, 1219. O'Brien trans., III, 313.

52. Renée Lang, ed., *Correspondance Rainer Maria Rilke–André Gide* (Paris: Corrêa, 1952), p. 13.

53. Rolland, excerpt from the "Journal intime," early April, 1913, Archives Romain Rolland.

54. Letter from Rolland to Rainer Maria Rilke, April 14, 1913, Archives Romain Rolland.

55. Rolland, excerpt from the "Journal intime," 1926–1927, Archives Romain Rolland.

56. *Correspondance Rilke–Gide*, p. 121.

57. *Ibid.*, p. 121.

58. *Ibid.*, p. 124.

59. Rolland, *Journal des années de guerre*, pp. 618–619.

60. *Correspondance Rilke–Gide*, p. 258.

61. Gide, "Deux Rencontres avec Romain Rolland," *Littérature engagée*, pp. 124–125.

62. Rolland, excerpt from the "Journal intime," 1915, Archives Romain Rolland.

63. Letter from Rolland to André Bourguignon, June 21, 1941, Archives Romain Rolland.

64. Letter from Gide to Rolland, January 11, 1916, Archives Romain Rolland.

65. Letter from Gide to Rolland, January 25, 1916, Archives Romain Rolland.

66. Rolland, *Journal des années de guerre*, p. 665.

67. Wilfred Monod (1867–1943), pastor for a time of the Oratoire in Paris, also held a post as professor in the Paris Faculty of Theology.

68. Anton Kippenberg (1874–1950) was head of the Insel Verlag in Leipzig.

69. The painter Pierre Bonnard (1867–1947). He achieved a real degree of recognition only after 1935.

70. Eugène Druet held a comprehensive exposition of Pierre Bonnard's work in 1922.

71. Letter from Gide to Rolland, February 17, 1916, Archives Romain Rolland.

72. Rolland, *Journal des années de guerre,* p. 666.

73. Rolland, "Journal intime," September, 1933–June, 1934, Archives Romain Rolland.

74. Léon Bazalgette (1873–1928) praised Rolland's articles against the war. He was a translator of Walt Whitman and wrote studies of Whitman and Emile Verhaeren.

75. Rolland, excerpt from the "Journal intime," March 17, 1913, Archives Romain Rolland.

76. Letter from Rolland to Emile Verhaeren, October 17, 1914, Archives Romain Rolland.

77. Letter from Rolland to Emile Verhaeren, November 23, 1914, Archives Romain Rolland.

78. Stefan Zweig, *Romain Rolland* (Frankfurt: Rütten, 1921), p. 207.

79. Rolland, *Le Voyage intérieur* (Paris: Albin Michel, 1959), p. 133. Orig. ed. 1942.

80. Rolland, *Journal des années de guerre,* p. 156.

81. Gide, *Journal,* I, 543–544. End of February or early March, 1916. O'Brien trans., II, 131.

82. *Ibid.,* p. 544.

83. Fragments published in *Le Parthenon,* November 5, 1913, Archives Romain Rolland.

84. Gide, *Journal,* I, 551, 617. O'Brien trans., II, 138, 197.

85. Gide, "Réflexions sur l'Allemagne," *Œuvres complètes,* IX (1935), 115. Orig. ed. 1919.

86. Gide, "Journal sans dates," *Nouvelle Revue Française,* LXX (July 1, 1919), 278. O'Brien trans. of *Journal,* II, 237.

87. Jean Delay, ed., *Correspondance André Gide–Roger Martin du Gard* (Paris: Gallimard, 1968), I, 145.

88. *Ibid.,* pp. 145–146.

89. *Ibid.,* p. 146.

90. Henri Massis, *Jugements* (Paris: Plon-Nourrit, 1924), p. 137.

91. *Ibid.,* p. 246.

92. *Correspondance Gide–Martin du Gard,* I, 266.

93. *Ibid.,* p. 268.

94. Gide, *Journal,* I, 544.

95. *Correspondance Gide–Martin du Gard,* I, 268.

96. Rolland, *Mémoires* (Paris: Albin Michel, 1956), p. 128.

CHAPTER IV: Art and the Artist

1. Rolland, *L'Esprit libre* (Paris: Albin Michel, 1953), p. 69.

2. Rolland, *Journal des années de guerre* (Paris: Albin Michel, 1952), p. 1770.

3. *Ibid.,* p. 1770.

4. Letter from Rolland to Heinz Nonveiller, October 22, 1926, Archives Romain Rolland.

5. Rolland, "Le Devoir des intellectuels contre la guerre," *Avenir Social,* May 1, 1927, p. 143.

6. Rolland, "Journal intime," 1893–1902, Archives Romain Rolland.

7. Rolland, *Deux Hommes se rencontrent* (Paris: Albin Michel, 1964), p. 36.

8. *Ibid.*

9. *Ibid.*

10. *Ibid.,* p. 41.

11. Rolland, excerpts from the "Journal intime," 1893–1902, Archives Romain Rolland.

12. Gide, "Les Limites de l'art," *Prétextes* (Paris: Mercure de France, 1947), p. 38. Orig. ed. 1903.

13. Gide, "Propositions," *Nouvelle Revue Française,* XXXVI (December, 1911), 649.

14. *Ibid.,* p. 651.

15. Gide, "De l'évolution du théâtre," *L'Hermitage,* II (1904), 5.

16. Gide, "Souvenirs littéraires et problèmes actuels," *Feuillets d'automne* (Paris: Mercure de France, 1949), p. 187.

17. Gide, *Journal des Faux-Monnayeurs* (Paris: Gallimard, 1967), p. 53. Orig. ed. 1926.

18. Gide, *Thésée* (Paris: Gallimard, 1946), p. 10.

19. Gide, *Si le grain ne meurt* (Paris: Gallimard, 1945), p. 287.

20. Gide, *Œdipe, Théâtre* (Paris: Gallimard, 1947), pp. 283–284. Orig. ed. 1931.

21. Gide, *Le Retour de l'enfant prodigue* (Paris: Gallimard, 1948), p. 193. Orig. ed. 1907.

22. Arthur R. Levy, *L'Idéalisme de Romain Rolland* (Paris: A.-G. Nizet, 1946), p. 124.

23. Gide, *Prétextes,* p. 105.

24. Rolland, *Musiciens d'aujourd'hui* (Paris: Hachette, 1949), pp. 63–67. Orig. ed. 1908.

25. Letter from Rolland to Cosette Padroux, April 15, 1905, Archives Romain Rolland.

26. *Ibid.,* early 1905.

27. Jean Delay, *La Jeunesse d'André Gide* (Paris: Gallimard, 1956), II, 647.

28. Gide, Préface to *Les Fleurs du mal de Charles Baudelaire* (Paris: Pelletan, 1917), p. xii.

29. Gide, "De l'évolution du théâtre," p. 10.

30. Gide, Préface to *Les Fleurs du mal*, p. xii.

31. Gide, *Le Traité du Narcisse, Œuvres complètes*, I (1933), 217. Orig. ed. 1891.

32. *Ibid.*, p. 218.

33. Gide, *Prétextes*, p. 118.

34. Gide, *Journal*, Pléiade ed. (Paris: Gallimard, 1951–1954), I, 738. O'Brien trans., II, 306.

35. Rolland, *Le Théâtre du peuple* (Paris: Albin Michel, 1913), p. 33. Orig. ed. 1903.

36. Rolland, Letter to the Académie des Sciences d'Art, October 20, 1925, Archives Romain Rolland.

37. Gide, *Le Traité du Narcisse*, p. 216.

38. Rolland, *Jean-Christophe* (Paris: Albin Michel, 1956), pp. 1139–1140. Orig. ed. 1903–1912.

39. Robert Dvorak, *Das Ethische und das Ästhetische bei Romain Rolland* (Bottrop i. W.: Wilh. Postberg, 1933), p. 27.

40. Gide, *Les Faux-Monnayeurs* (Paris: Gallimard, 1965), p. 156. Orig. ed. 1926.

41. Christian Sénéchal, *Romain Rolland* (Paris: Editions de la Caravelle, 1933), p. 28.

42. Gide, *Journal des Faux-Monnayeurs*, p. 30.

43. Gide, "Conférences sur Dostoïevsky," *Œuvres complètes*, XI (1936), 220.

44. Rolland, *Deux Hommes se rencontrent*, pp. 99–100.

45. Rolland, *Le Voyage intérieur* (Paris: Albin Michel, 1959), p. 134.

46. *Ibid.*, p. 135.

47. Rolland, *Le Théâtre du peuple*, p. 146.

48. Gide, *Philoctète, Œuvres complètes*, III, 33. Orig. ed. 1899.

49. Gide, "À propos des Déracinés," *Œuvres complètes*, II (1933), 440.

50. Gide, "De l'influence en littérature," *Œuvres complètes*, II (1933), 262. Orig. ed. 1900.

51. *Ibid.*, p. 259.

52. Gide, "Nationalisme et littérature," *Œuvres complètes*, VI (1934), 4. Orig. ed. 1909.

53. *Ibid.*, p. 4.

54. *Ibid.,* p. 6.

55. Rolland, *Le Cloître de la rue d'Ulm* (Paris: Albin Michel, 1952), p. 112.

56. Rolland, *Le Théâtre du peuple,* p. 142.

57. Rolland, *Jean-Christophe,* p. 1031.

58. Rolland, *Le Théâtre du peuple,* p. 118.

59. Gabriel Monod (1844–1912), historian who in 1905 was appointed to a professorship at the Collège de France.

60. Letter from Rolland to Gabriel Monod, January 28, 1891, Archives Romain Rolland.

61. Rolland, *Printemps romain* (Paris: Albin Michel, 1954), p. 40.

62. Rolland, *Quinze Ans de combat* (Paris: Rieder, 1935), p. v.

63. Rolland, *Jean-Christophe,* p. 1424.

64. René Arcos, *Romain Rolland* (Paris: Mercure de France, 1950), p. 105.

65. R.-M. Albérès, "Gide considéré comme esthète," *Nouvelle Revue Française, Hommage à André Gide* (Paris: Gallimard, 1951), p. 100.

CHAPTER V: Romain Rolland and the *N.R.F.*

1. *Romain Rolland et le mouvement florentin de "La Voce"* (Paris: Albin Michel, 1966), p. 261.

2. Jean Schlumberger, "Eveils," *Œuvres complétes* (Paris: Gallimard, 1958–1961), VI, 368.

3. Schlumberger, "Notes et chroniques, 1909," *Œuvres complètes,* I, 139.

4. *Ibid.,* p. 140.

5. Schlumberger, "Eveils," p. 380.

6. *Ibid.,* p. 380.

7. *Ibid.,* p. 381.

8. Schlumberger, "Notes et chroniques, 1909," p. 139.

9. Schlumberger, "Eveils," p. 373.

10. Schlumberger, "Notes et chroniques, 1909," p. 139.

11. Rolland, excerpt from the "Journal intime," March 17, 1913, Archives Romain Rolland.

12. René Arcos, *Romain Rolland* (Paris: Mercure de France, 1950), pp. 84–85.

13. *Ibid.,* p. 85.

14. *Ibid.*

15. *Ibid.,* p. 84.

16. Rolland, excerpt from the "Journal intime," October, 1925, Archives Romain Rolland.

17. Letter from Rolland to Marcel Martinet, August 12, 1924, Archives Romain Rolland.

18. Letter from Rolland to J.-R. Bloch, September 6, 1924, Archives Romain Rolland.

19. Letter from Rolland to Jacques Robefrance, November 16, 1927, Archives Romain Rolland.

20. Letter from Rolland to Louis Laloy, September 4, 1930, Archives Romain Rolland.

21. Robert de Traz was the editor of the *Revue de Genève* between the two wars.

22. Letter from Rolland to J.-R. Bloch, January 20, 1925, Archives Romain Rolland.

23. Letter from Rolland to J.-R. Bloch, January 20, 1925, Archives Romain Rolland.

24. Letter from Rolland to J.-R. Bloch, March 7, 1927, Archives Romain Rolland.

25. Letter from Rolland to Marcel Martinet, November 15, 1930, Archives Romain Rolland.

26. Letter from Rolland to André Kapélès, June 1, 1930, Archives Romain Rolland.

27. Letter from Rolland to Marcel Martinet, November 15, 1930, Archives Romain Rolland.

28. Jean-Bertrand Barrère, *Romain Rolland par lui même* (Paris: Seuil, 1960), pp. 183–184.

29. Letter from Rolland to Mme E. Marchand, January 28, 1931, Archives Romain Rolland.

30. Letters from Rolland to J.-R. Bloch, August 26, 1935, and February 24, 1936, Archives Romain Rolland.

31. Letter from Rolland to Jacques Copeau, Easter Monday, 1912, Archives Romain Rolland.

32. Rolland, *Deux Hommes se rencontrent* (Paris: Albin Michel, 1964), p. 61.

33. Letter from Jacques Copeau to Rolland, April 3, 1912, Archives Romain Rolland.

34. Letter from Rolland to Copeau, Easter Monday, 1912, Archives Romain Rolland.

35. Letter from Rolland to Copeau, October 13, 1912, Archives Romain Rolland.

36. Letter from Copeau to Rolland, October 24, 1912, Archives Romain Rolland.

37. Letter from Rolland to Copeau, December 18, 1913, Archives Romain Rolland. René Morax, a Swiss writer, created the Théâtre du Jorat at Mézières, where subjects were taken from the Bible or from national tradition.

38. Letter from Rolland to Copeau, July 15, 1914, Archives Romain Rolland. Grazia Deledda, an Italian writer, wrote at first of the life and character of her native Sardinia, turning later to portray refined but tormented heroes of high society.

39. Albert Thibaudet, *"Jean-Christophe—La Nouvelle Journée* par Romain Rolland," *Nouvelle Revue Française,* L (February 1, 1913), 316.

40. Schlumberger, "Eveils," p. 378.

41. Gide, "Marcel Drouin," *La Table Ronde,* May, 1949, pp. 710–711.

42. Schlumberger, "Eveils," pp. 378–379.

43. Letter from Rolland to Copeau, November 2, 1915, Archives Romain Rolland.

44. Letter from Copeau to Rolland, November 19, 1915, Archives Romain Rolland.

45. Henri Guilbeau published his *Pour Romain Rolland* in response to Massis's *Romain Rolland contre la France.* In 1915 Rolland found him a position at the Prisoner of War Agency in Geneva, and Guilbeau soon thereafter founded the review *Demain,* which he sought to keep in line with Rolland's thinking.

46. Letter from Copeau to Henri Guilbeau, November 19, 1915, Archives Romain Rolland.

47. Rolland, *Journal des années de guerre* (Paris: Albin Michel, 1952), p. 577.

48. Letter from Copeau to Rolland, October 10, 1915, Archives Romain Rolland.

49. Rolland, *Journal des années de guerre,* p. 504.

50. Letter from Roger Martin du Gard to Rolland, July 10, 1919, Archives Romain Rolland.

51. Letter from Rolland to J.-R. Bloch, July 20, 1919, Archives Romain Rolland.

52. Letter from Rolland to Waldo Frank, September 8, 1919, Archives Romain Rolland.

53. Letter from Rolland to J.-R. Bloch, November 28, 1920, Archives Romain Rolland.

54. Letter from Rolland to J.-R. Bloch, October 12, 1920, Archives Romain Rolland.

55. Letter from Rolland to Jean Paulhan, August 25, 1928, Archives Romain Rolland.

56. Letter from Rolland to Paulhan, January 12, 1932, Archives Romain Rolland.

57. Letter from Rolland to Paulhan, October 31, 1939, Archives Romain Rolland.

58. Letter from Rolland to Paulhan, June 22, 1943, Archives Romain Rolland.

59. Letter from Rolland to Pierre Abraham, July 26, 1932, Archives Romain Rolland.

CHAPTER VI: God and Religion, Christ and Christianity

1. Jean Psichiari (1854–1929) was a writer and philologist who became professor of modern Greek at the Ecole des Langues Orientales in Paris.

2. Paul Claudel, Préface, *Correspondance entre Louis Gillet et Romain Rolland* (Paris: Albin Michel, 1949), p. 10.

3. Rolland, *Le Voyage intérieur* (Paris: Albin Michel, 1959), p. 93.

4. *Ibid.*, p. 93.

5. Rolland, *Le Cloître de la rue d'Ulm* (Paris: Albin Michel, 1952), p. 247.

6. Rolland, *Le Voyage intérieur*, p. 94.

7. *Ibid.*

8. Gide, *Les Cahiers et les poésies d'André Walter* (Paris: Gallimard, 1952), p. 27. Orig ed. 1891–1892.

9. Gide, *Les Nourritures terrestres* (Paris: Gallimard, 1964), p. 30. Orig. ed. 1897.

10. Letter from Rolland to Gabriel Monod, January 28, 1891, Archives Romain Rolland.

11. Gide, "Réflexions sur quelques points de littérature et de morale," *Œuvres complètes,* II (1933), 414.

12. Germaine Brée, *André Gide, l'insaisissable Protée* (Paris: Les Belles Lettres, 1953), p. 54.

13. Gide, *Les Nourritures terrestres*, p. 19.

14. Gide, *Œdipe, Théâtre* (Paris: Gallimard, 1947), p. 288.

15. Gide, *Les Nourritures terrestres*, p. 212.

16. Gide, *André Walter*, p. 112.

17. Gide, *Journal*, Pléiade ed. (Paris: Gallimard, 1951–1954), II, 310.

18. Gide, *Les Nourritures terrestres*, p. 21.

19. Gide, *Feuillets d'automme* (Paris: Mercure de France, 1949), p. 253.

20. Gide, "Réflexions sur quelques points de littérature et de morale," p. 415.

21. Gide, *Numquid et tu?* (Paris: Edition de la Pléiade, 1926), p. 13. Orig. ed. 1922.

22. Gide, "Deux Interviews imaginaires," *Feuillets d'automne,* pp. 253–254.

23. Pierre Teilhard de Chardin (1884–1954), philosopher, scientist, and theologian, was known especially for his work in the fields of geology and paleontology, and for his philosophical and scientific considerations of evolution.

24. Gide, "Feuillets," *Journal,* I, 725. O'Brien trans., II, 294.

25. Gide, *Feuillets d'automne,* pp. 257–259.

26. Gide, "Réflexions sur quelques points de littérature et de morale," p. 422.

27. Gide, *Journal,* II, 122–123. O'Brien trans., IV, 113–114.

28. Gide, *Feuillets d'automne,* p. 271.

29. *Ibid.,* pp. 271–273.

30. *Ibid.,* p. 272.

31. Gide, *Et nunc manet in te* (Neuchâtel: Ides et Calendes, 1947), p. 119.

32. Gide, *André Walter,* p. 71.

33. Gide, "Réflexions sur quelques points de littérature et de morale," p. 414.

34. Rolland, *Le Voyage intérieur,* p. 36.

35. *Ibid.*

36. *Ibid.,* p. 37.

37. Rolland, *Jean-Christophe* (Paris: Albin Michel, 1956), p. 264.

38. *Ibid.,* p. 1442.

39. Rolland, excerpt from the "Journal intime," May 1, 1922–December 31, 1923, Archives Romain Rolland.

40. Rolland, *Mémoires* (Paris: Albin Michel, 1956), p. 144.

41. Letter from Rolland to Frank Abauzit, February 23, 1914, Archives Romain Rolland.

42. Letter from Rolland to Raymond d'Estiveaud, August 8, 1920, Archives Romain Rolland.

43. Gide, *Journal,* I, 367.

44. Jean Delay, ed., *Correspondance André Gide–Roger Martin du Gard,* II, 426.

45. Letter from Rolland to Charles Bernard, February 26, 1931, Archives Romain Rolland.

46. Paul Claudel, "La Pensée religieuse de Romain Rolland," *La Revue* (des Deux Mondes), January 15, 1949, pp. 210–211.

47. Jacques Robichez, *Romain Rolland* (Paris: Hatier, 1961), p. 105.

48. Paul Claudel, "La Pensée religieuse de Romain Rolland," p. 195.

49. *Ibid.,* p. 211.

50. Rolland, *La Vie de Ramakrishna* (Paris: Stock, 1956), p. 186. Orig. ed. 1929.

51. Letter from Rolland to Leon Tolstoy, August 23, 1901, Archives Romain Rolland.

52. Rolland, *Pierre et Luce* (Paris: Albin Michel, 1958), pp. 149–150. Orig. ed. 1920.

53. Rolland, *Le Voyage intérieur,* p. 27.

54. *Ibid.*

55. Gide, *Si le grain ne meurt* (Paris: Gallimard, 1945), p. 290.

56. Gide, *André Walter,* p. 113.

57. Gide, *Numquid et tu?,* p. 14.

58. Gide, *Journal,* I, 675. O'Brien trans., II, 250.

59. *Ibid.,* p. 675. O'Brien trans., II, 250.

60. Gide, *Les Nourritures terrestres,* p. 200.

61. Gide, *Le Retour de l'enfant prodigue* (Paris: Gallimard, 1948), p. 181.

62. *Ibid.,* p. 181.

63. *Ibid.,* pp. 183–184.

64. *Ibid.,* p. 184.

CHAPTER VII: The Morality of Individualism

1. Justin O'Brien, *Portrait of André Gide: A Critical Biography* (New York: McGraw-Hill, 1964), p. 206. Orig. ed. 1953.

2. Gide, *Si le grain ne meurt* (Paris: Gallimard, 1945), p. 72.

3. Gide, *Les Nourritures terrestres* (Paris: Gallimard, 1964), p. 20.

4. Gide, *Les Faux-Monnayeurs* (Paris: Gallimard, 1965), p. 442.

5. Gide, *Journal,* Pléiade ed. (Paris: Gallimard, 1951–1954), I, 30.

6. Gide, *Œdipe, Théâtre* (Paris: Gallimard, 1947), p. 272.

7. Gide, *Les Cahiers et les poésies d'André Walter* (Paris: Gallimard, 1952), p. 72.

8. Gide, "Pages inédites," *Œuvres complètes,* XI (1936), 24.

9. Gide, *Les Nourritures terrestres,* p. 185.

10. Gide, *André Walter,* p. 111.

11. Gide, "Pages inédites," pp. 25–26.

12. Gide, *Les Nourritures terrestres,* p. 180.

13. *Ibid.,* p. 157.

14. *Ibid.,* p. 231.

15. Gide, *André Walter,* p. 112.

16. Gide, "Pages inédites," p. 30.

17. Gide, *Numquid et tu?* (Paris: Editions de la Pléiade, 1926), p. 19.

18. Gide, *Journal,* I, 1083. O'Brien trans., III, 196.

19. Gide, "Réflexions sur quelques points de littérature et de morale," *Œuvres complètes,* II (1933), 419.

20. Gide, *Les Nourritures terrestres,* p. 115.

21. *Ibid.*

22. *Ibid.,* p. 44.

23. Gide, *André Walter,* p. 27.

24. Gide, *Les Nourritures terrestres,* p. 105.

25. Gide, *Si le grain ne meurt,* p. 197.

26. Gide, *Journal,* I, 978.

27. *Ibid.,* I, 996. O'Brien trans., III, 118.

28. *Ibid.,* p. 729.

29. *Ibid.,* p. 1268.

30. Gide, *Le Traité du Narcisse, Œuvres complètes,* I (1933), 216.

31. Gide, *Le Retour de l'enfant prodigue* (Paris: Gallimard, 1948), p. 189.

32. Gide, *Si le grain ne meurt,* p. 287.

33. Gide, *Divers* (Paris: Gallimard, 1931), p. 207.

34. Gide, *André Walter,* p. 48.

35. Gide, *Le Retour de l'enfant prodigue,* p. 203.

36. *Ibid.,* pp. 207–208.

37. Gide, *Philoctète, Œuvres complètes,* III (1933), 32. Orig. ed. 1899.

38. Gide, *L'Immoraliste* (Paris: Mercure de France, 1964), p. 115. Orig. ed. 1902.

39. Gide, Préface de 1901 au *Roi Candaule, Théâtre,* p. 159.

40. Gide, *Paludes* (Paris: Gallimard, 1926), pp. 107–108. Orig. ed. 1895.

41. Gide, *Si le grain ne meurt,* p. 275.

42. *Ibid.*

43. Rolland, *Le Cloître de la rue d'Ulm* (Paris: Albin Michel, 1952), p. 239.

44. Rolland, *Jean-Christophe* (Paris: Albin Michel, 1956), p. 789.

45. *Ibid.,* p. 1536.

46. Rolland, "Tolstoy: l'esprit libre," *Les Cahiers Idéalistes Français,* X (November, 1917), 291.

47. Rolland, *Jean-Christophe,* p. 1536.

48. *Ibid.,* p. 1538.

CHAPTER VIII: Gide, Rolland, and Communism

1. *André Gide et notre temps* (Paris: Gallimard, 1935), p. 65.

2. Gide, *Journal,* Pléiade ed. (Paris: Gallimard, 1951–1954), I, 1044. O'Brien trans., III, 160.

3. The precise date of the text of July 27 and that of May 13 is not given in the *Nouvelle Revue Française,* where both are listed simply as having been written in 1931.

4. The text appears in the *Nouvelle Revue Française* as "une société sans cloisons" ("a society without divisions"). The version of the Pléiade edition has been retained here.

5. Gide, *Journal,* I, 1066. O'Brien trans., III, 179–180.

6. *André Gide et notre temps,* pp. 44–50.

7. Gide, *Jeunesse* (Neuchâtel: Ides et Calendes, 1945), p. 9.

8. *André Gide et notre temps,* pp. 50–51.

9. Gide, *Journal,* I, 870. O'Brien trans., III, 5.

10. Claude Mauriac, *Conversations avec André Gide* (Paris: Albin Michel, 1951), p. 193.

11. Gide, *Journal,* I, 1132. O'Brien trans., III, 237.

12. Rolland, *Mémoires* (Paris: Albin Michel, 1956), p. 68.

13. Letter from Rolland to Runham Brown, February 20, 1931, Archives Romain Rolland.

14. Letter from Rolland to Léon Pierre-Quint, December 21, 1932, Archives Romain Rolland.

15. Rolland, *Quinze Ans de combat* (Paris: Rieder, 1935), p. v.

16. *Ibid.,* p. 83.

17. Rolland, *L'Esprit libre* (Paris: Albin Michel, 1953), p. 211.

18. Rolland, *Quinze Ans de combat,* p. 80.

19. Gide, *Journal,* I, 1140. O'Brien trans., III, 244.

20. André Breton, *Misère de la poésie* (Paris: Editions Surréalistes, 1932), p. 3.

21. *Ibid.,* p. 29.

22. *Ibid.*

23. Félicien Challaye, sociologist who published studies on Nietzsche, Péguy, Jaurès, Japan, the Congo, etc.

24. Gide, *Littérature engagée* (Paris: Gallimard, 1950), pp. 15–16.

25. Rolland, *Par la révolution, la paix* (Paris: Editions Sociales Internationales, 1935), p. 31.

26. *Ibid.,* p. 48.

27. Gide, *Littérature engagée,* p. 15.

28. Rolland, *Par la révolution, la paix,* p. 56.

29. *Ceux qui ont choisi* (Paris: Association des Ecrivains et Artistes Révolutionnaires, 1933), pp. 3–5.

30. Gide, *Littérature engagée,* pp. 20–21.

31. *Ceux qui ont choisi,* p. 5.

32. *Ibid.,* p. 7.

33. *Ibid.*, p. 8.

34. *Ibid.*, p. 21.

35. Rolland, *Quinze Ans de combat*, p. 206.

36. Gide, *Littérature engagée*, p. 39.

37. Gide, *Journal*, I, 1182–1183. O'Brien trans., III, 281–282.

38. *Ibid.*, I, 1180. O'Brien trans., III, 280.

39. *Ibid.*, I, 1183. O'Brien trans., III, 282.

40. Gide, *Littérature engagée*, pp. 39–40.

41. *Ibid.*, p. 40.

42. Letter from Rolland to Henri Barbusse, February 2, 1922, Archives Romain Rolland.

43. *Ibid.*

44. *Ibid.*

45. Rolland, excerpt from the "Journal intime," December, 1932–September, 1933, Archives Romain Rolland.

46. Rolland, *Par la révolution, la paix*, p. 69.

47. Gide, *Littérature engagée*, p. 41.

48. *Ibid.*, pp. 113–114.

49. *Ibid.*, p. 83.

50. Letter from André Suarès to Rolland, February 19, 1933, Archives Romain Rolland.

51. Carl v. Ossietzky (1889–1938), German journalist who, as a pacifist, attacked secret military organizations that were forming after World War I and joined with supporters of the Soviet Union. In 1932 he was condemned to a year of prison and upon his release was again imprisoned in a concentration camp by the Nazis from 1933 to 1936. He was awarded the Nobel Peace Prize in 1935. He edited the antifascist, antimilitarist organ *Die Weltbühne* from 1926 until it was banned in Germany in 1933, after which it continued publication in Prague, Zurich, and Paris.

52. Draft of a letter from Rolland to Gide, Archives Romain Rolland.

53. The journalist Kurt Hiller was a socialist, though an opponent of Marxism. He was also an opponent of power politics and from 1926 to 1933 was the leader of a group of revolutionary pacifists.

54. Letter from Rolland to Gide, April 8, 1934, Bibliothèque Doucet.

55. Rolland, excerpts from the "Journal intime," September, 1933–June, 1934, Archives Romain Rolland.

56. Letter from Gide to Rolland, Archives Romain Rolland.

57. Gide, "Deux Rencontres avec Romain Rolland," *Littérature engagée*, pp. 125–126.

58. Ramon Fernandez (1894–1944), son of a Mexican diplomat and of a French mother, was the author of a number of literary portraits: Gide, Proust, Balzac. He became a strong Marxist supporter after 1934.

59. Paul Vaillant-Couturier (1892–1937) was a member of the directing committee of the French Communist party in 1921, a delegate from 1919 to 1928 and again in 1936 and from 1928 editor-in-chief of *l'Humanité*.

60. Palekh: a locality in the U.S.S.R. known from the eighteenth century for icon paintings. After the October Revolution ateliers were founded in Palekh for decorating and painting everyday objects, some of which were designed as lacquer ware.

61. Rolland, excerpts from the "Journal intime," September, 1933–June, 1934, Archives Romain Rolland.

62. Rolland, "Journal intime," end of January–early February, 1936, Archives Romain Rolland.

63. Letter from Rolland to Gide, February 5, 1936, Archives Romain Rolland.

64. Letter from Rolland to Maxim Gorki, July 30, 1935, Archives Romain Rolland.

65. Letter from Rolland to Christian Sénéchal, July 9, 1935, Archives Romain Rolland.

66. Letter from Rolland to Sénéchal, August 5, 1935, Archives Romain Rolland.

67. Mme Rolland's first marriage to the Russian, Prince Koudacheff, ended when her husband died.

68. Letter from Rolland to Charles Bernard, September 21, 1934, Archives Romain Rolland.

69. Rolland, excerpt from the "Journal intime," October, 1935–July, 1936, Archives Romain Rolland.

70. Gide, *Littérature engagée,* p. 134.

71. Gide, *Retour de l'U.R.S.S.,* suivi de *Retouches à mon Retour de l'U.R.S.S.* (Paris: Gallimard, 1950), p. 13. Orig. ed. 1936.

72. *Ibid.,* p. 15.

73. *Ibid.,* p. 32.

74. *Ibid.,* p. 34.

75. *Ibid.,* p. 43.

76. *Ibid.,* p. 44.

77. *Ibid.,* p. 69.

78. *Ibid.,* p. 56.

79. *Ibid.,* p. 76.

80. *Ibid.*, p. 80.

81. "Les Variations de M. André Gide," *Candide,* March, 1933.

82. François Mauriac, "Les Esthètes fascinés," *Echo de Paris,* September 10, 1932.

83. Z. Lvovsky, "Moscou répond à la conversion d'André Gide," *Nouvelles Littéraires,* December 24, 1932.

84. Thierry Maulnier, "Les Essais," *Revue Universelle,* April 15, 1934, pp. 243–244.

85. Gide, *Journal,* I, 1288.

86. Gide, *Littérature engagée,* p. 55.

87. Gide, *Journal,* I, 1116–1117. O'Brien trans., III, 224.

88. *Ibid.,* 1179–1180. O'Brien trans., III, 279.

89. Gide, *Littérature engagée,* p. 58.

90. Schlumberger, "Compagnons," *Œuvres complètes* (Paris: Gallimard, 1958–1961), VII, 199.

91. *Ibid.,* pp. 193–194.

92. *Ibid.,* p. 199.

93. Jean Delay, ed., *Correspondance André Gide–Roger Martin du Gard* (Paris: Gallimard, 1968), II, 86–87.

94. Victor Serge, *Mémoires d'un révolutionnaire* (Paris: Seuil, 1951), pp. 346–347.

95. Rolland, letter to J.-R. Bloch, March 3, 1938, Archives Romain Rolland.

96. Rolland, "Journal intime," August 1, 1936–April 15, 1937, Archives Romain Rolland.

97. Gide, *Journal,* I, 1241. O'Brien trans., III, 334.

98. Rolland, letter to J.-R. Bloch, March 19, 1936, Archives Romain Rolland.

99. Letter from Rolland to Bloch, November 8, 1936, Archives Romain Rolland.

100. Jean Grenier, "L'Âge des orthodoxies," *Nouvelle Revue Française,* April 1, 1936, p. 486.

101. *Ibid.,* pp. 484–489.

102. Gide, "Conférences sur Dostoïevsky," *Œuvres complètes,* XI (1936), 289.

103. *Ibid.,* p. 262.

104. Gide, *Journal,* I, 1180. O'Brien trans., III, 279.

105. Letter from Rolland to René Arcos, November 27, 1936, Archives Romain Rolland.

106. Letter from Rolland to Thérèse Pottecher, December 10, 1936, Archives Romain Rolland.

107. Pierre Naville, author of a number of works on Marx and the working class. A friend, too, of Leon Trotsky's and author of *Trotsky vivant*.

108. Gide, *Journal*, I, 1142. O'Brien trans., III, 246.

109. Gide, *Littérature engagée*, p. 37.

110. Claude Naville, *André Gide et le communisme* (Paris: Librairie du Travail, 1936), p. 11. Preface by Pierre Naville.

111. Victor Serge, *Mémoires d'un révolutionnaire*, p. 347.

112. *Correspondance Gide–Martin du Gard*, II, 87, 119.

113. Victor Serge, *From Lenin to Stalin* (New York: Pioneer, 1937), p. 56.

114. Gide, *Journal*, I, 1288. O'Brien trans., III, 375.

115. Victor Serge, *Mémoires d'un révolutionnaire*, p. 365.

116. Gide, *Littérature engagée*, pp. 155–156.

117. Isaac Deutscher, *The Prophet Outcast* (New York: Oxford University Press, 1963), pp. 327–328.

118. Leon Trotsky, "I Stake My Life!" *The Basic Writings of Trotsky*, ed. Irving Howe (New York: Random House, 1963), p. 288.

Gide's own account (of which Trotsky's statement is a paraphrase) appears in *Retour de l'U.R.S.S.* suivi de *Retouches à mon Retour de l'U.R.S.S.*, pp. 64–65:

Sur la route de Tiflis à Batoum, nous traversons Gori, la petite ville où naquit Staline. J'ai pensé qu'il serait sans doute courtois de lui envoyer un message, en réponse à l'accueil de l'U.R.S.S. où, partout, nous avons été acclamés, festoyés, choyés. Je ne trouverai jamais meilleure occasion. Je fais arrêter l'auto devant la poste et tends le texte d'une dépêche. Elle dit à peu près: "En passant à Gori au cours de notre merveilleux voyage, j'éprouve le besoin cordial de vous adresser..." Mais ici, le traducteur s'arrête: Je ne puis point parler ainsi. Le "vous" ne suffit point, lorsque ce "vous," c'est Staline. Cela n'est point décent. Il y faut ajouter quelque chose. Et comme je manifeste certaine stupeur, on se consulte. On me propose: "Vous, chef des travailleurs," ou "maître des peuples" ou... je ne sais plus quoi. Je trouve cela absurde; proteste que Staline est au-dessus de ces flagorneries. Je me débats en vain. Rien à faire. On n'acceptera ma dépêche que si je consens au rajout. Et, comme il s'agit d'une traduction que je ne suis pas à même de contrôler, je me soumets de guerre lasse, mais en déclinant toute responsabilité et songeant avec tristesse que tout cela contribue à mettre entre Staline et le peuple une effroyable, une infranchissable distance.

119. Pierre Naville, *Trotsky vivant* (Paris: Julliard, 1962), p. 96.

120. Gide, *Littérature engagée*, p. 155.

121. Nikolai Alexeïevitch Ostrovski (1904–1936), Soviet writer who, until his death, was the spiritual leader of the Communist youth movement.

122. *Völkischer Beobachter,* founded in 1886 as a rightist newspaper, became Hitler's national socialist daily. Published in Munich.

123. Rolland, "L'U.R.S.S. en a vu bien d'autres," *l'Humanité,* January 18, 1937.

124. Louis Guilloux, "D'un voyage en U.R.S.S.," *Nouvelle Revue Française, Hommage à André Gide* (Paris: Gallimard, 1951), pp. 248–249.

125. I am obliged to paraphrase this text since Mme Rolland did not give me permission to copy it verbatim.

126. Rolland, excerpt from the "Journal intime," August 1, 1936–April 15, 1937, Archives Romain Rolland.

127. Rolland, excerpt from the "Journal intime," August 1, 1936–April 15, 1937, Archives Romain Rolland. I am obliged to paraphrase this text since Mme Rolland did not give me permission to copy it verbatim.

128. Rolland, excerpt from the "Journal intime," August, 1936–April, 1937, Archives Romain Rolland.

129. Gide, *Retour de l'U.R.S.S.,* suivi de *Retouches à mon Retour de l'U.R.S.S.,* p. 107.

130. Rolland, excerpt from the "Journal intime," June 29, 1937, Archives Romain Rolland.

131. Victor Basch, philosopher born in Budapest. He was given the chair in esthetics that had been created at the Sorbonne in 1918. At Rennes he founded the first provincial section of the Ligue des Droits de l'Homme and became its president in 1926. In this capacity he was a supporter of antifascist politics and was assassinated during the German occupation in World War II.

132. Paul Langevin, physicist who was given the chair in general and experimental physics at the Collège de France in 1909. In 1904 he had succeeded Pierre Curie at the Ecole de Physique et de Chimie and in 1925 became its director.

133. Albert Bayet was a teacher of sociology at the Sorbonne. His concern for republican rights and freedoms led him to collaborate with many radical socialist newspapers.

134. Andrée Viollis, pseudonym for Andrée Françoise Caroline d'Ardenne de Tizac. She accompanied Pierre Herbart on a trip to China and wrote several books on China.

135. Rolland, excerpt from the "Journal intime," June 29, 1937, Archives Romain Rolland.

136. Max Beloff, *The Foreign Policy of Soviet Russia, 1929–1941* (New York: Oxford University Press, 1949), II, 30–31.

137. Claude Mauriac, *Conversations avec André Gide,* pp. 13–14.

138. *Ibid.,* p. 14.

139. *Ibid.,* p. 19. The anthropologist Paul Rivet created the Musée de l'Homme in 1937. He participated in political life as the Conseiller Municipal de Paris and Conseiller Général de la Seine in 1935.

140. Jean Guéhenno, "Lettre ouverte à André Gide," *Vendredi,* December 17, 1937.

141. Black Shirts: popular name given to Italian fascist groups, the first of which was established in Milan in 1919. Moroccans: a nationalist movement against France was gaining strength at this time in Morocco.

142. Gide, "Lettre à *Vendredi,*" *Vendredi,* December 24, 1937.

143. Guéhenno, "Réponse à André Gide," *Vendredi,* December 24, 1937.

144. *Retour de l'U.R.S.S.,* p. 160.

145. *Ibid.,* pp. 160–174.

146. *Ibid.,* p. 174.

147. Claude Mauriac, *Conversations avec André Gide,* pp. 212–213.

148. Jacques Robichez, *Romain Rolland* (Paris: Hatier, 1961), p. 102.

149. *Correspondance Gide–Martin du Gard,* II, 154–155.

150. René Cheval, *Romain Rolland, l'Allemagne et la guerre* (Paris: Presses Universitaires de France, 1963), p. 723.

151. *Correspondance Gide–Martin du Gard,* II, 288.

CHAPTER IX: *Conclusion*

1. Gide, *Retour de l'U.R.S.S.,* suivi de *Retouches à mon Retour de l'U.R.S.S.* (Paris: Gallimard, 1950), p. 14.

2. Rolland, *L'Âme enchantée* (Paris: Albin Michel, 1966), I, 109. Orig. ed. 1922–1923.

3. *Ibid.,* p. 163.

4. *Ibid.,* p. 164.

5. Letter from Rolland to Harold Bobe, November 12, 1936, Archives Romain Rolland.

6. Paul Iseler, *Les Débuts d'André Gide vus par Pierre Louÿs* (Paris: Editions du Sagittaire, 1937), p. 82.

7. Rolland, *Retour au Palais Farnèse* (Paris: Albin Michel, 1956), p. 358.

8. Gide, *Feuillets d'automme* (Paris: Mercure de France, 1949), pp. 273–274.

9. *Ibid.*, p. 273.

10. Gide, *Si le grain ne meurt* (Paris: Gallimard, 1945), p. 87.

11. Gide, *Les Faux-Monnayeurs* (Paris: Gallimard, 1965), p. 387.

12. Gide, *Les Cahiers et les poésies d'André Walter* (Paris: Gallimard, 1952), p. 60.

13. Klaus Mann, *André Gide, die Geschichte eines Europäers* (Zurich: Steinberg, 1948), p. 28.

FRENCH TEXTS

Pages 3–4:

Rolland et Gide ne pouvaient pas se souffrir. Ce "cafard" disait l'un et l'autre "ce faux artiste."

Page 8:

Mon cher Gide

Jeudi prochain à 4 heures et quart, Romain Rolland vous donne rendez-vous dans son cabinet de l'amphithéâtre Turgot. Il m'indique, dans sa lettre, le chemin qui nous y mènera. Voulez-vous, à 3 heures et demie, vous trouver sous les Galeries de l'Odéon. Nous nous y rencontrerons et nous rendrons ensemble à la Sorbonne. Heureux de vous revoir bientôt. Très à vous

E. Verhaeren

Page 9:

Je me souviens du jour où je fis sa connaissance. C'était nombre d'années avant la guerre. Romain Rolland faisait alors un cours sur la musique ancienne au Collège de France. Je souhaitais le voir et l'entendre, et me laissai très volontiers entraîner par Verhaeren avec qui j'étais intimement lié. Tous deux nous écoutâmes avec recueillement, ainsi que le nombreux auditoire, la voix chaude et vibrante du maître, jeune encore mais déjà célèbre, dont la grave et cordiale autorité s'exerçait comme involontairement par le simple effet d'une conviction profonde et d'une dignité naturelle. Son cours était coupé d'exemples qu'il donnait lui-même au piano, avec une éloquence grave et persuasive. Nul souci personnel de se faire valoir lui-même, mais bien seulement le musicien (je ne sais plus lequel) qu'il interprétait. À la fin du cours, Verhaeren et moi, nous nous approchâmes de lui. Il nous parla avec cette même simplicité qui, déjà, faisait de son cours une sorte de causerie amicale.

Page 10:

Vous pouvez classer les écrivains selon que leur réponse à votre enquête commencera par "afin de," "pour" ou par "parce que."

Il y aura ceux pour qui la littérature est surtout un but, et ceux pour qui surtout un moyen.

Quant à moi, j'écris parce que j'ai une bonne plume, et pour être lu par vous... Mais je ne réponds jamais aux enquêtes.

Page 11:

Oubliez ma lettre. Ce n'était qu'une de ces discussions amicales, òu involontairement on outre un peu sa pensée.

Page 11:

sauf la forme — il y a beaucoup moins à apprendre dans la littérature parisienne d'aujourd'hui que dans la littérature du reste de l'Europe; et il y a beaucoup moins à apprendre dans la littérature européenne que dans le reste de la vie des hommes européens. L'art, qui jadis fut prophète, est aujourd'hui distancé par la vie.

Pages 11–12:

Très sincèrement je ne vois pas bien comment l'amour de Tolstoy et de Whitman peut s'accorder avec celui de l'art à la façon de Gide ou de Duhamel. Je n'énonce aucune critique contre ceux-ci. Mais s'ils peuvent, à la rigueur, s'harmoniser tous ensemble dans une intelligence purement critique, contemplative et statique, ils ne le peuvent pas (à mon sens) dans un esprit créateur et constructeur.

Page 12:

ces belles monographies de Romain Rolland

Page 13:

qui est un de nos meilleurs écrivains. Les fragments que j'ai lus de lui dans la *Nouvelle Revue Française* m'ont paru aussi fort beaux.

CHAPTER III: War

Page 14:

Je suis accablé. Je voudrais être mort. Il est horrible de vivre au milieu de cette humanité démente, et d'assister, impuissant, à la faillite de la civilisation. Cette guerre européenne est la plus grande catastrophe de l'histoire, depuis des siècles, la ruine de nos espoirs les plus saints en la fraternité humaine.

Page 15:

Journée d'attente angoissée. Pourquoi ne mobilise-t-on-pas? Tout le temps qu'on diffère est autant de gagné pour l'Allemagne.

Page 15:

Europe, élargis-toi ou meurs.

Pages 15–16:

L'idéal qui s'en va est la patrie nationale qui veut être et rester la première. . . .

L'idéal qui vient est la Patrie humaine qui demande à toutes les autres de se consentir des sacrifices mutuels, afin de s'harmoniser et de coopérer à la grande œuvre commune: la maîtrise de la Nature par le genre humain.

Page 16:

il faut briser avec un passé, certainement vénérable, mais qui a fait suffisamment ses preuves de sa malfaisance et de son incapacité sanglante.

Page 16:

terre de l'humanité et terre de l'Esprit, terre de Sacrifice et de la Clarté

Page 17:

Ce triomphe moral, nous devons tous vouloir qu'elle le garde jusqu'au bout, qu'elle reste jusqu'au bout juste, lucide et humaine. Je n'ai jamais pu distinguer la cause de la France de celle de l'humanité. . . . Je veux que la France soit aimée, je veux qu'elle soit victorieuse non seulement par le droit . . . , mais par la superiorité de son grand cœur généreux. Je veux qu'elle soit assez forte pour combattre sans haine et pour voir, même dans ceux qu'elle est forcée d'abattre, des frères qui se trompent et dont il faut avoir pitié, après les avoir mis dans l'incapacité de nuire.

Pages 17–18:
ce n'était pas seulement le cœur de la France que je voulais entendre. C'était le cœur de ma vraie patrie: l'Europe. Si j'étais resté en France, jamais les battements de ce cœur ne seraient parvenus jusqu'à moi. En Suisse, et seulement en Suisse, je pouvais recevoir directement les confidences de l'un et de l'autre camps. En Suisse seulement, je pouvais juger impartialement: car là, et là seulement, je pouvais réunir tous les éléments du procès.

Page 18:
  La guerre a beau avoir fini, dit-on, depuis trois mois, jamais la compression de la pensée n'a été pire. La censure des lettres est intolérable. La moitié de ma correspondance de France est supprimée; le reste, caviardé à tour de bras.

Page 19:
En arriver à penser cela, voici qui est grave.

Page 20:
  Je ne suis pas, Gerhart Hauptmann, de ces Français qui traitent l'Allemagne de barbare. Je connais la grandeur intellectuelle et morale de votre puissante race. Je sais tout ce que je dois aux penseurs de la vieille Allemagne; et encore à l'heure présente, je me souviens de l'exemple et des paroles de *notre* Goethe — il est à l'humanité entière — répudiant toute haine nationale. . . . J'ai travaillé toute ma vie, à rapprocher les esprits de nos nations; et les atrocités de la guerre impie qui les met aux prises, pour la ruine de la civilisation européenne, ne m'amèneront jamais à souiller de haine mon esprit.

Quelques raisons que j'aie donc de souffrir aujourd'hui par

votre Allemagne et de juger criminels la politique allemande et les moyens qu'elle emploie, je n'en rends point responsable le peuple qui la subit et s'en fait l'aveugle instrument.

Page 21:

Une Française qui est en Russie me reproche d'être un mauvais Français. Un Allemand qui est à Saint-Moritz me reproche d'être un Français aveuglé par le sentiment national. Les deux lettres m'arrivent par le même courrier.

Pages 21–22:

Mon cher Romain Rolland

Habitant avec Copeau chez des amis communs, et angoissé autant que lui au sujet de Jacques Rivière, il était naturel que Copeau me montrât votre lettre. Vous comprendrez sans peine, je l'espère, l'émotion avec laquelle je l'ai lue: À plus d'une reprise déjà j'ai failli vous écrire, depuis que s'est ouvert cet abominable conflit — et surtout après avoir lu dans les journaux votre lettre à Hauptmann. Je vous supplie d'oublier un instant ce qui peut vous déplaire dans mes livres; c'est un homme de bonne foi qui vous parle, et que les événements font plus proche de vous; quelqu'un qui comme vous avait des amis en Allemagne, et qu'il ne parvient pas à haïr.

Vous semblez garder quelque espoir, sinon de les convaincre, du moins de les renseigner. Ils ignorent tout, dites-vous, des cruautés de leur armée... Mais quel étrange résultat espérez-vous en leur éclairant ces horreurs? Leur faire prendre en dégoût leur patrie? Non; c'est de tout leur cœur qu'ils ont besoin de la défendre, besoin de s'illusionner sur tous ses défauts monstrueux.

Ah! combien j'aimerais parler avec vous de ces choses! Si vous rentriez à Paris, faites le moi savoir [sic], je vous en prie — et croyez à ma bien vive sympathie.

André Gide

J'allais fermer ma lettre lorsque me parvient un mot d'un de mes meilleurs amis, Paul Laurens, dont le frère a dû tomber entre les mains de l'ennemi. Il a dû télégraphier hier à Monsieur Ador, mais vous serait profondément reconnaissant si vous pouviez veiller de votre côté à ce que les démarches nécessaires aient été faites pour obtenir quelques renseignements au sujet du *Sergent Pierre Laurens* — 25° reg territoriale 8° Com^nie blessé le 26 ou le 27 Sept^bre dans la région d'Arras et présumé disparu.

Savez-vous quelque chose de Bachelin?

A.G.

Pages 23–25:

— Votre lettre m'a ému, mon cher Gide. Cette abominable guerre a ceci de bon, du moins, qu'elle rapproche beaucoup d'esprits qui vivaient un peu à l'écart les uns des autres. — Vous le dirai-je? Elle m'a même rapproché de nos "ennemis" d'Allemagne. Elle dévoile le plus profond du cœur.

Vous me demandez ce que j'attends de ces entretiens. J'attends qu'en éclairant les autres, ils m'éclairent moi-même. Je ne cherche pas à leur faire mépriser leur patrie, mais à leur fournir les moyens de la faire estimer, en connaissant les crimes qu'on lui reproche et en les condamnant, ou en m'apportant la preuve que ces crimes sont inventés par une presse mensongère et des témoins hallucinés. La France est enveloppée, mon cher ami, de presque autant de mensonges que l'Allemagne. C'est comme une mer de brouillards. Et l'Europe en est couverte. . . . Comment est-il possible qu'on laisse un Richepin écrire, dans le *Petit Journal,* que les Allemands ont coupé la main droite à 4000 jeunes garçons de 15 à 17 ans, — et d'autres sottises scélérates de ce genre! Est-ce que de telles paroles ne risquent pas, d'amener, de notre part, des cruautés réelles? Depuis le commencement de la guerre, chaque trait de barbarie . . . a été amplifié cent fois; et naturellement il en a fait naître d'autres. C'est une suite de représailles. Jusqu'où n'iront-elles pas. . . ? Il faut que les hommes comme nous, dans le haut intérêt non seulement de l'esprit européen, mais de leur peuple même, se dégagent vigoureusement de cette atmosphère mortelle. Il faut que nous qui avons le privilège de connaître les meilleurs de l'Allemagne intellectuelle et d'être connus d'eux, nous restions en relations étroites avec eux, que nous usions de la confiance qu'ils ont toujours en nous. . . . Nous devons loyalement tâcher de les entendre: ce n'est pas dans des *Adresses* officielles et marquées du visa de la police prussienne que leur vraie pensée s'exprime;

elle s'exprime dans leurs lettres . . . ; elle s'exprimerait encore mieux dans des entretiens, si je pouvais, comme je m'y efforce, faire venir un certain nombre d'entre eux à Genève . . . afin de s'expliquer. Il est possible que j'y réussisse. . . . Je voudrais qu'on pût reconstituer, au cœur même de la tourmente, l'unité morale de l'élite européenne. Je voudrais essayer du moins. . . . En tout cas, je ne m'accommoderai jamais, pour ma part, de la haine. Je sais qu'elle se trompe. Tout ce dont nous souffrons ne vient pas de la seule Allemagne. . . .

Pages 26–27:

Dans le fléau d'aujourd'hui, nous avons tous notre part: les uns par volonté, les autres par faiblesse; et ce n'est pas la faiblesse qui est la moins coupable. Apathie du plus grand nombre, timidité des honnêtes gens, égoïsme sceptique des veules gouvernants, ignorance ou cynisme de la presse, gueules avides des forbans, peureuse servilité des hommes de pensée qui se font les bedeaux des préjugés meurtriers qu'ils avaient pour mission de détruire; orgueil impitoyable de ces intellectuels qui croient en leurs idées plus qu'en la vie du prochain et feraient périr vingt millions d'hommes, afin d'avoir raison; prudence politique d'une Eglise trop romaine, où saint Pierre le pêcheur s'est fait le batelier de la diplomatie; pasteurs aux âmes sèches et tranchantes comme un couteau, sacrifiant leur troupeau afin de la purifier; fatalisme hébété de ces pauvres moutons — Qui de nous n'est pas coupable? Qui de nous a le droit de se laver les mains du sang de l'Europe assassinée?

Page 27:

l'Europe n'est pas libre. La voix des peuples est étouffée.

Page 27:

je n'en ai jamais douté. Elle porte tout à l'excès. Sa caractéristique constante est le déséquilibre, dans le mal comme dans le bien.

Page 27:

"Laissez-moi parachever l'œuvre des morts" (c'est-à-dire tuer la France entière). 377 voix contre 110. L'héroïsme meurtrier, — meurtrier de soi-même. L'héroïsme pris pour but, quand il ne

devrait jamais être que l'instrument d'un but, le serviteur d'une tâche. Ce fut toujours l'erreur d'idéal de la France. Elle en meurt. Un peuple meurt toujours de l'erreur de ses vertus.

Page 28:

Je déplore que sa longue pièce sur Romain Rolland use d'arguments souvent douteux.

Page 28:

c'est un mot de ralliement. Et lorsque nous entendons que "la Patrie est en danger," l'important c'est que nous nous levions et unissions pour la défendre.

Pages 29–30:

Mon cher Romain Rolland

Suroccupé par l'œuvre du "foyer franco-belge," j'ai dû renoncer, mais bien à regret, à la longue lettre que je voulais vous écrire, en réponse à l'article du journal de Genève que vous m'avez si aimablement envoyé. Un autre article de vous, lu depuis, dans ce même journal (12 oct.) répond par avance à plusieurs objections que je m'apprêtais à vous faire. À ce second article, j'ai la joie de pouvoir m'associer pleinement et de n'avoir plus à faire les réserves auxquelles m'obligeait le premier. Dans ce premier article, la générosité de votre pensée m'apparaissait hélas! trop chimérique, et trop dangereux ce désir de vouloir demeurer, si j'ose ainsi dire — à la fois neutre et français. Oui, certes, nos journaux éclairent les événements (et d'une manière générale toute la face de cette guerre) avec une partialité systématique qui m'en rend parfois la lecture extrêmement pénible; ne croyez point que j'en sois dupe. Mais l'important aujourd'hui est de créer et de maintenir un état d'esprit qui nous permette de triompher. Je ne sais rien de ceux que je connaissais en Allemagne — non point même de Rainer Maria Rilke que j'aimais tendrement et dont la traduction de mon Enfant Prodigue devait paraître en Octobre à la . . . [sic] Verlag. Je ne puis croire qu'il m'ait enlevé son affection, non plus que je ne lui enlève la mienne.

J'ai eu l'occasion de lire et de donner à lire cet article du 12 oct. à plusieurs qui n'avaient pu connaître votre pensée que par les citations savamment interrompues qu'en avaient faites certains journaux de manière à la dénaturer traîtreusement. Malheureusement j'ai dû rendre ce n° du journal de Genève à l'ami qui me l'avait prêté. Ne vous serait-il pas possible de m'en procurer un autre exemplaire? Et si quelque autre article de vous paraît encore, envoyez le moi [*sic*] je vous en prie — car il m'est odieux de vous entendre méjuger; donnez moi [*sic*] donc toutes les armes pour vous défendre — mais faites en sorte que je puisse vous défendre jusqu'au bout et ne parlez plus de vous expatrier, le jour où la France vivrait sous un régime oppressif; car c'est alors surtout que la présence d'un esprit comme le vôtre, deviendrait nécessaire. Quant à cette . . . [*sic*] de conciliabule que votre lettre me dit souhaiter, qui réunirait je ne sais sur quel pic de Suisse les esprits supérieurs des pays ennemis... non déjà j'en suis sûr, vous ne le croyez plus possible. Vous voyez bien qu'*ils* out refusé de reconnaître la commission des Etats-Unis. On ne pourra discuter avec eux qu'après qu'on les aura vaincus. Il ne faut même pas tenter aujourd'hui d'abréger la durée de la guerre: elle recommencerait demain plus terrible.

Conduisant ici des réfugiés belges, j'ai quitté Paris pour deux jours; j'attendais ce moment pour vous écrire et le conseil d'un grand paysage apaise. Si je restais ici plus longtemps je vous aurais écrit plus longuement et ma lettre aurait pris une autre forme, de manière à pouvoir paraître dans le Journal de Genève ou ailleurs, mais je suis surmené et trop fatigué pour mener à bonne expression ma pensée. Je vous attends au delà du tunnel; alors il sera bon de causer. Mais déjà maintenant croyez que je vous écoute de tout mon cœur.

André Gide

Je sais que Copeau a correspondu avec vous au sujet de Rivière; mais moi aussi je veux vous remercier du zèle que vous apportez dans cette affaire. Vous savez sans doute que Madame Rivière a reçu de son mari une seconde lettre. Peut-être bientôt pourrons-nous nous assurer que sa captivité n'est pas trop éprouvante [?—illegible] car il était de santé très délicate et je ne sais comment il va supporter l'hiver — Toujours rien de Pierre Laurens.

Page 31:

frères de France, frères d'Angleterre, frères d'Allemagne, nous ne nous haïssons pas. Je vous connais, je nous connais. Nos peuples ne demandaient que la paix et que la liberté.

Page 32:

Il est d'une gaieté folle. La guerre (qui l'eût cru!) est son élément. Elle est, selon ses paroles, l'état de nature. . . . Cet état de gaieté belliqueuse lui donne une santé comme il n'en a jamais eu. Il boit et mange comme quatre. Chose curieuse, Gide est devenue intime avec lui et partage son ivresse.

Page 32:

Extrêmement (et peu s'en faut que je ne dise: déplorablement) accessible à la sympathie, j'ai laissé retenir mon esprit, durant la guerre, sur une pente naturelle qui l'eût entraîné fort loin, et ne sus opposer de résistance (je me le reproche suffisamment aujourd'hui) aux enthousiasmes irréfléchis des amitiés qui me circonvenaient alors. Chez les Van Rysselberghe, dans la constante société de Verhaeren, de Copeau, de Ghéon, de Schlumberger, de Vincent d'Indy, sans emboîter le pas précisément, je n'eus point la force de protester. Du moins je jugeai prudent de me taire et donnai tout mon temps et presque toutes mes pensées à l'œuvre des réfugiés dont je pouvais m'occuper sans compromissions.

Pages 33–34:

Et tout cela parce qu'il n'a pu faire parvenir son terme de loyer!

Page 34:

J'apprends une nouvelle qui me navre et à laquelle vous ne pouvez manquer d'être sensible, ainsi que Gide. Le bon, l'inoffensif Rilke, qui habitait à Paris, 18 rue Campagne-Première, a été avisé que tous ses meubles, tous ses manuscrits, toutes ses lettres ont été brusquement vendus et dispersés. C'est une perte irréparable pour l'art, et un coup d'une cruauté sans raison, à l'égard du doux penseur et poète. J'en souffre non seulement pour lui, mais pour le renom français. Voulez-vous voir aussi promptement que possible, s'il ne reste aucun moyen de sauver les épaves du naufrage. Faites ce que vous pourrez pour l'honneur de la France!

Pages 34–35:

Je restai longtemps sans revoir Romain Rolland. La querre vint. Il m'écrivit de Suisse, au sujet du séquestre de Rainer Maria Rilke. Averti trop tard, je ne pus empêcher, hélas! la dispersion de la bibliothèque et du mobilier de notre ami, ni même assister au simulacre de vente qui, comme furtivement, permit à des forbans et à des hommes de paille de s'emparer à vil prix d'objets précieux, de tableaux et de dessins de grande valeur et d'une quantité de livres rares — que, par la suite, je fis de vains efforts pour rassembler. Je raconterai cela quelque jour. J'ai gardé tous les documents relatifs à cette farce tragique, au rôle complaisant du séquestre, et la correspondance que j'échangeai avec Romain Rolland à ce sujet.

Pages 35–36:

Mon cher Romain Rolland

Oui, je sais bien que j'étais suroccupé; je sais bien que Rilke aurait dû nous écrire, qu'un simple mot à son concierge aurait évité cela... N'importe! je ne me pardonne pas de n'avoir pas prévu et agi en conséquence alors qu'il était encore temps. À vrai dire je ne pensais pas que cela fût possible, et je doute si le séquestre a agi ici comme il devait...

Au reçu de votre mot, j'ai couru avec Copeau rue Campagne-Première: il n'est que trop vrai que tout a été vendu (dispersé?) il y a près d'un an, dit la concierge — une excellente femme qui pleurait en nous racontant ceci et qui est parvenue à mettre à l'abri dans des malles les lettres et les manuscrits — tous les papiers, semble-t-il, qui n'étaient pas "de vente." Ces malles, sont, pour l'instant, dans un atelier, ou hangar, non loué, mais qui peut être occupé d'un jour à l'autre — la concierge me préviendrait dans ce cas — Je n'ai pu parvenir à voir aujourd'hui le séquestre, mais ne perds pas espoir, s'il est de bon vouloir — avec ses indications, de parvenir à rassembler et recueillir quelques uns [sic] des livres ou objets auxquels Rilke, vraisemblablement pouvait tenir le plus. Je vous récrirai à ce sujet — J'aurais — j'ai pour Rilke une affection très vive; deux fois j'étais passé (il y a six mois environ) pour tâcher d'avoir quelques nouvelles; mais la loge de la concierge était fermée — Non, je ne puis me consoler, me pardonner de ne pas avoir su faire à temps, pour un ami, ce que j'aurais été si profondément heureux de faire.

Croyez à mes sentiments bien cordiaux.

André Gide

Pages 36–37:

Mon cher Romain Rolland

Oui, j'ai bien reçu votre lettre — vos deux lettres. J'attendais, pour vous récrire d'avoir un peu plus à vous raconter: voici où j'en suis:

J'ai été voir le séquestre. Sans doute ai-je marqué un peu trop mon... étonnement devant la manière sommaire dont s'était effectuée cette vente: il m'a parlé avec une insolence, une fureur des plus pénibles. Mais du moins ai-je pu apprendre le nom de l'avoué qui s'était occupé de la vente — avoué qui par une heureuse chance, se trouve être membre du Comité du Foyer Franco-Belge dont je suis vice-président — avoué également de Mrs. Edith Wharton qui s'occupe elle aussi de notre œuvre, et connaissait Rilke personnellement. Je l'ai mise au courant de l'histoire, qui l'a indignée autant que nous. Par l'avoué j'ai su le nom du commissaire-priseur; et par le commissaire-priseur le nom de trois principaux acheteurs des livres repartis par lots.

Au total la vente — tant de livres que du mobilier a produit je crois 538 fr. C'est un honteux escamotage... Aujourd'hui même (je n'ai le nom des acheteurs que depuis hier) j'ai couru à ce que je pensais être leur boutique — Mais ce sont des bouquinistes sans magasin (?) qui n'étaient pas chez eux (rue de Seine ou rue Guénégaud) et qu'on ne trouve qu'en leur donnant rendez-vous, (m'a dit le concierge); ce que je vais faire.

Je voudrais tant pouvoir rassurer Rilke au sujet de ses manu-scrits. Etant donné le mauvais vouloir du séquestre, il me sera extrêmement difficile d'obtenir de regarder ses papiers. Il faudrait pour cela sans doute un mot de Rilke lui-même... attendez pour cela que je demande à l'avoué la marche à suivre. J'espérais d'abord pouvoir prendre moi-même ces deux malles de papiers, chez moi, sous ma garde — mais il vaut peut-être mieux les laisser sous la garde du séquestre, qui, bien qu'insolent, est sans doute honnête. J'aime à croire que *tous* ses papiers personnels ont été preservés.

Je ne puis comprendre — ni me consoler — que Rilke n'ait écrit, ni à vous, ni à moi, ni à sa concierge qu'il savait si dévouée. Le moindre mot de lui eût si facilement évité tout cela. Il devait pourtant se douter que s'il restait plus d'un an sans payer son loyer, il risquait une saisie... il n'y a eu là rien d'illégal, à proprement parler — et le fait ne nous paraît monstrueux que parce que nous savons quel être inoffensif et douloureux était Rilke.

Ne pouvez-vous atteindre Rilke qu'à travers Zweig? Je le déplore — car il me faut bien vous dire ici, si pénible que cela me soit d'avoir à le dire *à vous* qui certainement allez me croire aveuglé par la haine — que je tiens Zweig pour un parfait chenapan et que j'ai des raisons pour cela.

Au revoir. Croyez à mon dévouement

André Gide

Pages 38–41:

Mon cher Romain Rolland

J'attendais pour vous récrire, d'avoir du nouveau à vous apprendre au sujet de Rilke.

J'ai obtenu du commissaire-priseur l'indication des quatre acheteurs principaux. Le plus important est "en voyage." Deux autres sont insaisissables: ce sont des bouquinistes sans boutique, qu'on ne trouve chez eux que sur rendez-vous. Le quatrième est un misérable petit revendeur qui ne se souvient de rien, et, si on lui parle de "livres allemands" ne veut plus rien savoir.

Craignant, si j'écrivais aux deux autres, de les voir se dérober et m'échapper définitivement, craignant aussi, dans le cas où ils ne connaîtraient pas encore la valeur des livres achetés par eux, de leur ouvrir les yeux et les éclairer par ma démarche et les questions qu'elle entraînerait, j'ai jugé plus prudent de recourir à un intermédiaire, à l'éditeur F. de la rue de Seine, qui, voulant aussi des livres allemands, aurait moins risqué d'éveiller les soupçons que le particulier que je suis. Ne le connaissant pas personnellement, j'ai voulu d'abord me renseigner sur son honorabilité, savoir si l'on pouvait se fier à lui, etc. Mon intention aurait été, est encore de lui confier le soin de racheter, si possible, le meilleur, ou du moins ce que nous jugerions le plus précieux au point de vue sentimental, et le plus irremplaçable, de la bibliothèque de Rilke; et de lui demander de bien vouloir garder en dépôt ces livres, dans l'espoir de pouvoir les remettre à Rilke plus tard. Visites, démarches, présentation, tout cela a pris du temps et ce n'est qu'hier que j'ai pu entrer en rapport avec F. — Celui qui me présentait à F., le pasteur Wilfred Monod que je ne connaissais pas précédemment, mais avec qui j'ai pu entrer facilement en rapports, semble prendre à cœur cette affaire et voudrait m'aider à examiner si cette vente a bien été régulièrement effectuée, si tout a été fait selon les règles, s'il n'y a pas eu là une sorte d'escamotage ("Avec un boche ça n'est pas la peine de se gêner.") pour le plus grand profit de quelques malins — Je veux occuper un avocat, de cette affaire, — et, s'il découvre une irrégularité — ne pensez-vous pas qu'on pourrait en parler à Mathias Morhardt, qui, au nom de la ligue des droits de l'homme pourrait prendre l'affaire en main? —

Ne pourrais-je avoir un catalogue (si incomplet fût-il) de la bibliothèque de R. — des livres auxquels il tenait le plus? Quant aux papiers, manuscrits, correspondances, etc. vous l'aurez déjà rassuré, n'est-ce pas. J'ai confiance que, grâce à la concierge, cela du moins a été préservé — et, tout de même, c'est le principal.

Mais, à côté de la question Rilke, un mot de ma dernière lettre a fait naître entre nous une question Zweig, au sujet de laquelle vous me demandez des explications. Tout ce que je vais pouvoir faire aujourd'hui, c'est de poser quelques jalons: Voici:

Franz Blei, un autre juif allemand, que vous connaissez peut-être, tout au moins de nom, mon principal traducteur en Allemagne (c'est du moins lui qui signe les traductions de sa femme et d'autres) s'est toujours montré pour moi de la plus grande gentillesse, et si mon nom est un peu connu là-bas, c'est à lui d'abord que je le dois. Dans le (Revue) [*sic*] avait paru, il y a déjà longtemps de cela, une traduction de mon *Prométhée mal enchaîné* — signée de sa femme — que plusieurs années ensuite il me proposa de faire paraître en volume, signé de lui. Kippenberg (était-ce déjà Kippenberg?) parla d'illustrations.

J'acceptai à condition qu'on me laissât choisir mon dessinateur, auquel fut promis, par l'entremise de Blei une somme d'à peu près 100 francs par dessin (il y en avait 5). C'est à Bonnard que je m'adressai pour ce travail, qui fut livré à date voulue. — Mais ce qui ne fut pas livré du tout, ce fut la somme promise — que je sortis alors de ma poche, laissant croire à Bonnard qu'elle m'avait été remise pour lui, par l'éditeur ou par Blei, désireux tout à la fois de couvrir Blei, et de ne point laisser Bonnard souffrir de ce manque de parole. — Du reste je n'en voulus pas autrement à Blei, que je savais peu fortuné et réduit souvent aux expédients. Je lui prouvai ma non rancune, à quelque temps de là, en m'occupant à réunir pour lui des dessins que devait reproduire une nouvelle revue qu'il fondait; je lui adressai un certain nombre de photographies de dessins inédits, que Druet mit aimablement à ma disposition, et ajoutai un très beau dessin original de Van Rysselberghe — qu'il était bien convenu que je lui prêtai seulement — mais que Blei eut soin "d'égarer" au lieu de la confier à la reproduction. Le dessin m'avait été confié par Van Rysselberghe, de sorte que je fus extrêmement ennuyé par cet escamotage. — Il y eut peu après un autre escamotage (?) de recette d'une représentation de mon *Roi Candaule*... Je n'ai jamais pu tirer l'affaire parfaitement au clair.

   — Mais Zweig, dans tout ceci?

   — Dans tout ceci, Zweig n'a absolument rien à voir. Mais l'affaire Zweig ne m'appartient pas et j'ai promis de n'en point parler. Bien que de même ordre, exactement, (et n'ayant donc absolument rien à voir avec la guerre) elle est beaucoup plus grave — grave même jusqu'à l'invraisemblance, de sorte que jusqu'avant la guerre on eût voulu douter encore; on doutait. Je consens à douter encore; mais il est bien certain que ce n'est pas maintenant, que nous pouvons chercher à nous éclairer et à mettre la chose au point. Dans le doute je me tais; mais dans le doute je préfère n'avoir aucun rapport avec Zweig — Il en serait exactement de même si nous n'étions pas en guerre avec l'Allemagne et la situation d'aujourd'hui n'incline en rien mon jugement.

   C'est donc à défaut de l'histoire Zweig que je vous raconte l'histoire Blei (qu'à mon tour je vous prie de garder pour vous, trouvant peu décent d'ajouter des griefs personnels à tant de griefs supérieurs).

Au demeurant je ne crois pas Zweig incapable de certain dévouement amical — très juif en cela, très agent de liaison, très prévenant, très officieux. Je ne suis entré en rapports avec lui que peu de temps avant la guerre. Je ne puis dire à quel point et combien profondément il m'a déplu. Naturellement je ne donne pas pour une raison mon impression... mais, tout de même, quand ensuite j'ai appris l'histoire, je me suis expliqué mon impression. Et comme je me défie des *impressions,* et que, celle-ci, je n'étais pas seul à l'avoir... pour un peu je dirais que c'est ce qui m'aide à douter de l'histoire. Excusez-moi de ne parler point plus nettement. Il m'en coûte et particulièrement vis-à-vis de vous que j'estime — mais, encore une fois, je suis lié.

Excusez la longeur de cette lettre — et croyez-moi bien cordialement

André Gide

Page 41:

Il répond aujourd'hui, mais en se dérobant. Il me conte longuement les petites canailleries d'un autre écrivain allemand, qui s'est fait le barnum de ses œuvres en Allemagne, et qui l'a volé, dit-il. Après quoi, passant à mon ami, il fait une pirouette et se dégage. C'est, dit-il, une affaire du même ordre; mais "elle ne lui appartient pas, et il a promis de n'en point parler..." Alors, pourquoi en a-t-il parlé, et dans ces termes outrageants? Je le lui reproche, avec quelque sévérité.

(N.B. — Il ne l'a pas oublié.)

Page 42:

Ce qui me tient surtout à cœur, ce qui me paraît notre devoir essentiel, c'est de fonder moralement, intellectuellement, l'unité européenne.

Page 43:

Les plus excellentes gens sont aussi les plus dupes.

Page 43:

Non, ne haïssez-pas. La haine n'est pas faite pour vous, — pour nous — défendons-nous de la haine plus que de nos ennemis.

Page 44:

Ne croyez pas que j'aie un faible pour les Allemands. Ma
situation est paradoxale. L'amour de la musique m'a fait entrer
dans la peau de Jean-Christophe. Une fois là, il m'a bien fallu
y rester jusqu'à ce qu'il fût mort. Mais Christophe lui-même
n'aime pas trop les Allemands; et moi, je ne pourrais vivre six
mois de suite en Allemagne. . . .

Pages 44–45:

Je reprends par le commencement Jean-Christophe et fais de
grands efforts de sympathie sans que ma considération pour
Romain Rolland, pour son livre du moins, soit accrue.

On y respire une sorte de cordialité fruste, de vulgarité, de
bonhomie — dont lui saura gré le lecteur pour qui l'artiste n'est
qu'un faiseur d'embarras. Passons.

Ce qui me confond, c'est l'aisance, l'inconscience, avec laquelle
il fait de son héros un Allemand — ou, si l'on veut, il fait d'un
Allemand son héros. Cela est, que je sache, sans exemple; car
même Stendhal a soin d'indiquer que son Fabrice était né de
père français. Que faut-il donc y voir davantage? Le germanisme
de ses goûts, de ses tendances, de ses réactions, de ses volontés,
qui permet à Romain Rolland de peindre Jean-Christophe sinon
précisément à son image, tout au moins de l'aimer par sympathie
— ou bien l'illusion d'un cerveau, généreux mais incapable de
critique, qui crée en Jean-Christophe, abstraitement, un être non
plus allemand que français, un musicien, un être vague, à qui il
prête toutes les sensations, les émotions qu'il veut?

Ah! que cette insuffisance psychologique est donc germaine
encore! Que cela est peu signifiant!

Pages 45–46:

La question des origines germaniques de Jean-Christophe
voudrait une longue réponse. — J'ai eu plus d'une raison pour
choisir les pays rhénans comme patrie de mon héros. D'abord,
son génie musical: c'est une plante qui, jusqu'ici n'a pas trouvé
chez nous de conditions propices pour se développer vigoureusement. Puis, comme vous dites très bien, mon dessin d'observer
la France avec des yeux tout neufs de Huron candide et barbare.
Mais, j'avais une autre raison secrète, et plus profonde: ce sera

une réponse aux harangues des pangermanistes qui viennent de
fêter avec fracas l'anniversaire de la "Bataille des Nations."

. . . Le pays de Beethoven et de Jean-Christophe ne sera
jamais pour moi un pays étranger. Je ne suis pas de ces
lamentables Français qui, dans la rage qu'ils mettent à appauvrir
la France, afin de la réduire à eux et à leurs amis, ne seraient
pas loin de la ramener aux limites du domaine de leur Philippe-
Auguste, et qui traitent d'étranger le genevois Jean-Jacques. Je
ne tiens pas plus compte de leur nationalisme rétréci que de
l'arrogance de l'impérialisme allemand qui, par droit de conquête,
s'étale impudemment dans des terres qu'il a volées. À la barbe
de l'un et de l'autre, je m'annexe avec tranquillité la rive gauche
du Rhin, la Vallonie, Genève et les pays romands. J'y plante
notre drapeau.

. . . Le Rhin est une coulée de lumière qui mûrit les coteaux
et les âmes d'occident. Elle n'est pas plus à vous, Allemands,
qu'elle n'est à nous: elle est à l'Europe. Elle ne nous divise point,
elle nous réunit. Qu'il en puisse être de même de mon Christophe,
votre fils et le nôtre.

Page 46:

Je commence le quatrième cahier. J'avoue que, par instants,
les premiers avaient triomphé de mes préventions; une certaine
grâce un peu fruste, une justesse de ton, suppléaient au défaut
de style; mais la troisième partie de *l'Adolescence* (Ada) est
déplaisante à l'excès dans la gaucherie de sa franchise, et d'une
pénible insuffisance dans les moyens d'expression. Ces longueurs,
ou plutôt ces traînasseries, ce lyrisme épais et rudimentaire,
germanique on dirait — me sont intolérables. Et jusqu'à la
constante évidence de l'*intention,* qui me choque comme une
impudeur artistique, une indélicatesse.

Mais je comprends qu'un tel livre se fasse des amis, et de
nombreux.

Pages 46–47:

Je reprends Jean-Christophe: *le Buisson ardent,* où j'en suis
arrivé et dont le début est certainement remarquable. Il m'ap-
paraît parfois que ce livre barbare, mal équarri, sans art, sans
grâce et de qualités en apparence si peu françaises, reste ce qui

a été produit en France de plus important, ou du moins de plus typique, par notre génération.

Page 47:

si je n'avais si mal à la tête

Page 47:

de toute notre littérature, il me semble que le livre que l'on imaginerait le plus facilement écrit en Allemagne c'est *Jean-Christophe* et de là sans doute son succès d'Outre-Rhin.

Pages 47–48:

Evidemment ce qui me choque dans le cas de Romain Rolland, c'est qu'il n'a rien à perdre par le fait de la guerre: son livre (*Jean-Christophe*) ne paraît jamais meilleur que traduit. Je vais plus loin: il ne peut que gagner au désastre de la France, que gagner à ce que la langue française n'existe plus, ni l'art français, ni le goût français, ni aucun de ces dons qu'il nie et qui lui sont déniés. Le désastre final de la France donnerait à son *Jean-Christophe* sa plus grande et définitive importance.

Il est de si parfaite bonne foi que parfois presque il vous désarme. C'est un ingénu, mais un ingénu passionné. Il a tôt fait de prendre pour vertu sa franchise, et, comme elle est quelque peu sommaire, il a pris pour hypocrisie ce que d'autres avaient de moins rudimentaire que lui. Je m'assure que trop souvent ce qui permit son attitude, c'est le peu de sentiment et de goût, de compréhension même qu'apporte son esprit à l'art, au style, et à cette sorte d'atticisme qui n'a plus d'autre patrie que la France. Rien n'est plus informe que son livre; c'est un kugelhof où parfois croque un bon raisin. Aucun apparat, aucun artifice; j'entends bien que c'est par là qu'il plaît à certains.

Page 48:

Comment avez-vous pu porter sur Romain Rolland et les dix volumes de son *Jean-Christophe,* sur Romain Rolland et l'art de France, sur Romain Rolland et la Grande Guerre, ce jugement de vingt lignes, brutal comme un coup de poignard?

Page 48:

la force secrète de son œuvre mais surtout pour la pureté de sa foi

Page 49:

Vous ne l'avez pas voulu; et je me demande avec une angoisse vaine ce qui a pu vous pousser à un geste si rudimentaire et si définitif?

Page 49:

Tout ce que je puis répondre à votre lettre, c'est que je vous sais le plus grand gré, de m'avoir écrit ainsi.

L'*étude* que vous déplorez de ne voir point en place de cette exécution sommaire (et Jacques C.[opeau] vous aura dit peut-être que, pénétré déjà par moi-même du sentiment que vous m'exprimez, j'ai voulu au dernier moment m'en ressaisir) — l'étude que j'aurais pu écrire, ne vous eût sans doute pas beaucoup satisfait, car je ne parviens pas à découvrir en Jean-Christophe tout ce que vous y voyez — mais du moins le ton y eût été, et votre lettre précisément m'indique celui qu'il aurait fallu prendre.

Page 49:

Fais l'impossible pour supprimer le passage de mon Journal concernant Romain Rolland: quitte à laisser en blanc la page avec mention censure prendrais à ma charge frais de retirage mieux vaudrait léger retard

Page 50:

Le dilettantisme n'est point nécessairement frivole. Parfois pour nous donner le change, il s'enveloppe de gravité et prend une allure austère.

Page 50:

s'est servi de moi contre Rolland

Page 50:

Très perplexe. Et même à peu près décidé à me compromettre là-dedans, par probité, en somme, et par gratitude. Et puis un peu aussi avec l'idée qu'étant si fortement raciné à la N.R.F. mon geste réparerait bien des injustices, et notamment toutes les vôtres! qui avez jugé R.R. *sans l'avoir lu!* Oui!

Pages 50–51:

Maintenant, permettez-moi de protester lorsque je vous entends dire que je juge Romain Rolland sans l'avoir lu. J'ai vécu, à

Cuverville, quatre mois avec *Jean-Christophe* que j'ai lu, dans les *Cahiers de la Quinzaine* sinon complètement, du moins aux quatre cinquièmes... après quoi je n'ai plus pu triompher de mon inappétence. Il m'est sans doute arrivé plus d'une fois de louer une œuvre de confiance, sans la connaître, ou la connaître suffisamment. Mais de critiquer, non.

Page 51:

le plus souvent les relectures ne font que m'enfoncer dans mon opinion première. . . .

Pages 51–52:

J'ai lu plus tard, dans le *Journal* d'un écrivain, qui a cru prendre les devants, pour se défendre, en m'attaquant, — (bien que je ne songeasse point à l'attaquer, car, à vrai dire, je ne songe pas à lui, il ne tient point de place dans ma pensée) — que "Romain Rolland a tôt fait de prendre pour vertu sa franchise, et que, comme celle-ci est quelque peu sommaire, il a pris (ou prend) pour hypocrisie ce que d'autres ont de moins rudimentaire que lui."

Il se peut bien que je sois "rudimentaire." L'Apôtre Paul l'était aussi, qui ne goûtait guère "ceux qui ont en eux oui oui, et puis non non... Car le Fils de Dieu, qui est véritable, n'a pas été oui et non, mais il a toujours été oui en lui."

Le jeune Christophe que j'étais, au retour de Rome, était furieusement "oui en lui"; et il haïssait l'amphibisme de la pensée, cette mixture de oui et de non, qui empuantit les âges sans foi et sans vertèbres. Au lieu d'y voir ce qu'elle est, une maladie de l'âme dévirilisée, qui, impuissante à se garder sa propre foi, se complaît à se trahir soi-même, je la nommais duplicité. . . .

Chapter IV: Art and the Artist

Page 54:

Par loyalisme aveugle, par coupable confiance, ils se sont jetés tête baissée dans les filets que leur tendait leur impérialisme. Ils ont cru que le premier devoir pour eux était, les yeux fermés, de défendre l'honneur de leur Etat contre toute accusation. Ils n'ont pas vu que le plus noble moyen de le défendre était de réprouver ses fautes et d'en laver leur patrie.

Page 54:

La guerre a jeté le désarroi dans nos rangs. La plupart des intellectuels ont mis leur science, leur art, leur raison, au service des gouvernements. Nous ne voulons accuser personne, adresser aucun reproche. Nous savons la faiblesse des âmes individuelles et la force élémentaire des grands courants collectifs. . . .

Pages 54–55:

Point de privilège entre les hommes! Nul homme — (qu'il soit artiste, ou non) — n'a droit à vivre, s'il ne se fait pas le serviteur de l'humanité; et le plus grand a le plus de devoir.

Page 55:

L'art actuel . . . ne doit nous endormir dans un charme voluptueux (comme notre art parisien d'aujourd'hui). *Il faut qu'il nous inquiète.* En une époque de perfection comme la Grèce de Sophocle, l'art peut être une lumière sereine. Dans notre société en ruines, où chacun souffre et fait souffrir, où chacun est victime et coupable, l'art doit être un sévère directeur de consciences qui nous montre nos fautes, le moyen de les racheter, et nous force à l'action.

Pages 55–56:

Je ne crois pas non plus que ce soit en lisant de la littérature parisienne que vous arriverez à sortir du malaise. Vous me dites que les Blum, les Gourmont, les Gide (je ne cite que les plus intelligents) "perçoivent le malaise." Ils ne le perçoivent pas seulement. Ils sont le malaise.

Page 56:

On est sain ou malsain.

Page 56:

On ne practise pas avec la peste. . . .

Page 56:

il y a partout à apprendre

Page 56:

Ne croyez pas que je regarde Gide, ni Gourmont, pour des médiocres. Il s'en faut de beaucoup. Mais il y a en eux un principe de mort.

Page 56:

les pensées des autres sont misérables, leur vie est mesquine.

Page 57:

[L'œuvre d'art] doit trouver en soi sa suffisance, sa fin et sa raison parfaite; formant un tout, elle doit pouvoir s'isoler et reposer, comme hors de l'espace et du temps, dans une satisfaite et satisfaisante harmonie.

Page 57:

Je ne reproche point à Gautier cette doctrine de "l'Art pour l'art," en dehors de quoi je ne sais point trouver raison de vivre; mais d'avoir réduit l'art à n'exprimer rien que si peu.

Je ne lui reproche point d'avoir proclamé roi le poète, mais au contraire d'avoir si misérablement rétréci son domaine.

Je lui sais gré d'avoir honni l'art utilitaire, mais je ne puis lui pardonner de n'avoir reconnu qu'utilitaire la pensée, ou de ne l'avoir pas connue du tout.

Page 58:

L'école symboliste. Le grand grief contre elle, c'est le peu de curiosité qu'elle marqua devant la vie. . . . La poésie devint pour eux un refuge; la seule échappatoire aux hideuses réalités. . . .

Page 58:

Il s'agit d'abord de bien comprendre qui l'on est . . . ensuite il conviendra de prendre en conscience et en main l'héritage.

Page 58:

Chacun de nous, adolescent, rencontre au début de sa course, un monstre qui dresse devant lui telle énigme qui nous puisse empêcher d'avancer. Et, bien qu'à chacun de nous, mes enfants, ce sphinx particulier pose une question différente, persuadez-vous qu'à chacune de ses questions la réponse reste pareille; oui, qu'il n'y a qu'une seule et même réponse à de si diverses questions;

et que cette réponse unique c'est: l'Homme; et que cet homme unique, pour un chacun de nous, c'est Soi.

Page 59:

> — Je ne veux plus y songer: Rien — moi-même.
> — que cherchais-tu?
> — Je cherchais... qui j'étais.

Page 59:

l'art véritable est celui qui tâche d'unir les hommes entre eux, ou directement par la puissance de l'amour, ou indirectement en combattant tout ce qui s'oppose à cette union, cette fraternité.

Pages 59–60:

ce n'est que là où la vie surabonde que l'art a chance de commencer. L'art naît par surcroît, par pression de surabondance, il commence là, où vivre ne suffit plus à exprimer la vie.

Page 61:

Il ya bien d'autres êtres en moi.

Page 62:

Le romancier authentique crée ses personnages avec les directions infinies de sa vie possible; le romancier factice les crée avec la ligne unique de sa vie réelle. Le génie du roman fait vivre le possible, il ne fait pas vivre le réel.

Page 62:

cette harmonie des contours et des sons, où l'art du poète se joue.

Page 62:

La beauté ne sera jamais une production naturelle; elle ne s'obtient que par une artificielle contrainte.

Page 62:

l'orgueil du mot ne supplante pas la pensée.

Page 63:

Les raisons qui me poussent à écrire sont multiples, et les plus importantes sont, il me semble, les plus secrètes. Celle-ci peut-être surtout: mettre quelque chose à l'abri de la mort — et c'est là ce qui me fait, dans mes écrits, rechercher, entre toutes qualités, celles sur qui le temps ait le moins de prise, et par quoi ils se dérobent à tous les engouements passagers.

Page 63:

Un peuple, à la rigueur, se passe de beauté; il ne doit pas, il ne peut pas se passer de vérité.

Page 63:

Quelles que soient mes sympathies ou mes antipathies pour un régime politique et social, elles n'ont rien à voir avec ma conception de l'Art. Mon art est libre de tous les partis et contre tous les partis: car sa fonction même est de maintenir contre eux tous la liberté. La beauté nue. L'entière vérité.

Pages 63–64:

La question morale pour l'artiste, n'est pas que l'Idée qu'il manifeste soit plus ou moins morale et utile au grand nombre; la question est qu'il la manifeste bien.

Page 64:

Les écrivains d'aujourd'hui s'évertuent . . . à décrire des raretés humaines, ou bien des types qui n'existent que dans des groupes anormaux, en marge de la grande société des hommes agissants et sains. Puisqu'ils se sont mis d'eux-mêmes à la porte de la vie, laisse-les et va où sont les hommes. Aux hommes de tous les jours, montre la vie de tous les jours: elle est plus profonde et plus vaste que la mer.

Page 64:

Le roman s'est occupé des traverses du sort, de la fortune bonne ou mauvaise, des rapports sociaux, du conflit des passions, des caractères, mais point de l'essence même de l'être.

Page 65:

Ils peignent des panoramas, l'art est de faire un tableau.

Page 65:

Dickens et Dostoïewski sont de grands maîtres en cela. La lumière qui éclaire leurs personnages n'est presque jamais diffuse. Dans Tolstoï, les scènes les mieux venues paraissent grises parce qu'elles sont également éclairées de partout.

Page 66:

Il y a toujours un moment où ils se mêlent et se nouent dans une sorte de vortex; ce sont des tourbillons où les éléments du récit — moraux, psychologiques, et extérieurs — se perdent et se retrouvent. Nous ne voyons chez lui aucune simplification, aucun épurement de la ligne. Il se plaît dans la complexité; il la protège. Jamais les sentiments, les pensées, les passions ne se présentent à l'état pur. Il ne fait pas le vide à l'entour.

Page 66:

Je viens de passer l'après-midi avec deux vieux amis intimes de Tolstoy, un Français et un Russe. Le Français me racontait qu'un jour il apporta à Tolstoy une œuvre de Gide dont il était enthousiaste. Tolstoy, très friand de nouveautés artistiques, se mit à l'écouter. Au bout de cinq minutes, il criait de colère, et il ne décolérait plus jusqu'à la fin de la lecture. Ensuite, par respect pour l'opinion de son ami, il reprenait le livre, et le relisait, seul; il sortait de cette seconde lecture encore plus irrité. — Et tandis que le Français s'étonnait, devant moi, que Tolstoy ne goutât point cette œuvre, je m'étonnais bien plus qu'on eût pu croire, un instant, que Tolstoy pût goûter Gide, sans cesser d'être Tolstoy.

Encore une fois, je ne critique point Gide. Si je le nomme, c'est à cause de son talent même. Son art peut être de tout premier ordre. Mais il est contradictoire avec celui de Tolstoy.

Page 67:

À partir de cet instant, j'appris à dégager mon esprit de mon cœur.

Page 67:

je fis de mes passions mêmes les servantes de mon art.

Page 67:

je les laissais jeter leur premier feu; et je les attachais ensuite à ma charrue.

Page 67:

Faute d'être appelées par *de l'étrange,* les plus rares vertus pourront rester latentes; irrévelées pour l'être même qui les possède; ou n'être pour lui que cause de vague inquiétude, germe d'anarchie.

Page 67:

devenir le plus humain possible

Page 68:

Il est possible d'imaginer un peuple sans littérature . . . , mais comment imaginer une parole qui ne soit pas l'expression de quelqu'un? une littérature qui ne soit pas l'expression d'un peuple? . . . les œuvres les plus humaines, celles qui demeurent d'intérêt le plus général, sont aussi bien les plus particulières, celles où se manifeste le plus spécialement le génie d'une race à travers le génie d'un individu.

Page 68:

La verité . . . c'est que, s'il y a des frontières en art, elles sont moins des barrières de races que des barrières de classes. Je ne sais pas s'il y a un art français et un art allemand; mais il y a un art des riches et un art de ceux qui ne le sont pas.

Page 69:

on ne réalisera la fraternité des hommes dans l'art, qui doit être le but du théâtre populaire, on ne réalisera même aucun art véritablement universel qu'après avoir brisé la stupide suprématie de l'orchestre et des loges, et l'antagonisme des classes que provoque l'inégalité blessante des places dans nos salles de spectacles.

Page 69:

l'art est trop noble et trop grand pour souffrir le partage avec quoi que ce soit. Où il est, il est tout; où il n'est pas, il n'est rien.

Pages 69–70:

c'est toujours l'idée de la tranquillité future, de l'inaction rêveuse et artistique, qui me soutient quand je travaille et que j'agis maintenant. Mon but, c'est le doux isolement, plus tard, avec des personnes chères, en Dieu et en l'art. Aujourd'hui, je me remplis de souvenirs, d'observations et de pensées, pour les digérer pendant le reste de ma vie, sans plus avoir besoin du monde, et sans lui donner de droits sur moi. Je paye donc depuis

quelques années, et pour quelque temps encore, mon écot à la
vie. Plus tard, je serai libre . . . ; comme mon caractère n'est
pas trop porté à l'action, mais y répugne plutôt, — je veux me
débarasser le plus vite possible de cette corvée de la vie active;
je double la dose tout de suite, pour que ce soit plus vite
fini. . . . Mais je voudrais que tu saches combien je me force
perpétuellement, même pour faire ce qui m'est agréable: je
n'aime pas *agir!*

Page 70:
il avait mêlé souvent à son art des préoccupations étrangères à
l'art: il lui attribuait une mission sociale.

Page 70:
C'est avec les bons sentiments que l'on fait la mauvaise littérature...

CHAPTER V: Romain Rolland and the *N.R.F.*

Pages 71–72:
    Avant d'être le groupe de la N.R.F., nous fûmes . . . (un)
groupe d'amis . . . très divers par leur formation, leurs dons et
leurs goûts, mais d'accord sur un certain nombre de choses
essentielles. . . . C'est ce qui fit le caractère original et la
solidarité de l'équipe. Notre entente ne s'établit pas autour d'un
programme; c'est notre programme qui fut l'expression de notre
entente.
    Nous n'apportions pas une formule nouvelle, ayant passé l'âge
ou l'on croit trouver le génie dans des mots magiques; mais
nous avions en commun quelques grandes admirations, doublées
d'énergique refus, et quelques principes qu'il faudrait qualifier
de moraux autant que d'esthétiques. Notre lien résida dans une
manière d'être, dans une éthique, plutôt que dans une manière
d'écrire; aussi notre unité n'eut-elle jamais rien d'uniforme.

Page 72:
d'une part, contre la littérature dite de boulevard ou de journal,
sans racines ni prolongements, de l'autre contre une littérature
traditionaliste qui s'enfermait dans des formules épuisées. . . .
    Ce qui a tant irrité contre nous les nationalistes et réaction-
naires de tout poil . . . c'est qu'un goût si bizarre s'accompagnât

chez nous de jugements critiques parfaitement raisonnables. Ce mélange de bon sens et de non-conformisme brouillait à leurs yeux les catégories du bien et du mal et leur faisait juger notre influence comme particulièrement dangereuse. Ils nous en voulaient de savoir, s'il le fallait, parler aussi pertinemment qu'eux-mêmes de Racine ou de l'art florentin; notre respect du langage leur semblait un empiétement sur leur domaine réservé, et notre accueil aux littératures étrangères achevait de les convaincre que nous introduisions un cheval de Troie au cœur d'une France démantelée.

Page 73:

il aurait été lui-même porter les numéros chez les abonnés.

Page 73:

Je ne doute pas que si Gide se fut chargé de conduire à lui seul la revue, il n'en eût fait quelque chose de plus particulier. Le rare et l'éxquis y eussent côtoyé l'étrange; il eût créé un laboratoire de style et d'idées, où il aurait fait place à tout ce qui lui semblait curieux et friand; mais où n'aurait pu prendre naissance une discipline commune, un mouvement littéraire.

Page 74:

fonder, à 3 ou 4, une sorte de Correspondance littéraire, comme celle de Grimm et Diderot, qui rayonnerait sur l'Europe, et grouperait en un faisceau les pensées les plus significatives des grands pays d'Occident.

Page 74:

notre éternel ballon d'oxygène.

Page 74:

Ne craignez pas d'y mettre un accent personnel. Et surtout, de *l'accent*. Ayez l'air d'y croire. Faites mieux: croyez-y. . . . Ayez du culot. Et soyez sûr que je suis avec vous dans ce que vous allez faire.

Page 74:

Finalement, *Europe* devait l'emporter. Et la revue parut — avec son appui moral et sous le signe de l'indépendance de l'Esprit, — auquel nous étions tous solidement attachés.

Page 75:

Mais j'en reste tout à fait indépendant. Et si je me suis établi en Suisse, c'est afin de bien marquer que mon centre de pensée n'est pas en France, mais en dehors des nations, dans un "Weltbürgertum" qui embrasse les hommes libres de toutes les races et de tous les pays.

Page 75:

Je trouve Paris (littérairement) somnifère.

Page 75:

je m'en désintéresse.

Page 75:

de braves gens et de bons artistes

Page 76:

Une revue qui n'est pas une "personne morale," nettement individualisée, et distincte de toute autre, n'est pour moi qu'une boîte aux lettres.

Page 76:

Comment *Europe* serait-elle rien de plus, quant les plus éminents de ses collaborateurs écrivent aujourd'hui à *Clarté* bolchevike, demain à la revue De Traz qui nous a dénoncés pendant la guerre et n'a point désarmé, un jour au *Mercure,* un autre aux *Marges* et un troisième à la *N. Revue française,* sans parler de la *Revue Européenne?*

Page 76:

Je ne puis pas écrire où je ne respire pas bien.

Page 77:

toujours la même impression, quand je lis un n° de la *Nouvelle Revue Française.* J'étouffe. Beaucoup de talent, mais pas d'air.

Page 78:

Je désire . . . m'excuser auprès de vous de ce que la *Nouvelle Revue Française* n'ait point encore saisi l'occasion de manifester la haute estime où elle tient votre personne et vos écrits. De ce silence, que plus d'un nous a reproché, voici la raison: depuis très longtemps j'ai demandé à l'un de nos collaborateurs, qui me semblait pour cela le mieux qualifié, de nous donner une étude d'ensemble sur votre œuvre. Il n'a pas encore eu le loisir de la mener à bien. Et, cependant, chaque fois que paraissait un de vos livres, nous ajournions d'en parler, afin de ne pas déflorer l'étude en question. Telle est l'explication toute banale d'un mystère qui, faute d'être éclairci, risquait de passer à vos yeux pour une inconvenance... En attendant que notre collaborateur s'acquitte enfin de sa tâche (ce qui ne saurait tarder) puis-je vous demander, Monsieur, s'il vous plaîrait d'honorer la *Nouvelle Revue Française* — et de faire cesser l'équivoque, fâcheuse pour nous seuls, que peut accréditer notre silence involontaire — en y publiant quelques pages? Je songe tout particulièrement à tel fragment ou à la totalité d'une "Vie" de grand musicien, de grand peintre ou de grand écrivain.

Page 80:

Jean-Christophe est terminé. De l'œuvre solide, totale, vue de la racine au sommet, depuis la terre qui la nourrit jusqu'à la lumière qui chante en elle, un autre parlera ici. Un autre, en attendant peut-être Romain Rolland lui-même.

Page 80:

Ce qu'il accomplissait le lendemain ou l'année suivante le dispensait de s'appesantir sur ce qu'il n'accomplissait pas le jour même.

Page 80:

J'en venais, vers la fin des vacances, à ne plus oser lui parler de ses projets avortés. . . . Mais, à chaque printemps, ses ferveurs renaissent; il parlait alors de nouveaux projets avec une éloquence si persuasive qu'elle emportait crédit neuf et de nous tous et de lui-même.

Page 80:

Avec combien d'auteurs ne nous brouilla-t-il pas . . .

Pages 80–81:

Notamment Romain Rolland, sur l'œuvre duquel il promettait toujours la grande étude qui aurait mis toute chose au point —

étude toujours promise pour les plus proches vacances et toujours
différée sous de nouveaux prétextes — si bien que, par son
incompréhensible silence, la *N.R.F.* parut nourrir à l'égard de
Romain Rolland une hostilité foncière. Les explications que
nous pûmes donner après coup ne dissipèrent jamais le mal-
entendu. L'ouvrage magistral sur Péguy, reçu aussitôt après la
mort de Rolland, me fit sentir, non sans chagrin, combien il eût
été facile de trouver des points d'entente avec un esprit si mani-
festement loyal et soucieux d'équité.

Page 81:

Et je crois fermement que nous devons nous interdire tout
mouvement — j'allais dire tout sentiment — qui soit capable
de nous diviser entre nous. Il n'est pas question de faire appel
à nous sentiments, ni même à nos convictions, mais seulement à
toute notre force, à toute notre patience, pour vaincre. Jusqu'à
la victoire tous les Français ne peuvent occuper qu'une position,
celle du combat.

Page 82:

J'ai simplement remarqué qu'il pourrait être fâcheux pour
Romain Rolland que des jeunes gens avec lesquels on lui connaît
des attaches tinssent de tels discours.

Page 82:

Voyez-vous, cher Romain Rolland, ce qu'il y a de triste et de
dégoûtant dans de tels malentendus c'est qu'on ne parvient
jamais à s'en dépêtrer tout à fait, à les remettre au point rigou-
reusement, c'est que plus on argumente plus on s'embrouille, et
qu'une petite salissure peut tâcher malgré tout les cœurs les
mieux disposés à l'oubli.

Page 83:

indigne de lui autant qu'elle l'est de vous.

Page 83:

Je ne suis pas surpris de cette malveillance dont j'ai été plus
d'une fois l'objet depuis 5 ans, de la part de l'un ou l'autre de
ces mm. de la *N.R.F.* Et toujours sous les formes d'une courtoise
sournoiserie. J'aime mieux de francs ennemis.

Page 84:

Mais que cette *N. Revue f.* m'est donc antipathique! En voilà
pour qui la théorie est le tout de la vie! Comme ils ne peuvent
rien (ou si peu) créer par eux-mêmes, ils fabriquent des boîtes,
des boîtes, — avec l'acharnement maniaque de guêpes détraquées
qui maçonneraient des cellules sans jamais rien y mettre. Et
comme ils sont fiers de leurs boîtes! Si du moins ils savaient en
renouveler un peu la forme de l'ornementation, avec l'ingéniosité
de ces artisans d'orient et d'Extrême Orient. Mais point. Ils
mettent leur orgueil à répéter des poncifs, en les démarquant.
Noblement. Pompeusement. Ce sont des esprits très distingués. —
La France est bien gardée. Ouf! que je suis aise d'être dehors!

CHAPTER VI: God and Religion, Christ and Christianity

Pages 86–87:

Je vois en lui le représentant, le héros le plus typique de cette
génération, disons plutôt de cette "levée" à l'aurore d'un siècle
nouveau. . . . Une génération à qui plus que nulle autre s'ap-
plique cette parole du prophète Amos: Voici que je vous enverrai
la faim, non point la faim de pain, mais la faim de la parole
de Dieu. La génération de Péguy et de Psichari, mais aussi, et
je cite pêle-mêle, celle d'André Gide, de Francis Jammes, d'André
Suarès, de Bourget, de Barrès, de Huysmans, de Brunetière. . . .
Un seul trait commun entre eux: c'est qu'aucun d'eux ne devait
rien à l'Eglise de leur nativité et que ceux d'entre eux qui
tardivement s'en rapprochèrent ne trouvèrent chez elle, intérieur
ou extérieur, aucun encouragement.

Page 87:

j'ai respiré . . . les vapeurs de l'abîme.

Page 87:

Dieu était mort.

Page 87:

C'est une vilenie de la part de Dieu. Bon pour nous, artistes,
qui pouvons mourir pour une minute d'extase, car elle tue la
mort!... Mais lui, lui qui n'est qu'autant qu'il sera, — lui, qui

n'aura pas été s'il n'est pas complètement... c'est une chose atroce que cette mort, qui le tue tout entier.

Page 87:

Ce fut mon acte le plus religieux. "Dieu! je suis franc avec toi! Je ne vais plus à ta Messe. . . . Je ne crois pas en toi."

Page 88:

j'ai dû réédifier sur de nouvelles bases mon être tout entier.

Page 89:

Ne souhaite pas, Nathanaël, trouver Dieu ailleurs que partout. Chaque créature indique Dieu, aucune ne le révèle.

Dès que notre regard s'arrête à elle, chaque créature nous détourne de Dieu.

Page 89:

Que chercher près d'un Dieu? Des réponses? Je me sentais moi-même une réponse à je ne savais encore quelle question.

Page 89:

Dieu me tient; je le tiens; nous sommes. Mais en pensant ceci, je ne fais qu'un avec la création entière; je me fonds et m'absorbe dans la prolixe humanité.

Page 89:

Par delà les phénomènes aux pluralités contingentes, contempler les vérités ineffables.

Page 90:

Ma foi ne dépend en rien de cela.

Page 90:

Je trouve plus d'apaisement à considérer Dieu comme une invention, une création de l'homme, que l'homme compose peu à peu, tend à former de plus en plus, à force d'intelligence et de vertu. C'est à Lui que la création parvient, aboutit, et non point de Lui qu'elle émane. Et comme le temps n'existe pas pour l'Eternel, cela revient au même pour Lui.

Page 90:

Toute évolution doit aboutir à Dieu.

Page 91:

Cette dernière parole du Christ me retiendrait de confondre le Christ avec Dieu, si déjà ne m'avertissait tout le reste.

Pages 91–92:

Dès l'instant que j'eus compris que Dieu n'était pas encore, mais devenait, et qu'il dépendait de chacun de nous qu'il devînt, la morale, en moi fut restaurée. Nulle impiété, nulle présomption dans cette pensée; car je me persuadais à la fois que Dieu ne s'accomplissait que par l'homme et qu'à travers lui; mais que si l'homme aboutissait à Dieu, la création, pour aboutir à l'homme, partait de Dieu; de sorte que l'on retrouvait le divin aux deux bouts, au départ comme à l'arrivée, et qu'il n'y avait eu de départ que pour en arriver à Dieu. Cette pensée bivalve me rassurait et je ne consentais plus à dissocier l'un de l'autre: Dieu créant l'homme afin d'être créé par lui; Dieu fin de l'homme; le chaos soulevé par Dieu jusqu'à l'homme, puis l'homme se soulevant ensuite jusqu'à Dieu. N'admettre que l'un: quelle crainte, quelle obligation! N'admettre que l'autre: quelle infatuation! Il ne s'agissait plus d'obéir à Dieu, mais de l'animer, de s'éprendre de lui, de l'exiger de soi par amour et de l'obtenir par vertu.

Page 92:

Nous n'en sommes pas encore là. Cet état d'athéisme complet, il faut beaucoup de vertu pour y atteindre; plus encore pour s'y maintenir.

Page 92:

Dieu est à venir. Je me persuade et me redis sans cesse que: Il dépend de nous. C'est par nous que Dieu s'obtient.

Page 93:

Mais il faut remarquer que par la série des causes et des êtres réels, je n'entends point ici la série des choses particulières et changeantes, mais seulement la série des choses fixes et éternelles.

Pages 93–94:

Vertige!... Vin de feu!... Ma prison s'ouvre. Voilà donc la réponse, obscurément conçue dans la douleur et dans le désespoir, appelée par des cris de passion aux ailes brisées, obstinément cherchée, voulue, dans les meurtrissures et les larmes de sang, la voilà rayonnante, la réponse à l'énigme du Sphinx, qui m'étreint depuis l'enfance, — à l'antimonie accablante entre l'immensité de mon être intérieur et le cachet de mon individu, qui m'humilie et qui m'étouffe!... *"Nature naturante"* et *"nature naturée"*... C'est la même. "Tout ce qui est, est en Dieu." Et moi aussi, je suis en Dieu! De ma chambre glacée, où tombe la nuit d'hiver, je m'évade au gouffre de *la Substance,* dans le soleil blanc de l'Être.

Page 94:

Je ne puis tomber qu'en Lui. J'ai la paix.

Page 94:

Christophe, halluciné, tendu de tout son être, frémit dans ses entrailles... Le voile se déchira. Ce fut un éblouissement. À la lueur de l'éclair, il vit, au fond de la nuit, il vit — il fut le Dieu. Le Dieu était en lui: Il brisait le plafond de la chambre, les murs de la maison; Il faisait craquer les limites de l'être; Il remplissait le ciel, l'univers, le néant. Le monde se ruait en Lui, comme une cataracte. Dans l'horreur et l'extase de cet effondrement, Christophe tombait aussi, emporté par le tourbillon qui broyait comme des pailles les lois de la nature. Il avait perdu le souffle, il était ivre de cette chute en Dieu... Dieu-abîme! Dieu-gouffre, Brasier de l'Être! Ouragan de la vie! Folie de vivre, — sans but, sans frein, sans raison — pour la fureur de vivre!

Page 95:

"Dieu a créé l'homme," dit-on. Mais l'homme le lui rend bien! Il est loin d'avoir fini de créer Dieu!

Page 95:

Je suis parfaitement rassuré sur la permanence du divin dans la pensée humaine et sur le lent enfantement pour l'humanité de nouvelles formes religieuses.

Page 95:

cette abominable agonie qui suffirait à faire maudire Dieu, s'il existait; — mais heureusement, il n'existe pas; — du moins sous la forme du Maître tout puissant et conscient, qu'on offre à nos imaginations d'enfant. Le pauvre Dieu, s'il existe — (il existe sûrement en nous) — souffre et lutte avec nous; et l'issue du combat n'est ni moins que certaine. [*sic*] C'est ce qui fait que nous ne devons pas l'abandonner — ni le combat, ni le Dieu (qui a besoin de nous) — même aux heures du plus amer désespoir.

Page 96:

Est-il vrai que Romain Rolland, agonisant, ait reçu visite de Claudel; à la suite de laquelle l'irréductible athée aurait fait venir un prêtre, reçu les derniers sacrements, etc. C'est ce que je lis, non sans stupeur, dans un journal italien qui m'arrange à la sauce piquante et souhaite que Romain Rolland me serve de bon exemple.

Page 96:

Voici ma seule profession de foi:

Depuis l'âge de quinze ans, je vis libre de toutes les religions établies. Mais je respecte la liberté de tous ceux qui croient, — dans la mesure où leur croyance n'est pas intolérante, ou oppressive pour les autres. Mon respect ne va pas à une forme de pensée — avec ou sans Dieu ou Dieux — mais aux hommes, personnellement, dignes de respect.

Page 97:

Il a écrit lui-même, et je l'ai sous les yeux, à ce moment la relation de cette étonnante expérience. Il a trois "visions," c'est lui-même qui emploie le mot, dont il faudra bien, un jour ou l'autre, que je parle. "J'allais mourir, dit-il, je me savais sur l'extrême seuil de l'abîme. À ce moment je me sentis soutenu et réconforté par la prière de tous ces amis, spécialement de mes amis catholiques, qui s'élevait à Dieu pour moi. Je sentais cette brûlante communion des âmes chrétiennes, venant au secours de l'une d'elles en danger, et les liens dont elles entourent Dieu qui, lui-même, aspire à cette réciprocité d'amour. Tout cela pénétrait la solitude desséchée de la fièvre; c'était comme l'affectueuse pression d'une main amie. Sublime idée d'un Dieu fait homme qui se sacrifie à tout instant par amour pour tous et pour chacun, et de la communauté des fidèles qui s'associent à ce sacrifice, et, dans la mesure de leurs forces, y participent. Quel

soulagement pour le cœur qui, dans ces heures de détresse, ne
trouve rien pour lui dans le panthéïsme glacé, qui suffisait aux
jours de santé! Pauvreté morale du panthéïsme! Un Être en qui
tous les êtres sont absorbés. Quel intérêt si Lui et eux sont
impersonnels? Cela ne rend aucun compte du vrai problème qui
est le moi — les moi (au pluriel) cette infinité de mois [*sic*]."

Pages 97–98:

Malgré tout il se tient sans le franchir, sur le seuil de la
croyance. . . . Son cœur, d'un mouvement puissant, le porte vers
la foi. Mais la foi ne satisfait pas son exigeance religieuse de
vérité.

Page 98:

Les conceptions religieuses de Romain Rolland n'étaient pas
celles de la foi catholique, mais jamais il n'a été un ennemi de
l'Eglise qui les professe.

Page 98:

"Etrange dualité de ma nature! Une raison ferme, tranquille,
inflexible, qui ne croit pas, et sur laquelle aucun argument de
foi ne mord. Un instinct du cœur, qui s'abandonne aux élans de
la prière — et peut-être surtout au puissant courant du fleuve
invisible, coulant sous terre des siècles d'âmes croyantes qui
m'ont précédé et engendré. Nous cheminons, ainsi sur deux
chemins parallèles, sans rien pouvoir l'un sur l'autre, mais sans
nous heurter." "Ma raison se refuse à croire, dit-il ailleurs, le
mot de refus est d'ailleurs inexact, elle ne peut pas."

Pages 98–99:

si religieux que nous soyons, et si convaincus que tout homme
porte en lui la lumière divine, nous ne pouvons admettre que
le point de vue de la raison, — justement parce que la raison
nous paraît le rayonnement de Dieu en nous.

Page 99:

Mais il reste un ami toujours pour ceux qu'il a reçus une fois
à sa table.

Page 99:

Oui, j'aimerais bien aller avec toi, à l'église, en ce jour. . . .
En étant près de lui, on est plus près l'un de l'autre.

Page 99:

J'ai toujours vécu, parallèlement deux vies, — l'une celle du personnage que les combinaisons des éléments héréditaires m'ont fait revêtir, dans un lieu de l'espace et une heure du temps, — l'autre, celle de l'Être sans visage, sans nom, sans lieu, sans siècle, qui est la substance et le souffle de toute vie.

Page 99:

Je ne dis pas adieu au Christ sans une sorte de déchirement; de sorte que je doute à présent, si je l'avais vraiment quitté.

Page 100:

Je ne sais pas — je ne sais rien. Tu m'as demandé, je suis venu. Je ne te connais pas; je ne sais pas qui tu es ni même si tu es; mais je suis venu à toi, pour que ton divin cœur ne se dolente pas à cause de moi, si parfois tu étais et tu me désires.

Page 100:

Le catholicisme a lié à la figure du Christ et à son enseignement tout un cortège d'idées et tout un jeu d'attitudes, si étroitement, qu'il soit aujourd'hui très difficile de repousser les uns sans repousser l'autre à la fois. . . .

Page 100:

Pourtant ces attaques contre le christianisme, le Christ ne les a pas méritées; mais l'Eglise; et tout ce que je pense aujourd'hui contre elle, c'est avec Lui.

Page 100:

La Maison, ce n'est pas Vous, mon Père.

Pages 100–101:

Ah! Vous n'avez pas dit cela, mais mon frère. Vous, Vous avez construit toute la terre et la Maison et ce qui n'est pas la Maison. La Maison, d'autres que Vous l'ont construite; en Votre nom, je sais, mais d'autres que Vous.

Page 101:

Père, je vous l'ai dit, je ne vous aimai jamais plus qu'au désert. Mais j'étais las, chaque matin, de poursuivre ma subsistance. Dans la maison, du moins, on mange bien.

Page 101:

Mais écoute: C'est moi qui t'ai formé; ce qui est en toi, je le sais. Je sais ce qui te poussait sur les routes; je t'attendais au bout. Tu m'aurais appelé... j'étais là. — Va maintenant; rentre dans la chambre que j'ai fait préparer pour toi.

CHAPTER VII: The Morality of Individualism

Page 102:

tout respect comporte un aveuglement dont il faut s'affranchir pour progresser vers la lumière.

Page 103:

La réponse me paraît simple: c'est de trouver cette règle en soi-même; d'avoir pour but le développement de soi.

Page 103:

C'est un appel à la vaillance, que de ne connaître point ses parents.

Page 103:

Je n'ai jamais eu de bonheur que ma raison ne désapprouve.

Page 104:

C'est au défaut de la logique que je prends conscience de moi. O ma plus chère et ma plus riante pensée! qu'ai-je affaire de chercher plus longtemps à légitimer ta naissance.

Page 104:

agir selon la plus grande sincérité.

Page 104:

Nathanaël, ah! satisfais ta joie quand ton âme en est souriante — et ton désir d'amour quand tes lèvres sont encore belles à baiser, et quand ton étreinte est joyeuse.

Page 104:

Je ne sentis bientôt plus mon âme que comme une volonté aimante . . . palpitante, ouverte à tout venant, pareille à tout, impersonnelle, une naïve incohésion d'appétits, de gourmandises, de désirs. . . . Je m'abandonnai donc à ce désordre plus sincère et naturel, qui s'organiserait de soi-même, pensais-je, et du reste estimant que le désordre même était moins dangereux pour mon âme, qu'un ordre arbitraire et nécessairement factice puisque je ne l'avais pas inventé.

Page 105:

étant autrefois sans loi, je vivais.

Page 105:

tout doit être remis en question.

Page 105:

Nathanaël, je t'enseignerai que toutes choses sont divinement naturelles.

Page 105:

Commandements de Dieu, vous avez endolori mon âme. . . .
Enseignerez-vous qu'il a toujours plus de choses défendues?
De nouveaux châtiments promis à la soif de tout ce que j'aurai trouvé beau sur la terre?
Commandements de Dieu, vous avez rendu malade mon âme.

Page 105:

Nathanaël, je ne crois plus au péché.

Page 105:

La vie intense — voilà le superbe.
Être me devenait énormément voluptueux.

Page 105:

Laissez les morts ensevelir les morts.

Page 106:

Tout phénomène est le Symbole d'une Vérité. Son seul devoir est qu'il la manifeste. Son seul péché; qu'il se préfère. . . . Tout homme qui ne manifeste pas est inutile et mauvais.

Page 106:

Au nom de quel Dieu, de quel idéal me défendez-vous de vivre selon ma nature?... Jusqu'à présent j'avais accepté la morale du Christ, ou du moins certain puritanisme que l'on m'avait enseigné comme étant la morale du Christ. Pour m'efforcer de m'y soumettre, je n'avais obtenu qu'un profond désarroi de tout mon être. . . . Mais j'en viens alors à douter si Dieu même exigeait de telles contraintes.

Page 107:

Enfin, tu as renoncé à être celui que tu voulais être.

Page 107:

tu emportes tous mes espoirs. Sois fort; oublie-nous; oublie-moi. Puisses-tu ne pas revenir.

Page 107:

On a peur de se trouver seul: et l'on ne se trouve pas du tout. . . . Ce que l'on sent en soi de différent, c'est précisément ce que l'on possède de rare, ce qui fait à chacun sa valeur; et c'est là ce que l'on tâche de supprimer. On imite. Et l'on prétend aimer la vie.

Page 107:

Je me persuadais que chaque être, ou tout au moins que chaque élu, avait à jouer un rôle sur la terre, le sien précisément, et qui ne ressemblait à nul autre; de sorte que tout effort pour se soumettre à une règle commune devenait à mes yeux trahison; oui, trahison, et que j'assimilais à ce grand péché contre l'Esprit — qui ne serait point pardonné, — par quoi l'être particulier perdait sa signification précise, irremplaçable, sa — saveur — qui ne pouvait lui être rendue.

Page 108:

La vie! voilà le fond de ma nature, ce qui la définit, et ce qui la rend inexplicable aux autres qui m'entourent, voilà ce qui me remplit! Elle est ma foi, mon art, ma volonté. La beauté, la bonté, sont pour moi égales à la vie.

Page 108:

tous les hommes étaient partout les mêmes; il fallait en prendre son parti; et ne pas s'obstiner dans une lutte enfantine contre le monde; il fallait être soi-même, avec tranquillité.

Page 108:

Le premier devoir est d'être ce qu'on est. Oser dire: "Ceci est bien, cela est mal." On fait plus de bien aux faibles, en étant fort, qu'en devenant faible comme eux.

Page 109:

Trouve tes lois. Cherche en toi.

Chapter VIII: Gide, Rolland, and Communism

Page 110:

J'ai été longtemps convaincu que la question morale était plus importante que la question sociale. Je disais et j'écrivais: "L'homme est plus important que les hommes." . . . J'ai cru cela pendant quarante ans: je n'en suis plus aussi sûr aujourd'hui.

Page 111:

Mais surtout j'aimerais vivre assez pour voir le plan de la Russie réussir, et les Etats d'Europe contraints de s'incliner devant ce qu'ils s'obstinaient à méconnaître.

Page 111:

Je voudrais crier très haut ma sympathie pour la Russie; et que mon cri soit entendu, ait de l'importance. Je voudrais vivre assez pour voir la réussite de cet énorme effort; on succès que je souhaite de toute mon âme, auquel je voudrais travailler. Voir ce que peut donner un état sans religion,* une société sans famille. La religion et la famille sont les deux pires ennemis du progrès.

* Sans religion? Non, peut-être. Mais une religion sans mythologie.

Pages 111–112:

Quand on songe à l'enseignement du Christ et qu'on voit ce qu'en a fait le monde moderne, on est navré. . . . J'estime que le christianisme a fait banqueroute. J'ai écrit et je pense profondément que si le christianisme s'était imposé, si l'on avait accepté l'enseignement du Christ tel quel, il ne serait pas question aujourd'hui de communisme. Il n'y aurait même pas de question sociale.

Page 112:

comment ne pas se sentir une âme communiste?

Page 113:

communiste, de cœur aussi bien que l'esprit, je l'ai toujours été; même en restant chrétien; et c'est bien pourquoi j'eus du mal à séparer l'un de l'autre et plus de mal encore à les opposer. Je n'y serais jamais parvenu tout seul. Il a fallu gens et événements pour m'instruire. Ne parlez pas ici de "conversion"; je n'ai pas changé de direction; j'ai toujours marché de l'avant; je continue; la grande différence c'est que, pendant longtemps, je ne voyais rien devant moi, que de l'espace et que la projection de ma propre ferveur; à présent, j'avance en m'orientant vers quelque chose; je sais que quelque part mes vœux imprécis s'organisent et que mon rêve est en passe de devenir réalité.

Au demeurant parfaitement inapte à la politique. Ne me demandez donc point de faire partie d'un Parti.

Pages 113–114:

Mes idées sociales n'allaient pas plus loin. Jaurès n'avait pas encore fait pénétrer la pensée socialiste dans la jeunesse bourgeoise de France. Notre éducation laissait beaucoup à désirer. Mon socialisme n'était que d'instinct. — Mais en peu d'années tout allait changer.

Pages 114–115:

Je vous remercie de vos aimables paroles. — et sur et dans [*sic*] votre livre. Je viens de le parcourir avec intérêt, et je le lirai attentivement. Mais je ne puis tarder pour protester contre une erreur invraisemblable qui me concerne.

p. 323 vous écrivez:

"N'est il pas frappant *qu'à la même heure* (donc en 1932!) Romain Rolland (je passe les épithetès) arrive, *presqu'en même temps* que Gide, à des conclusions analogues aux siennes? *C'est en des termes bien proches de ceux dont Gide s'est servi* que R.R. s'est déclaré en faveur de la grande expérience russe."

Ces lignes dénotent une telle méconnaissance — (inconnaissance) — de mon action ininterrompue, depuis *quinze ans,* pour la Révolution Russe, qu'elles me révoltent. J'ai beau connaître la désinvolture, qu'affichent également les écrivains français d'après-guerre, à l'égard de l'histoire. Ceci passe la mesure.

Faut-il vous rappeler que, moins de trois mois après la révolution russe, — le 1er mai 1917, j'envoyais de Genève un *Salut "à la Russie libre et libératrice"* (voir *"Les Précurseurs"*) — qu'en août-septembre 1918, j'affirmais mes sentiments de *"solidarité internationale avec le bolchevisme russe"* — qu'en août 1919, dans ma Déclaration d'indépendance de l'esprit, je déclarais que "la pensée russe est l'avant-garde de la pensée du monde" — que depuis, inlassablement, pendant douze ans, j'ai écrit et publié pour célébrer ou pour défendre la Révolution Russe —. . . . Si j'ai gardé ma liberté de discussion avec mes amis, les communistes russes, et si j'ai engagé, dans leurs journaux, en Russie même, plus d'une libre controverse avec les théoriciens bolcheviks, sur tel ou tel point de la doctrine, j'ai toujours combattu pour la Révolution Russe et pour l'œuvre héroïque de Lénine et de Staline.

Page 115:

il y a peu de chances pour que l'on soit instruit de ce que je pense et de ce que j'écris. Mais il n'est pas un communiste en U.R.S.S. qui l'ignore. . . .

Je suis habitué à bien des inexactitudes, à mon sujet, de la part des écrivains français; et je ne perds pas mon temps à y répondre. Mais de vous, que j'estime, je ne laisserai point passer sous silence une assertion qui dénature ainsi, ou qui supprime, quinze ans de ma vie. Il est énorme de me représenter, vis-à-vis de la Révolution Russe, comme un suiveur de votre homme de la onzième heure, — dont j'apprécie d'ailleurs le ralliement.

Page 116:

Ce n'est qu'en août 1914 que je suis entré, bien malgré moi, dans la politique. Jusqu'alors, j'étais imprégné de l'idéologie de mon temps et de ma classe, que je dénonce . . . l'idéologie de l'*homme abstrait*, détaché l'on disait alors, libéré des contingences de la vie politique et sociale. Il n'eût pas semblé digne d'un écrivain de s'en occuper.

Page 116:

Frères de Russie, qui venez d'accomplir votre grande Révolution, nous n'avons pas seulement à vous féliciter; nous vous remercions. Ce n'est pas pour vous seuls que vous avez travaillé, en conquérant votre liberté, c'est pour nous tous, vos frères du vieil Occident.

Pages 116–117:

Quand j'avais commencé ce nouveau carnet, je m'étais pourtant promis de n'y plus traiter ces questions. Ce qui fit simplement que je restai plusieurs semaines sans y rien écrire. Ces questions m'occupent presque exclusivement; j'y reviens sans cesse et n'en peux détourner ma pensée. Oui, vraiment, je ne pense à peu près à rien d'autre.

Page 117:

L'inculpation d'Aragon pour son poème "Front Rouge" paru dans la revue *Littéraire de la Révolution Mondiale,* inculpation qui l'expose à une peine de cinq ans de prison, constitue en France un fait sans précédent.

Nous nous élevons contre toute tentative d'interprétation d'un texte poétique à des fins judiciaires et réclamons la cessation immédiate des poursuites.

Page 118:

pourquoi demander l'impunité pour la littérature?. . . . La pensée est aussi dangereuse que des actes. Nous sommes des gens dangereux. C'est un honneur que d'être condamné sous un tel régime.

Page 118:

pour l'honneur même d'Aragon et des Surréalistes.

Page 118:

Nous sommes des combattants. Nos écrits sont nos armes. Nous sommes responsables de nos armes comme nos compagnons ouvriers ou soldats. Au lieu de les renier, nous sommes tenus de les revendiquer. Que chacun de nous soit jugé, individuellement, pour celles qu'il emploie.

Page 119:

Je vous prie de joindre mon nom aux signatures de ceux qui, sans distinction de patries, de partis et de religions, se déclarent prêts à s'opposer de toutes leurs forces à la guerre; sous quelque forme que celle-ci se présente, sous quelque forme que ceux-ci qui mènent l'opinion jugent habile de nous la présenter.

Page 119:

l'action est le but de la pensée.

Page 119:

rappelons l'adhésion adressée au Congrès par une élite d'intellectuels français au premier rang desquels . . . André Gide, dont les récentes déclarations ont soulevé l'émoi de la bourgeoisie de tous les pays. . . .

Page 120:

Bien que malade, je ne veux pas que ma voix soit absente de votre meeting de protestation contre les bourreaux de l'Allemagne. Que ces meurtriers, ces tortureurs soient souffletés par le poing géant des masses révolutionnaires du monde! Ces frénétiques, en quelques semaines, ont fait retomber l'Occident de plusieurs siècles en arrière. . . .

Page 120:

La lutte sociale est pour tous les pays la même, et les peuples qu'on envoie se battre pour des raisons qui leur échappent, et que souvent ils désapprouveraient s'ils les connaissaient vraiment, ces peuples ont chacun le même intérêt profond dont ils commencent à se rendre compte.

Page 121:

car tout impérialisme enfante nécessairement la guerre

Page 121:

dans le terrorisme allemand, je vois une reprise, un resaisissement du plus déplorable passé. Dans l'établissement de la société soviétique, une illimitée promesse de l'avenir.

Page 121:

L'avenir vous éclairera — trop tard — sur votre erreur meurtrière, dont la seule excuse est le délire de désespoir où l'aveuglement et la dureté de vos vainqueurs de Versailles avaient jeté votre peuple depuis quinze ans.

Pour moi, je maintiendrai, en dépit de vous, et contre vous, mon attachement à l'Allemagne — à la vraie Allemagne, — que les forfaits et les aberrations du fascisme hitlérien déshonorent.

Page 122:

En cet automne de 1933, devant l'arrogant redressement des nationalismes, devant la glorification des vieilles idoles au nom desquelles on mène les peuples au combat, l'anniversaire de la révolution russe prend une particulière importance. Il nous faut en profiter pour resserrer notre union.

L'on prétend voir aujourd'hui la propagande de Moscou dans chaque soulèvement populaire; dans quelque pays que ce soit; qu'il y ait propagande, il va sans dire, mais peut-être pas à la façon que l'on croit. L'événement dont nous célébrons aujourd'hui le seizième anniversaire a, par lui-même et par son seul exemple, une force de persuasion suffisante, bien autrement émouvante que les subsides et les discours; aucune compression ne pourra rien contre cela. La principale force de cette propagande, c'est qu'elle favorise une aspiration légitime. L'exemple des journées d'octobre a réveillé les peuples de l'accablement où l'oppression capitaliste les maintenait. Le grand cri poussé par l'U.R.S.S. a réveillé tous les espoirs; mais n'aurait point trouvé d'écho s'il ne répondait point, pour tant de cœurs, à tant de gémissements étouffés; pour tant d'esprits, à tant d'évidentes faillites.

Il y eut un temps où c'était vers la France, après 89, que se tournaient tous les regards. Mais la cause qui nous tient à cœur aujourd'hui n'est plus celle d'un seul pays. L'ennemi reste le même, aussi bien en France que partout; c'est contre lui que nous devons nous unir pour lutter. Que l'U.R.S.S. ait encore à triompher de difficultés très grandes et de tous ordres, il se peut; mais ceux qui crient à l'échec se réjouissent un peu trop vite; il importe de le leur prouver.

Page 123:

Il me paraît que le Congrès Mondial qui se prépare doit tenir à cœur tout particulièrement d'honorer les jeunes gens qui refusent de se prêter au jeu de la guerre, étudiants d'Angleterre ou d'Amérique, instituteurs français, "objecteurs" de tous pays; de les laver de cette perfide accusation de lâcheté par laquelle on s'efforce de les discréditer et de disqualifier leur conduite.

Il importe de leur faire connaître, en réponse à ces calomnies, que nous leur donnons notre estime, souvent même notre admiration, sachant bien qu'il faut plus de réel courage pour s'opposer isolément à un entraînement collectif que pour emboîter le pas, fût-ce pour affronter la mort; sachant tout ce que ce courage singulier comporte encore d'initiative et qu'il entraîne, en plus des sanctions matérielles, celles, pour certains plus redoutables encore, de l'opinion.

Il appartient à ce Congrès de proposer à la jeunesse cette nouvelle forme de l'héroïsme.

Page 123:

Ma réponse aux "objecteurs de conscience" traîne depuis quinze jours sur ma table; je n'ai pu me résoudre à l'envoyer. Non que ma pensée (j'allais dire ma conviction) reste, sur ce point, incertaine; mais me retient la crainte qu'on en puisse tirer parti pour me forcer à jouer un rôle politique pour lequel je me sens on ne peut moins qualifié.

Page 124:

Croyez-moi très sensible à la cordialité de votre lettre. Mais... non! Ne m'annoncez pas, je vous en prie. Si, ensuite, je ne paraissais pas à cette réunion, ce serait pour décevoir. Mais si je paraissais, je décevrais plus encore; et plus encore si je prenais la parole. Je ne suis pas fait pour les réunions publiques.

Page 124:

J'ai déjà déclaré ma sympathie (et le mot *sympathie* me paraît bien faible) pour les idées qui vous inspirent. Je trouverai d'autres occasions de la déclarer encore. Mais persuadez-vous que je ne vaux rien dans les réunions, que je n'ai pas la voix qu'il faut pour parler en public et suis fort mal qualifié pour présider quoi que ce soit. Ce rôle n'est pas fait pour moi, ne me convient pas et je n'y ferais que décevoir. Veuillez donc ne pas faire figurer mon nom sur les prospectus du congrès, s'il n'est pas déjà imprimé, et me croire néanmoins bien cordialement avec vous. Laissez-moi tranquillement écrire ce que j'ai encore à écrire; c'est ainsi que je pourrai le mieux et le plus durablement vous aider.

Page 125:

Notre ennemi, Barbusse, c'est la violence oppressive de la
société humaine, telle qu'elle existe à présent. Mais contre cette
violence, vous armez une violence adverse. À mon sens . . . la
méthode ne mène qu'à la destruction mutuelle.

Page 125:

La révolution, c'est la maison de tous ceux qui veulent une
humanité plus heureuse et meilleure. Elle est donc aussi mienne.

Page 125:

je ne dis pas: la non-résistance: car, ne vous y trompez pas,
c'est la suprême résistance. Refuser son consentement et son
concours à l'Etat criminel est l'acte le plus héroïque qui puisse
être accompli par un homme de notre temps; il exige lui —
de lui, un individu, seul, en face de l'Etat colosse, qui peut
l'étrangler, froidement, entre quatre murs, il exige une énergie
et un esprit de sacrifice incomparablement plus grands que
d'affronter la mort, en mêlant son haleine et sa sueur d'agonie à
celles du troupeau. Une telle force morale n'est possible que si
l'on réveille au cœur des hommes — de chaque homme, individuellement, — le feu de la conscience, le sens quasi mystique du
divin qui est en chaque esprit, et qui a soulevé aux heures
décisives de l'histoire les grandes races, jusqu'aux astres.

Page 126:

Tout peut et doit servir dans le combat commun. . . . Il
serait un pauvre conducteur d'hommes ou d'armées, celui qui ne
saurait point employer également les ressources d'actions variées
qui lui sont offertes.

Page 126:

Je trouve coupables gravement certains de vos chefs qui vous
laissent des illusions sur ce point et vous leurrent de l'espoir que
la guerre s'arrêtera devant des bras croisés. Elle s'arrêtera —
oui! — mais après qu'elle aura passé sur les corps de ceux qui
barrent le chemin. Elle s'arrêtera devant le soulèvement de
l'opinion du monde, provoqué par le sacrifice des Résistants
passifs. C'est ce sacrifice seul qui peut annoncer — ou préparer —

la victoire à venir de l'humanité, le salut des futures générations. Mais ce sacrifice ne pourra pas être évité.

Page 127:

Je m'associe de tout cœur à la sympathie et à l'admiration de Romain Rolland pour le courage de Dimitrov, de ses compagnons bulgares et de Torgler.

Page 129:

Mon cher Romain Rolland

Profiterai-je de mon passage à Bex pour causer avec vous? Mais je saurai respecter votre retraite et ne souhaiterai cette rencontre que si je sais que vous la souhaitez également.

De grand cœur avec vous

André Gide

Page 130:

Le temps passa. Il y a deux ans, me trouvant en Suisse, appelé à X..., non loin de Villeneuve, où je savais que vivait Romain Rolland, j'eus le vif désir de le revoir. Je souhaitais lui marquer ma haute estime. Il me fit savoir qu'il me recevrait volontiers et je pense qu'il comprit avec quelle émotion, lorsque je le revis, je répondis à sa chaleureuse accolade. De l'entretien que nous eûmes alors, je ne trouve rien à rapporter. Dans ce qu'il me disait je me sentais en grande communion de cœur avec lui. La constance et la résolution de sa pensée avaient empreint de noblesse les traits creusés de son visage. Emerson dit dans un de ses *Essais* que la grandeur morale d'un homme se manifeste dans ses moindres gestes et que le rayonnement de sa personnalité est sensible aussitôt, dès la première approche. Je ne sais si cela est toujours bien vrai; mais du moins je pensai ce jour-là que Romain Rolland ne faisait pas mentir Emerson.

L'attitude de Romain Rolland, prise au moment de la guerre et conservée durant toute sa vie avec une constance admirable, nous est d'un grand enseignement. Il était d'abord seul ou presque; durant longtemps, il eut à supporter les blâmes, les moqueries, les injures. Ceux qui le méprisaient, et, par patriotisme, le haïssaient le plus alors, doivent reconnaître aujourd'hui que la figure de Romain Rolland est de celles en qui s'incarnent l'honneur et la gloire de la France et de toute l'humanité.

Page 135:

"Vendredi" du 24 janvier et "L'Humanité" du 26 publient des pages de témoignages de mes confrères écrivains; j'ai l'heureuse surprise d'y voir au premier rang, André Gide. . . .

Page 137:

Il est absurde de parler de persécution contre la foi chrétienne en U.R.S.S. La liberté de cultes est assurée. . . . Il y a seulement une forte propagande antireligieuse, mais qui est tenue par les lois de respecter les locaux de culte. Qui ferait de scandale dans une église serait condamné. — Si nombre d'églises ont été fermées, c'est que le principe est établi (et je l'approuve) que les lieux de culte et les desservants doivent être entretenus par les croyants. S'ils ne sont pas assez nombreux ou assez généreux, pour subvenir à ses dépenses, l'Etat n'a pas à s'en charger.

Page 138:

en étant révolutionnaire l'écrivain n'est plus un opposant

Page 138:

J'ai déclaré, il y a trois ans, mon admiration pour l'U.R.S.S., et mon amour. . . .

Si je me suis trompé d'abord, le mieux est de reconnaître au plus tôt mon erreur; car je suis responsable, ici, de ceux que cette erreur entraîne. Il n'y a pas, en ce cas, amour-propre qui tienne; et du reste j'en ai fort peu. Il y a des choses plus importantes que l'U.R.S.S.: c'est l'humanité, c'est son destin, c'est sa culture.

Page 138:

Ce que j'admire en Léningrad, c'est Saint Pétersbourg.

Page 138:

Dans cette foule, je me plonge; je me plonge; je prends un bain d'humanité.

Page 139:

Le bonheur de tous ne s'obtient qu'en désindividualisant chacun. Le bonheur de tous ne s'obtient qu'aux dépens de chacun; Pour être heureux, soyez conformes.

Page 139:

De sorte que, chaque fois que l'on converse avec un Russe, c'est comme si l'on conversait avec tous.

Page 139:

En U.R.S.S., pour belle que puisse être une œuvre, si elle n'est pas dans la ligne, elle est honnie. La beauté est considérée une valeur bourgeoise. Pour génial que puisse être un artiste, s'il ne travaille pas dans la ligne l'attention se détourne, est détournée de lui: ce que l'on demande à l'artiste, à l'écrivain, c'est d'être conforme; et tout le reste lui sera donné par-dessus.

Page 140:

André Gide est communiste. Pour combien de temps?

Page 140:

Nous nous en voudrions de détruire un si bel enthousiasme, mais la presse soviétique se trompe, si elle prend André Gide pour un interprète des vertus bourgeoises, et si elle s'imagine que, dans ce récent avatar, il les trahit pour la première fois.

Eh, du reste, M. André Gide n'appartiendra jamais qu'à son propre parti.

Page 141:

Le communisme ne saura s'imposer qu'en tenant compte des particularités de chaque individu. Une société où chacun ressemblerait à tous n'est pas souhaitable; je dirai même qu'elle est impossible; une littérature, bien plus encore. Chaque artiste est nécessairement individualiste, si fortes que puissent être ses convictions communistes et son attachement au parti.

Page 141:

Un communisme bien compris a besoin de favoriser les individus de valeur, de tirer parti de toutes les valeurs de l'individu, d'obtenir le meilleur rendement de chacun. Et l'individualisme bien compris n'a pas à s'opposer à ce qui mettrait tout à sa place et en valeur.

Pages 141–142:

lorsque j'écris que je ne reconnais point pour essentiellement inconciliables un communisme "bien compris" et un individualisme "bien compris," j'entends: tels que je les comprends moi-même. Il faut donc que j'explique comment je les comprends. Il est certain que je ne vois point un communisme égalitaire, ou du moins que je ne vois l'égalité de conditions que pour le départ; qu'il n'impliquerait pour chacun que des chances égales, mais nullement une uniformité des qualités, une uniformisation — que j'estime à la fois impossible et fort peu souhaitable, aussi bien pour l'individu que pour la masse. Et, de même, une inter-nationalisation des intérêts économiques, n'impliquerait nulle-ment la suppression et la méconnaissance des particularités raciales ou géographiques, les différences heureusement irréduc-tibles des cultures et des traditions. La diversité même des exécutants fait la richesse et la beauté de la symphonie, et souhaiter que tous les instruments, cuivres, violons, hautbois ou clarinettes rendent le même son, serait aussi absurde que de penser que chaque instrument jouerait mieux s'il s'émancipait de l'ensemble de l'orchestre et n'observait plus la mesure.

Page 142:

Que la littérature, que l'art puissent servir la révolution, il va sans dire; mais il n'a pas à se préoccuper de la servir. Il ne la sert jamais si bien que quand il se préoccupe uniquement du vrai. La littérature n'a pas à se mettre au service de la révolution. Une littérature asservie est une littérature avilie, si noble et légitime que soit la cause qu'elle sert. Mais comme la cause de la vérité se confond dans mon esprit, dans notre esprit, avec celle de la Révolution, l'art, en se préoccupant uniquement de vérité, sert nécessairement la Révolution. Il ne la suit pas; il ne s'y soumet pas; il ne la reflète pas. Il l'éclaire.

Page 143:

Me voilà renseigné.

Page 143:

Ce qu'il y avait de stupéfiant, c'est la brusquerie avec laquelle la foi s'était évanouie. On ne sentait rien de chagrin, de la blessure, de la colère, que cause une grande déception. Pas d'arrachement. Une foi sans racines. Le mirage utopique s'était dissipé, sans laisser de traces.

Page 144:

Le communisme, à présent, fait fausse route; il ne peut se sauver qu'en cessant de se mettre à la remorque de Moscou. La foi dans l'U.R.S.S. est ébranlée; il y eut, à la suite du procès des 16, quantité d'exclusions du parti. Vous pensez bien que je suis cela de près.

Pages 145–146:

Non, il serait faux de dire que mes opinions, mes pensées, n'ont pas changé, et je serais de mauvaise foi de le prétendre. Mais le grand, le très important changement est celui-ci; j'avais cru, jusqu'à ces derniers temps, qu'il importait d'abord de changer l'homme, les hommes, chaque homme; et que c'était par là qu'il fallait commencer. C'est pourquoi j'écrivais que la question morale m'importait plus que la question sociale.

Je me laisse persuader aujourd'hui que l'homme même ne peut changer que d'abord les conditions sociales ne l'y invitent et ne l'y aident — de sorte que ce soit d'elles qu'il faille d'abord s'occuper.

Mais il faut s'occuper des deux.

C'est aussi, c'est beaucoup la bêtise et la malhonnêteté des attaques contre l'U.R.S.S. qui font qu'aujourd'hui nous mettons quelque obstination à la défendre. Eux, les aboyeurs, vont commencer à l'approuver lorsque précisément nous cesserons de le faire; car ce qu'ils approuveront ce seront ses compromissions, ses transigeances et qui feront dire aux autres: "Vous voyez bien!" mais par où elle s'écartera du but que d'abord elle poursuivait. Puisse notre regard, en restant fixé sur ce but, ne point être amené, par là même, à se détourner de l'U.R.S.S.

Page 146:

de singulières incertitudes, très inquiétantes. . . . Je n'ai pas grande confiance dans la durée de ses sentiments soviétiques.

Pages 147:

Le socialisme au lieu d'être un rétrécissement de l'esprit devrait en être un élargissement. . . .

Pourtant c'est une entreprise d'abaissement intellectuel qu'on travaille aujourd'hui, sous prétexte de répandre une nouvelle culture, qui serait la véritable. . . . Répandez la culture oui, mais n'assurez pas, après le triomphe de l'esprit primaire dans la bourgeoisie le triomphe de l'esprit primaire chez les ouvriers.

Pages 147–148:
cette félicité qui ne s'obtient que par le renoncement de ce qui est en nous d'individuel; car c'est l'attachement à nous-mêmes qui nous retient de plonger dans l'Eternité, d'entrer dans le royaume de Dieu et de participer au sentiment confus de la vie universelle.

Page 148:
L'individu triomphe dans le renoncement de l'individualité: Celui qui aime sa vie, qui protège sa personnalité, la perdra. . . . Résurrection dans la vie totale, oubli de tout bonheur particulier.

Page 148:
Et comme je crois, au surplus, que la personnalité ne s'affirme jamais plus qu'en se renonçant, il me paraît que . . . seules peuvent s'inquiéter du communisme les personnalités indécises, ou ceux qui croient ne pouvoir s'affirmer qu'aux dépens d'autrui.

Page 150:
Terrible désarroi après lecture des manifestations trotzkistes confiées par Pierre Naville. Mais, si bien fondées que puissent me paraître certaines critiques, il me semble que rien ne peut être plus préjudiciable que les divisions du parti.

Page 150:
Vous savez que je ne suis pas trotzkiste, et, ce que je reproche ici, ce n'est pas de mécontenter les trotzkistes mais bien de leur donner de si bonnes raisons d'être furieux contre la *N.R.F.* (et cela pour le contentement de personne... que je sache).

Page 150:
Nous avons alors ouvert devant lui le dossier de la répression anti-marxiste, anti-prolétarienne, dans l'U.R.S.S. qu'il s'apprête à visiter.

Page 151:
à présent où l'U.R.S.S. en est-elle? La bureaucratie redoutée, le mécanique administrative n'a jamais été plus forte.

Pages 151–152:

Je pensais faire beaucoup à Moscou, pour beaucoup de victimes...
J'ai vu tout de suite qu'il n'y avait absolument rien à faire...
On m'a comblé de banquets — comme si je venais là pour
banqueter!...

Page 152:

C'est pour avoir dénoncé ces compromissions que Trotsky est
traité d'ennemi public (alors qu'il ne l'est que des compromissions
de Staline) et, du coup, assimilé au fascisme, ce qui est vraiment
par trop simple. Il est beaucoup plus l'ennemi du fascisme que
Staline lui-même et c'est en tant que révolutionnaire et que
antifasciste qu'il dénonce les compromissions de ce dernier. Mais
allez donc faire comprendre cela à un peuple aveuglé!

Page 154:

je prétends que l'on peut ne pas approuver Staline, sans devenir
aussitôt trotskyste pour cela.

Pages 154–155:

Chers camarades,

Je comprends votre indignation au sujet du livre d'André Gide.
Ce mauvais livre est, d'ailleurs, un livre médiocre, étonnamment
pauvre, superficiel, puéril et contradictoire. S'il a eu un grand
retentissement, ce n'est certes pas à sa valeur qu'il le doit; elle
est nulle. C'est au bruit fait autour du nom Gide, et à l'exploitation de sa célébrité par les ennemis de l'U.R.S.S., toujours aux
aguets et prêts à se servir contre elle de toutes les armes qui
s'offrent à leur méchanceté.

Je réagis à la façon d'Ostrovsky. J'en veux à Gide, moins de
ses critiques, qu'il aurait pu faire ouvertement, quand il était
en U.R.S.S., s'il avait été franc, que du double jeu, qu'il a joué,
prodiguant en U.R.S.S. des protestations d'amour et d'admiration,
et, aussitôt rentré en France, portant à l'U.R.S.S. un coup dans
le dos, tout en protestant de sa "sincérité"!

J'entends dire ici que Gide prétend ne pas avoir voulu faire
tort à l'U.R.S.S. et à la Révolution, et qu'il se plaint que toute
la presse ennemie de l'U.R.S.S. se serve contre elle de son livre!
Ce n'est pourtant pas faute d'avoir été averti! Je sais que des amis

l'avaient prévenu du mal qu'il ferait, et l'avaient instamment prié d'y réfléchir. Il n'en a tenu aucun compte, et s'est hâté de publier son livre, à gros tirage, à bas prix. Qu'à présent il proteste contre les félicitations, et les panégyriques humiliants des suppôts de la réaction et jusque du *Voelkischer Beobachter* — je conçois qu'il s'en trouve gêné! Ce sont autant d'actes d'accusation contre lui. Mais il est bien tard pour s'en apercevoir! Le mal est fait. Aura-t-il la force de le défaire? J'en doute... S'il avait seulement la volonté! Les mois prochains nous le diront.

Mais encore une fois, comme Ostrovsky, "Je ne veux plus parler de lui." Ce n'est pas lui, ni qui que ce soit, ni quoi que ce soit, qui pourra jamais arrêter la marche de l'histoire et le développement de l'U.R.S.S. L'U.R.S.S. en a vu bien d'autres!

Mais il faut, chers camarades, que chacun de ceux qui combattent pour la Révolution . . . veille de son mieux à ce que le travail dont il est responsable soit accompli le mieux possible.

. . . La vie est une lutte perpétuelle pour progresser, pour avancer. Luttons donc tous, ne nous estimons jamais satisfaits des buts atteints, poursuivons-en de toujours plus hauts! . . .

Et Staline lui-même — je n'ai pas besoin de dire: "le maître des peuples," comme Gide prétend qu'on l'a obligé de dire, qu'on ne peut en U.R.S.S. appeler Staline "camarade," ou lui dire simplement "vous"!, ce que pourtant je lui ai dit couramment dans nos entretiens au Kremlin, et chez Gorki, et dans la *Pravda* du 23-7-35 — Staline lui-même a, jadis, écrit, dans ses *Problèmes du Léninisme* que *"la modestie est l'ornement du vrai bolchevik."*

Soyons donc vrais et modestes mais inébranlables dans nos combats, dans nos efforts continuels pour enrichir, pour embellir la grande patrie universelle des travailleurs, que la Révolution d'Octobre a fondée!

Et ne nous laissons pas affecter par les haines aboyantes des ennemis, ou par les défaillances des amis trop débiles, qui ne peuvent nous suivre! Réjouissons-nous des peines fécondes (elles sont joies) de notre glorieux et difficile travail présent, et de l'heureux avenir qu'elles bâtissent.

Je vous serre les mains à tous, fraternellement.

Romain Rolland

Page 156:

nous attendions de grandes nouvelles. Nous dinâmes sans Gide — que nous ne revîmes que le lendemain. Il était bien allé au Kremlin en effet, mais il n'avait pas vu Staline. Son mentor l'avait conduit à un concert. Voilà ce que je puis vous dire sur ce point, que je me suis interdit de dire jusqu'au présent par la crainte qu'on fît de tels faits un usage malveillant. C'est si facile! Mais enfin, je les dis aujourd'hui puisqu'on doit la vérité à ses contemporains. On dit ensuite, au cours du voyage (mais quand?) que Gide aurait eu l'intention de parler à Staline des nouvelles lois promulgées en U.R.S.S., très sévères, disait-on, contre l'homosexualité et que c'était pour cela que Staline n'aurait pas voulu voir Gide. Il ne s'agit peut-être, après tout, que des racontars. Gide ne parlait jamais, du moins ne l'ai-je jamais entendu parler devant moi, de cette visite ratée.

Page 158:

Je ne l'ai pas voulu, car leur Message était outrageant pour André Gide, et je ne voulais pas avoir l'air de m'abriter derrière eux pour attaquer Gide.

Page 159:

La publication de mon *Retour de l'U.R.S.S.* m'a voulu nombre d'injures. Celles de Romain Rolland, m'ont peiné. Je n'ai jamais goûté ses écrits; mais du moins je tiens sa personnalité morale en haute estime. Mon chagrin vient de là: combien sont rares ceux qui atteignent la fin de leur vie avant d'avoir montré l'extrémité de leur grandeur. Je crois que l'auteur de *Au-dessus de la mêlée* jugerait sévèrement Rolland vieilli. Cet aigle a fait son nid; il s'y repose.

Pages 161–162:

Il a soudain un autre visage; les dents serrées sur un sourire étrange et dur, les yeux incandescents, il dit: "Je préfère la méthode hitlérienne. L'assassinat de Roehm était une chose monstrueuse, mais accomplie face à l'univers. Hitler niait la justice directement. Il n'avait pas honte de la loi honteuse dont il usait. Tandis que rien n'est plus abominable que les simulacres

des staliniens. Ils jugent ceux qu'ils ont condamnés d'avance.
Spectacle dérisoire, mascarade. . . .

Page 162:

Cinq intellectuels français ont envoyé le télégramme suivant
au gouvernement Negrin-Prieto: Demandons instamment au
gouvernement espagnol d'assurer à tous accusés politiques ga-
ranties de justice et particulièrement franchise et protection de la
défense. Avec nos sentiments très attentifs. André Gide, Georges
Duhamel, de l'Académie Française; Roger Martin du Gard,
François Mauriac, de l'Académie Française; Paul Rivet.

Page 162:

Rappelez-vous cette conversation que nous avons eue l'autre
soir. Vous décidiez que *Vendredi* n'était pas libre puisqu'il
refusait de s'engager à votre suite dans une querelle entre vous
et les *Isvestia,* à propos des communistes et des anarchistes
espagnols. Je vous expliquais qu'il s'en fallait de tout ce que
j'écrive et publie moi-même dans *Vendredi* tout ce qu'il me
plairait d'y écrire ou d'y publier. C'est que je ne me préfère pas à
Vendredi.

Page 162:

Devons-nous épouser toutes vos querelles?

Page 163:

M'entendre traiter de "nouveau allié des Marocains et des
Chemises Noires" m'est insupportable; et, puisque Guéhenno se
pique d'être particulièrement sensible à ce qu'il appelle "l'engage-
ment amical," permettez-moi de vous dire que je trouve, devant
une telle accusation, que c'était à *Vendredi* d'abord de protester;
à *Vendredi* qui publiait récemment ma déclaration d'attachement
indéfectible au Gouvernement Espagnol (inutile d'ajouter: Ré-
publicain; ce serait en reconnaître un autre).

Page 163:

Nous n'avions pas à poser la question difficile et encore pour
nous pleine d'obscurité des rapports entre les divers partis
républicains espagnols à propos de vous, encore moins à paraître
à trancher comme vous-même paraissez les trancher.

Page 163:

Je crois plus volontiers l'amour que la haine.

Pages 163–164:

L'U.R.S.S. n'est pas ce que nous espérions qu'elle serait, ce qu'elle avait promis d'être, ce qu'elle s'efforce encore de paraître; elle a trahi nos espoirs. . . . Mais nous ne détournerons pas de toi nos regards, glorieuse et douloureuse Russie. Si d'abord tu nous servais d'exemple, à présent hélas! tu nous montres dans quels sables une révolution peut s'enliser.

Page 164:

Ce matin, il mourait d'envie de nous accompagner à Vézelay, c'était visible; mais dans le même moment, se l'interdisait pour d'obscures raisons qui sont bien dans son personnage.

CHAPTER IX: Conclusion

Page 167:

J'ai toujours professé que le désir de demeurer constant avec soi-même comportait trop souvent un risque d'insincérité; et j'estime que s'il importe d'être sincère c'est bien lorsque la foi d'un grand nombre, avec la nôtre propre, est engagée.

Page 167:

On ne peut pas donner ce qui n'est pas à nous, — mon âme libre.

Page 167:

Comme la vie est mal faite! On ne peut pas se passer d'affection mutuelle, et on ne peut pas se passer non plus d'indépendance. L'une est aussi sacrée que l'autre.

Page 168:

Ah! chère maman, maman aimée, ce n'est pas tel amour ou telle amitié qui peut te rendre jalouse; au contraire, ils pourraient te servir, en m'attachant à la vie quotidienne; mais ton plus grand ennemi, c'est Dieu, c'est l'art, c'est l'idéal impersonnel, et ma solitude trop aimée. . . . Je ne puis pas aimer comme tout le monde, aimant au travers de Dieu, en qui je vois tout ce qui est. Dieu *est* d'abord, *puis* vous et moi. Qu'y faire? À peine si je parviens à oublier Dieu, dans mes moments de passion, de colère, ou d'attachement violent à ma personnalité et à d'autres. (Quand j'ai souffert il y a quelque temps, je l'avais oublié.) Ce que je te dis, tu penseras que je ferais mieux de ne pas te le dire; car il t'afflige. N'importe, je suis ce que je suis; Je préfère les Idées aux êtres; et la Vérité, la Beauté, le Bien éternels, à moi comme à ceux que j'aime. Ah! je ne les en aime pas moins autant ou plus que les jeunes gens ordinaires. Mais j'aime l'idéal avant tout, et je ne perds mon idéalisme que dans mes crises d'égoïsme piqué, ou de passion dont je ne suis pas maître.

Je t'embrasse... en Dieu.

Page 168:

Devant le moindre acte du don de soi, de sacrifice de soi pour autrui, pour un devoir abstrait, pour une idée, je m'agenouille. S'il doit aboutir à cela, tout le reste du monde n'est pas de trop: toute l'immense misère des hommes.

Page 169:

Voilà la gêne et l'angoisse; l'âme qui palpite et voudrait que l'autre le sache, — et qui ne peut pas, qui se sent enfermée. . . . Cela n'est rien encore: la pire souffrance est celle de deux âmes qui ne peuvent pas s'approcher.

Selected Bibliography

WORKS BY ANDRÉ GIDE

"À propos des déracinés." *Œuvres complètes,* II (1933), 473–444.
Amyntas. Paris: Gallimard, 1925. Orig. ed. 1906.
L'Arbitraire. Paris: L'Air du Temps, 1947.
Attendu que. Algiers: Charlot, 1943.
"Au service de l'Allemagne par Maurice Barrès." *L'Hermitage,* XI
   (July–December, 1905), 41–44.
"Auguste Bréal." *Le Figaro,* February 22, 1941.
Les Cahiers et les poésies d'André Walter. Paris: Gallimard, 1952,
   Orig. ed. 1891–1892.
Les Caves du Vatican. Paris: Gallimard, 1964. Orig. ed. 1914.
"Chroniques de l'Ermitage." *Œuvres complètes,* IV (1933), 377–396.
"Conférences sur Dostoïevsky." *Œuvres complètes,* XI (1936), 157–311.
"Conversation avec un Allemand." *Œuvres complètes,* IX (1935), 133–
   143.
Correspondance Paul Claudel–André Gide. Ed. Robert Mallet. Paris:
   Gallimard, 1949.
Correspondance Francis Jammes–André Gide. Ed. Robert Mallet. Paris:
   Gallimard, 1948.
Correspondance André Gide–Roger Martin du Gard. Ed. Jean Delay.
   2 vols. Paris: Gallimard, 1968.
Correspondance Rainer Maria Rilke–André Gide. Ed. Renée Lang.
   Paris: Corrêa, 1952.

Correspondance André Gide–André Suarès. Ed. Sydney D. Braun. Paris: Gallimard, 1963.

Correspondance André Gide–Paul Valéry. Ed. Robert Mallet. Paris: Gallimard, 1955.

"Corydon." *Œuvres complètes,* IX (1935) 177–347. Orig. ed. 1911.

"De l'évolution du théâtre." *L'Hermitage,* II (1904), 5–22.

"De l'importance du public." *L'Hermitage,* III (July, 1903), 81–95.

"De l'influence en littérature." *Œuvres complètes,* III (1933), 251–273. Orig. ed. 1900.

"Deux Interviews imaginaires." *Feuillets d'automne.* Paris: Mercure de France, 1949. Orig ed. 1943.

"Deux Rencontres avec Romain Rolland." *Littérature engagée,* pp. 124–126. Paris: Gallimard, 1950.

Divers. Paris: Gallimard, 1931.

Dostoïevsky d'après sa correspondance." *Grande Revue,* May 25, 1908. Clipping in the Bibliothèque Doucet.

L'Ecole des femmes. Paris: Gallimard, 1964. Orig. ed. 1929–1930.

"Education." *Cahiers des Saisons,* November, 1956. Clipping in the Bibliothèque Doucet.

"El Hadj." *Œuvres complètes,* III (1933) 67–95.

Eloges. Neuchâtel: Ides et Calendes, 1947.

"Enquête sur le marriage." *La Plume,* June 15, 1901, p. 445. Clipping in the Bibliothèque Doucet.

Essai sur Montaigne. Paris: Jacques Schiffrin, 1929.

Et nunc manet in te. Neuchâtel: Ides et Calendes, 1947.

Les Faux-Monnayeurs. Paris: Gallimard, 1965. Orig. ed. 1926.

"Feuillets." *Œuvres complètes,* II (1933), 457–475; VIII (1935), 347–352; XIII (1937), 405–445; XV (1939), 503–528.

Feuillets d'automne. Paris: Mercure de France, 1949.

"Feuillets inédits." *Œuvres complètes,* IX (1935), 351–373.

L'Immoraliste. Paris: Mercure de France, 1964. Orig. ed. 1902.

Incidences. Paris: Gallimard, 1951. Orig. ed. 1924.

"Isabelle." *Œuvres complètes,* VI (1934), 171–282. Orig. ed. 1911.

Jacques Rivière. Paris: Les Editions de la Belle Page, 1931.

Jeunesse. Neuchâtel: Ides et Calendes, 1945.

Journal. Bibliothèque de la Pléiade. 2 vols. Paris: Gallimard, 1951–1954. Vol. I: *Journal 1889–1939.* Vol. II: *Journal 1939–1949, Souvenirs.* Trans. into English with introd. and notes as *The Journals of André Gide* by Justin O'Brien. 4 vols. New York: Alfred A. Knopf, 1949–1951.

Journal des Faux-Monnayeurs. Paris: Gallimard, 1967. Orig. ed. 1926.

"Journal sans dates." *Nouvelle Revue Française,* LXX (July 1, 1919), 278–286.

"Justice ou charité." *Le Figaro,* February 25–26, 1945. Clipping in the Bibliothèque Doucet.

"Lettre à *Vendredi.*" *Vendredi,* December 24, 1937. Clipping in the Bibliothèque Doucet.

"Lettres." *Œuvres complètes,* XIV (1938), 399–412.

"Lettres à Angèle." *Œuvres complètes,* III (1933), 163–247. Orig. ed. 1900.

"Lettres à Christian Beck." *Mercure de France,* MXXXII (August 1, 1949), 616–637.

Littérature engagée. Paris: Gallimard, 1950.

"Nationalisme et littérature." *Œuvres complètes,* VI (1934), 3–20. Orig. ed. 1909.

Les Nourritures terrestres, suivi des *Nouvelles Nourritures.* Paris: Gallimard, 1964. Orig. eds. 1897 and 1935.

Numquid et tu? Paris: Editions de la Pléiade, 1926. Orig. ed. 1922.

Œdipe. Théâtre, pp. 249–327. Paris: Gallimard, 1947. Orig. ed. 1931.

Œuvres complètes. 15 vols. Paris: Gallimard, 1932–1939.

"Pages du journal de Lafcadio." *Œuvres complètes,* XI (1936), 15–19.

"Pages inédites." *Œuvres complètes,* XI (1936), 23–31.

Paludes. Paris: Gallimard, 1926. Orig. ed. 1895.

"Paradoxes." *Vie Nouvelle,* I (March, 1900), 28–29. Clipping in the Bibliothèque Doucet.

"Petites Gens." *Œuvres complètes,* I (1932), 272–273.

Philoctète. Œuvres complètes, III (1933), 17–63. Orig. ed. 1899.

"Le Poète." *Œuvres complètes,* I (1932), 271.

La Porte étroite. Paris: Mercure de France, 1964. Orig. ed. 1909.

Préface to *Les Fleurs du mal de Charles Baudelaire.* Paris: Pelletan, 1917.

Préfaces. Neuchâtel: Ides et Calendes, 1948.

Prétextes. Paris: Mercure de France, 1947. Orig. ed. 1903.

Le Procès. Paris: Gallimard, 1947. Adapted from Kafka with the collaboration of Jean-Louis Barrault.

"Promenade au salon d'automne." *Œuvres complètes,* IV (1938), 423–431.

Le Promethée mal enchaîné. Paris: Gallimard, 1949. Orig. ed. 1899.

"Propositions." *Nouvelle Revue Française,* XXXVI (December 1, 1911), 649–653.

"Proserpine." *Vers et Prose,* XXVIII (January–February–March, 1912), 19–21. Clipping in the Bibilothèque Doucet.

"La Querelle du Peuplier." *L'Hermitage,* III (1903), 222–228.

"Réflexions sur l'Allemagne." *Œuvres complètes,* IX (1935), 103–116. Orig. ed. 1919.

"Réflexions sur quelques points de littérature et de morale." *Œuvres complètes,* II (1933), 413–433. Orig. ed. 1897.

"Réflexions sur quelques points de morale chrétienne." *L'Art et la Vie,* September, 1896, pp. 595–560. Clipping in the Bibliothèque Doucet.

"Réponse à l'enquête: Pourquoi écrivez-vous?." *Littérature,* X (December, 1919). Clipping in the Bibliothèque Doucet.

"Réponse à une enquête sur l'influence allemande." *Œuvres complètes,* IV (1933), 413–414.

Le Retour de l'enfant prodigue. Paris: Gallimard, 1948. Orig. ed. 1907.

Retour de l'U.R.S.S., suivi de *Retouches à mon Retour de l'U.R.S.S.* Paris: Gallimard, 1950. Orig. ed. 1936 and 1937.

Le Roi Candaule. Théâtre, pp. 153–247. Paris: Gallimard, 1947. Orig. ed. 1901.

Saül. Théâtre, pp. 7–151. Paris: Gallimard, 1947. Orig. ed. 1903.

La Séquestrée de Poitiers. Paris: Gallimard, 1930.

Si le grain ne meurt. Paris: Gallimard, 1945. Orig. ed. 1920–1921.

"Souvenirs littéraires et problèmes actuels." *Feuillets d'automne.* Paris: Mercure de France, 1949.

"De Stremer et de l'individualisme." *L'Hermitage,* I (1900), 60–64.

"La Suisse entre deux langues." *Œuvres complètes,* VI (1934), 331–333.

La Symphonie pastorale. Paris: Gallimard, 1965. Orig. ed. 1919.

"La Tentative amoureuse ou le traité du vain désir." *Œuvres complètes,* I (1932), 223–243. Orig. ed. 1893.

Thésée. Paris: Gallimard, 1946.

Le Traité du Narcisse. Œuvres complètes, I (1932), 207–220. Orig. ed. 1891.

"Verlaine et Mallarmé." *Œuvres complètes,* VII (1934), 411–413.

Le Voyage d'Urien. Paris: Gallimard, 1929. Orig. ed. 1893.

Works by Romain Rolland

"À la Russie libre et libératrice." *L'Esprit libre,* pp. 211–212. Paris: Albin Michel, 1953.

L'Âme enchantée. Paris: Albin Michel, 1964–1966. Orig. ed. 1922–1933.

Une Amitié française. Paris: Albin Michel, 1955.

"Au-dessus de la mêlée," *L'Esprit libre,* pp. 76–89. Paris: Albin Michel, 1953.

"Aux jeunes." *Les Cahiers de la Jeunesse,* July 15, 1937, pp. 4–5. Clipping in the Archives Romain Rolland.

"Aux lycéens." *Les Cahiers de la Jeunesse,* December 15, 1938, pp. 17–18. Clipping in the Archives Romain Rolland.

Aux peuples assassinés. Paris: Ollendorf, 1916.

"Les Baglioni." Unpublished play, Archives Romain Rolland.

Un Beau Visage à tous sens. Paris: Albin Michel, 1967.

Beethoven. Paris: Albin Michel, 1966. Orig. ed. 1928–1943.

"Caligula." Unpublished play. Archives Romain Rolland.

Cette Âme ardente. Paris: Albin Michel, 1954.

Choix de lettres à Malwida von Meysenburg. Paris: Albin Michel, 1958.

Clerambault. Paris: Albin Michel, 1920.

Le Cloître de la rue d'Ulm. Paris: Albin Michel, 1952.

Colas Breugnon. Paris: Albin Michel, 1919.

Comment empêcher la guerre. Paris: Publications du Comité Mondial contre la Guerre et le Fascisme, 1937.

Compagnons de route. Paris: Albin Michel, 1961. Orig. ed. 1936.

Correspondence, unpublished. Archives Romain Rolland.

Correspondance entre Louis Gillet et Romain Rolland. Preface by Paul Claudel. Paris: Albin Michel, 1949.

"De deux maux, le moindre." *L'Esprit libre,* pp. 90–95, Paris: Albin Michel, 1953.

De la décadence de la peinture italienne. Paris: Albin Michel, 1957.

Deux Hommes se rencontrent. Paris: Albin Michel, 1964.

"Le Devoir des intellectuels contre la guerre." *Avenir Social,* May 1, 1927. Clipping in the Archives Romain Rolland.

"Empédocle." Unpublished play. Archives Romain Rolland.

Empédocle d'Agrigente. Paris: Sablier, 1931. Orig. ed. 1918.

"Enquête sur l'art chrétien." *L'Action Française,* July 15, 1912. Clipping in the Archives Romain Rolland.

"Enquête sur la séparation des beaux-arts et de l'état." *Les Arts et la Vie,* October 1904, pp. 250–251. Clipping in the Archives Romain Rolland.

L'Esprit libre. Paris: Albin Michel, 1953.

"La France a-t-elle une mission." *Les Cahiers de la Jeunesse,* July 15, 1938, pp. 15–16. Clipping in the Archives Romain Rolland.

Haendel. Paris: Albin Michel, 1951. Orig. ed. 1910.

Inde. Paris: Albin Michel, 1960. Orig. ed. 1951.

Jean-Christophe. Paris: Albin Michel, 1956. Orig. ed. 1903–1912.

"Jeanne de Piennes." Unpublished play. Archives Romain Rolland.

Le Jeu de l'amour et de la mort. Paris: Albin Michel, 1925.

Journal des années de guerre. Paris: Albin Michel, 1952.

"Journal intime." Unpublished. Archives Romain Rolland.

Les Léonides. Paris: Albin Michel, 1928.

Liluli. Paris: Albin Michel, 1926. Orig. ed. 1919.

Mahatma Gandhi. Paris: Stock, 1924. Orig. ed. 1923.

Mémoires. Paris: Albin Michel, 1956.

Musiciens d'aujourd'hui. Paris: Hachette, 1949. Orig. ed. 1908.

Musiciens d'autrefois. Paris: Hachette, 1912.

"Niobé." Unpublished play. Archives Romain Rolland.

"Opinion sur la liberté d'écrire." *Les Marges,* XXVI (February 15, 1923), 108–150.

"Orsino." Unpublished play. Archives Romain Rolland.

Pâques fleuris. Paris: Albin Michel, 1926.

Par la révolution, la paix. Paris: Editions Sociales Internationales, 1935.

Péguy. Paris: Albin Michel, 1948. Orig. ed. 1945.

Pierre et Luce. Paris: Albin Michel, 1958. Orig. ed. 1920.

"Pour la 'Fête de la Paix' à Lyon," November 10, 1928. Clipping in the Archives Romain Rolland.

"Pourquoi j'ai fait de mon Jean-Christophe un Allemand." Clipping in the Archives Romain Rolland. Published in excerpt in *Le Parthenon,* November 15, 1913.

Printemps romain. Paris: Albin Michel, 1954.

Quinze Ans de combat. Paris: Rieder, 1935.

"Réponse à l'enquête sur l'Allemagne." *Revue Européenne,* XXX (August 1, 1925), 58–59.

"Réponse à enquête sur l'anti-poésie." *Les Cahiers Idéalistes Français,* June, 1926. Clipping in the Archives Romain Rolland.

Retour au Palais Farnèse. Paris: Albin Michel, 1956.

Robespierre. Paris: Albin Michel, 1939.

Romain Rolland et le mouvement florentin de la Voce. Paris: Albin Michel, 1966.

"Savonarole." Unpublished play. Archives Romain Rolland.

"Siège de Mantoue." Unpublished play. Archives Romain Rolland.

Le Temps viendra. Paris: Albin Michel, 1938. Orig. ed. 1903.

"Le Théâtre actuel." *Montjoie,* Argenteuil, May 16, 1913. Clipping in the Archives Romain Rolland.

Théâtre de la révolution. Paris: Albin Michel, 1926. Orig. ed. 1909.

Le Théâtre du peuple. Paris: Albin Michel, 1931. Orig. ed. 1903.

"Tolstoy: l'esprit libre." *Les Cahiers Idéalistes Français,* November 17, pp. 291–293. Clipping in the Archives Romain Rolland.

Les Tragédies de la foi. Paris: Albin Michel, 1913.

Vie de Beethoven. Paris: Hachette, 1903.

Vie de Michel-Ange. Paris: Hachette, 1964. Orig. ed. 1906.

La Vie de Ramakrishna. Paris: Stock, 1956. Orig. ed. 1929.

Vie de Tolstoi. Paris: Hachette, 1959. Orig. ed. 1911.

Vie de Vivekananda. Paris: Stock, 1948. Orig. ed. 1930.

"La Volonté de la paix." *La Volonté de la Paix,* V (October–November, 1928). Clipping in the Archives Romain Rolland.

Le Voyage intérieur. Paris: Albin Michel, 1959. Orig. ed. 1942.

Voyage musical au pays du passé. Paris: Hachette, 1922.

Works About André Gide

Albérès, R.-M. *L'Odyssée d'André Gide.* Paris: La Nouvelle Edition, 1951.

Altman, Georges. "André Gide dans la foule." *Gros Plans,* March(?), 1933. Clipping in the Bibliothèque Doucet.

Amrouche, Jean. "André Gide communiste." *Mirages,* Tunis, December, 1932. Clipping in the Bibliothèque Doucet.

"André Gide et les écrivains soviétiques." *Journal de Rouen,* February 26, 1935. Clipping in the Bibliothèque Doucet.

André Gide et notre temps. Paris: Gallimard, 1935.

Archambault, Paul. *L'Humanité d'André Gide.* Paris: Bloud et Gay, 1946.

Articles concerning André Gide and communism. *Aux Ecoutes,* October 17, 1936. *Le Figaro,* October 24, 1936. Clippings in the Bibliothèque Doucet.

Brach, Sylbrandi. *André Gide et l'âme moderne.* Amsterdam: Kruyt, 1921.

Brachfeld, Georges I. *André Gide and the Communist Temptation.* Paris: Minard, 1959.

Brée, Germaine. *André Gide, l'insaisissable Prothée.* Paris: Les Belles Lettres, 1953.

Bronne, Carlo. *Rilke, Gide et Verhaeren.* Messein: Imprimerie Centrale de l'Ouest, 1955.

Cacambo. "Le Silence d'André Gide." *Candide,* May 9, 1935. Clipping in the Bibliothèque Doucet.

"Congrès international des écrivains." *Je suis partout,* June 29, 1935. Clipping in the Bibliothèque Doucet.

"La Conversion de M. Gide." *L'Action Française,* June 29, 1933. Clipping in the Bibliothèque Doucet.

Cordle, Thomas. *André Gide.* New York: Twayne, 1969.

Crossman, Richard. *The God that Failed.* London: Hamish Hamilton, 1950.

Curtius, Ernst Robert. *Die literarische Wegbereiter des neuen Frankreich.* Potsdam: Gutsav Kiepenheuer, 1919.

Dancourt, Louis. "André Gide communiste." *Le Cri du Jour,* October, 1935. Clipping in the Bibliothèque Doucet.

Dauvigny, Alain. *André Gide ou l'impossible morale.* Bordeaux: Samie, 1954.

Delay, Jean, *La Jeunesse d'André Gide.* Paris: Gallimard, 1956.

Demailly, Yves. A criticism of Léon Pierre-Quint's book, *André Gide.* *La Hune,* Spring, 1933, pp. 30–32. Clipping in the Bibliothèque Doucet.

Demeure, Fernand. "André Gide et l'Allemagne." *L'Ecole,* May 12, 1944.

Dervcre, Gaston. "Le 'Cas André Gide.' " *Le Merle Noir,* January 5, 1938. Clipping in the Bibliothèque Doucet.

Dobelle, Jean. "Un Apôtre de l'U.R.S.S." *La Faillite du Spirituel,* October 14, 1932. Clipping in the Bibliothèque Doucet.

Du Bos, Charles. *Le Dialogue avec André Gide.* Paris: Corrêa, 1947.

Duran, Lucien. "André Gide et l'U.R.S.S." *Mercure de France,* CCXLVI (August 15, 1933), 93–106.

"Un Ecrivain sans tribune." *Vu et Lu,* Paris, December 1, 1937. Clipping in the Bibliothèque Doucet.

"En U.R.S.S." *Le Progrès,* Lyon, March 6, 1937. Clipping in the Bibliothèque Doucet.

"Etude: Martin du Gard et Gide en appel." Supplement to *Le Monde,* March 23, 1968, pp. i-iv.

Fabre-Luce, Alfred. "Contre la manifestation Gide." *Pamphlet,* March 31, 1933. Clipping in the Bibliothèque Doucet.

Fabrègues, Jean de. "Une Révolution justifiée." *Combat,* January, 1938. Clipping in the Bibliothèque Doucet.

Fernandez, Ramon. *André Gide.* Paris: Corrêa, 1931.

———. "Notes sur l'évolution d'André Gide." *Nouvelle Revue Française,* CCXXXVIII (July 1, 1933), 129–135.

Fondande, Benjamin, *Le Nouveau Cahier Bleu.* May 10, 1934, pp. 356–360. Clipping in the Bibliothèque Doucet.

Fowlie, Wallace. *André Gide: His Life and Art.* New York: Macmillan, 1956.

Fréminville, Claude de. "Avec le recul de temps." *Populaire,* March 1, 1952. Clipping in the Bibliothèque Doucet.

Friedmann, Georges. "André Gide et l'U.R.S.S." *Europe,* CLXIX (January 15, 1937), 5–29.

———. *De la Sainte Russie à l'U.R.S.S.* Paris: Gallimard, 1938.

Gallois, Daniel. "La Conversion de l'enfant prodigue," November 24, 1932. Clipping in the Bibliothèque Doucet.

Guéhenno, Jean. "Lettre ouverte à André Gide." *Vendredi,* December 17, 1937. Clipping in the Bibliothèque Doucet.

————. "Réponse à André Gide." *Vendredi,* December 24, 1937. Clipping in the Bibliothèque Doucet.

Henriot, E. "André Gide communiste." *Le Temps,* October 10, 1932. Clipping in the Bibliothèque Doucet.

————. "L'Ecrivain juge ou partisan." *Le Temps,* December 17, 1934. Clipping in the Bibliothèque Doucet.

————. "Littérature et communisme." *Le Temps,* December 17, 1934. Clipping in the Bibliothèque Doucet.

Herbart, Pierre. *A la recherche d'André Gide.* Paris: Gallimard, 1952.

Hirsch, Charles-Henry. "Revues." *Mercure de France,* CCXL (November 15, 1932), 204–206.

Hommage à André Gide. Paris: Editions du Capitole, 1928.

Hytier, Jean. *André Gide.* Algiers: Charlot, 1938.

Ireland, G. W. *André Gide.* New York: Grove Press, 1963.

Iseler, Paul. *Les Débuts d'André Gide vus par Pierre Louÿs.* Paris: Editions du Sagittaire, 1937.

Lafille, Pierre. *André Gide romancier.* Paris: Hachette, 1954.

Lalou, René. "Culture et liberté." *Nouvelles Littéraires,* August 24, 1935. Clipping in the Bibliothèque Doucet.

Lambert, Jean. *Gide familier.* Paris: René Julliard, 1958.

Lang, Renée. *André Gide et la pensée allemande.* Paris: L.U.F. Egloff, 1949.

————. *Rilke, Gide et Valéry.* Boulogne-sur-Seine: Revue Prétecte, 1953.

La Rochelle, Drieu. "Nos Intellectuels devant Staline." *L'Emancipation Nationale,* September 26, 1936. Clipping in the Bibliothèque Doucet.

Le Brun, Henri. "Ceux qui n'aiment pas l'U.R.S.S." *Russie d'aujourd'hui,* June, 1935. Clipping in the Bibliothèque Doucet.

Loivey, Jean. "André Gide et le communisme." *La Revue du Siècle,* 1934, pp. 61–66. Clipping in the Bibliothèque Doucet.

Lvovsky, Z. "Moscou répond à la conversion d'André Gide." *Nouvelles Littéraires,* December 24, 1932. Clipping in the Bibliothèque Doucet.

"M. André Gide chez les communistes." *Candide,* November 1, 1934. Clipping in the Bibliothèque Doucet.

Mann, Klaus. *André Gide, die Geschichte eines Europäers.* Zurich: Steinberg, 1948.

Marchand, Max. *La Complexe Pédagogie et didactique d'André Gide.* Oran: Max Marchand, 1954.

Martin, Claude. *André Gide par lui-même*. Paris: Seuil, 1963.

Martin du Gard, Roger. *Notes sur André Gide*. Paris: Gallimard, 1951.

Massis, Henri. *D'André Gide à Marcel Proust*. Lyon: Lardanchet, 1948.

————. "Lectures." *Revue Universelle*, LVIII (September 15, 1934), 738–740.

Mauclair, Camille. "D'Oscar Wilde à Lénine." *Dépêche de Toulouse*, September 16, 1932. Clipping in the Bibliothèque Doucet.

Maulnier, Thierry. "Les Essais." *Revue Universelle*, LVII (April 15, 1934), 242–246.

————. "Réponse à M. André Gide." *Le Figaro Littéraire*, June 29, 1935. Clipping in the Bibliothèque Doucet.

————. "Sur une conversion." *L'Action Française*, November 10, 1932. Clipping in the Bibliothèque Doucet.

Mauriac, Claude. *Conversations avec André Gide*. Paris: Albin Michel, 1951.

Mauriac, François. "Deux Témoignages." *Temps Présent*, May 20, 1938. Clipping in the Bibliothèque Doucet.

————. "Les Esthètes fascinés." *Echo de Paris*, September 10, 1932. Clipping in the Bibliothèque Doucet.

————. "Gide et *Vendredi*." *Temps Présent*, December 31, 1937. Clipping in the Bibliothèque Doucet.

Millet, Raymond. "Au congrès international des écrivains: le communisme vaincra-t-elle la culture occidentale." *Le Temps*, June 23, 1935. Clipping in the Bibliothèque Doucet.

————. "Le Débat décisif du congrès international des écrivains. *Le Temps*, June 24, 1935. Clipping in the Bibliothèque Doucet.

"Naissance du XXe siècle." *Revue du Siècle*, May, 1944, pp. 53–60. Clipping in the Bibliothèque Doucet.

Naville, Claude. *André Gide et le communisme*. Paris: Librairie de Travail, 1936.

Nobécourt, R.-G. *Les Nourritures normandes d'André Gide*. Paris: Médicis, 1949.

Nöel, Maurice. "M. André Gide est nommé 'Ingénieur des Ames'." *Le Figaro*, October 27, 1934. Clipping in the Bibliothèque Doucet.

"Nouveau Converti," December 22, 1932. Clipping in the Bibliothèque Doucet.

Nouvelle Revue Française. Hommage à André Gide. Paris: Gallimard, 1951.

O'Brien, Justin. *Portrait of André Gide: A Critical Biography*. New York: McGraw-Hill, 1964. Orig. ed. 1953.

Painter, George. *André Gide*. London: Arthur Barker, 1951.

Pell, Elsie. *André Gide, l'évolution de sa pensée religieuse.* Paris: Henri Didier, 1936.

Pfleger, Charles. *Aux prises avec le Christ.* Mulhouse: Salvator, 1949.

Pierre-Quint, Léon. *André Gide.* Paris: Stock, 1952.

———. "Notes sur les idées de défense nationale et de patrie." *Cahiers du Sud,* CXLIX (March, 1933), 161–170.

Planche, Henri. *Le Problème de Gide.* Paris: Edition Tequi, 1952.

Porché, François. "André Gide, défenseur de l'Occident." *Nouvelles Littéraires,* April 26, 1930. Clipping in the Bibliothèque Doucet.

Putnam, Samuel. "André Gide and Communism." *Partisan Review,* I (November–December, 1934), 30–36.

Rauch, Erich. *Zum Freundschaftsproblem in Leben und Werk André Gides.* Jena: G. Meuenbahr, Universitätsbücherei, 1933.

Rivière, Jacques. "André Gide." *Chroniques des Lettres Françaises,* IV (1926), 145–168, 289–303.

Robert le Diable. "Causerie littéraire." *L'Action Française,* January 23, 1930. Clipping in the Bibliothèque Doucet.

Rousseau, André. Article concerning André Gide and communism. *Le Figaro,* May 4, 1935. Clipping in the Bibliothèque Doucet.

Roux, François de. "André Gide communiste." *Activités,* May, 1933, pp. 9–12. Clipping in the Bibliothèque Doucet.

Saillenfest, Jean. "Les Feuillets d'André Gide." *La Revue du Siècle,* May, 1934, pp. 53–60. Clipping in the Bibliothèque Doucet.

Saint-Chamont, Jean de. "André Gide et le communisme." *La Vie Intellectuelle,* October, 1935, pp. 334–341. Clipping in the Bibliothèque Doucet.

Schildt, Goran. *Gide et l'homme.* Paris: Mercure de France, 1949.

Schlumberger, Jean. "Adieux." *Œuvres complètes,* V, 335–381.

———. "Compagnons." *Œuvres complètes,* VII, 155–208.

———. "Eveils." *Œuvres complètes,* VI, 263–408.

———. *Madeleine et André Gide,* Paris: Gallimard, 1956.

———. "Notes et chroniques, 1909." *Œuvres complètes,* I, 137–153.

———. *Œuvres complètes.* 7 vols. Paris: Gallimard, 1958–1961.

Schwob, René. *Le Vrai Drame d'André Gide.* Paris: Bernard Grasset, 1932.

Simon, Pierre-Henri. "Correspondance d'André Gide et de Roger Martin du Gard introduite et publiée par Jean Delay." *Le Monde,* March 23, 1968, p. 1.

Souday, Paul. *André Gidé.* Paris: Simon Krâ, 1927.

Starkie, Enid. *André Gide.* New Haven: Yale University Press, 1954.

"Le Succès du camarade André Gide." *Aux Ecoutes,* March 25, 1933. Clipping in the Bibliothèque Doucet.

Thomas, Lawrence. *André Gide, the Ethic of the Artist.* London: Secker and Warburg, 1950.

Tregaro, Louis. "Quand Caliban fait de la politique." *Feuilles Libres,* January 25, 1938. Clipping in the Bibliothèque Doucet.

Vaillant-Couturier, P. "André Gide parlera ce soir, salle Cadet." *l'Humanité,* March 21, 1933. Clipping in the Bibliothèque Doucet.

Vanderem, F. "La Comédie littéraire." *Candide,* July, 1933. Clipping in the Bibliothèque Doucet.

Vandervelde, Emile. "La Conversion d'André Gide au communisme." *Le Dépêche,* Cherbourg, January 7, 1933. Clipping in the Bibliothèque Doucet.

"Les Variations de M. André Gide." *Candide,* March(?), 1933. Clipping in the Bibliothèque Doucet.

Works About Romain Rolland

Arcos, René. *Romain Rolland.* Paris: Mercure de France, 1950.

———. "Romain Rolland." *La Pensée,* July–August–September, 1945, pp. 29–39. Clipping in the Archives Romain Rolland.

———. "Souvenirs." Clipping in the Archives Romain Rolland.

Barrère, Jean-Bertrand. "Romain Rolland et les Catholiques." *Ecclesia,* August, 1951, pp. 97–100. Clipping in the Archives Romain Rolland.

———. *Romain Rolland, l'âme et l'art.* Paris: Albin Michel, 1966.

———. *Romain Rolland par lui-meme.* Paris: Seuil, 1960.

Beigbeder, Marc. "Il n'y a pas eu de Romain Rolland." *Esprit,* CXXXII (April, 1947), 605–625.

Bonnerot, Jean. *Romain Rolland.* Paris: La Nouvelle Revue Critique, 1921.

Cheval, René. *Romain Rolland, l'Allemagne et la guerre.* Paris: Presses Universitaires de France, 1963.

Claudel, Paul. "La Pensée religieuse de Romain Rolland." *La Revue* (des Deux Mondes), January 15, 1949, pp. 193–211.

Debram, Isabelle. *Monsieur Romain Rolland, initiateur du défaitisme.* Genève: Henri Jarrys, 1918.

Dvorak, Robert. *Das Ethische und das Ästhetische bei Romain Rolland.* Bottrop i. W.: Wilh. Postberg, 1933.

Europe. February, 1926. Special issue devoted to Romain Rolland.

Grappin, Pierre. *Le Bund "Neues Vaterland."* Paris: IAC, 1952.

Guéhenno, Jean. "Un Homme: Romain Rolland." *Le Figaro,* January 7, 1945. Clipping in the Archives Romain Rolland.

Guilbeaux, Henri. *Pour Romain Rolland.* Genève: J.-H. Jeheber, 1915.

"Hommage à Romain Rolland." *Le Disque-Vert,* March–April, 1954. Clipping in the Archives Romain Rolland.

Jourdain, Francis. "Souvenirs sur Romain Rolland." *La Pensée,* July–August–September, 1945, pp. 40–42. Clipping in the Archives Romain Rolland.

Jouve, Pierre-Jean. *Romain Rolland vivant.* Paris: Paul Ollendorff, 1920.

Kaempffer, Annemarie. *Romain Rollands Frauengestallten.* Charlottenburg: Gebrüder Hoffmann, 1931.

Kemp, Robert. "La Vie des livres: péchés d'orgueil." *Nouvelles Littéraires,* February 12, 1953. Clipping in the Archives Romain Rolland.

Kempf, Marcelle. *Romain Rolland et l'Allemagne.* Paris: Nouvelles Editions Debresse, 1962.

Kirchler, Walter. *Romain Rolland, Henri Barbusse, Fritz von Unruh.* Würzburg: Verlagsdruckerei, 1920.

Kobi, Emil E. *Die Erziehung zum Einzeln.* Frauenfeld: Huber, 1966.

Krakowski, Ber. *La Psychologie des peuples allemands et juifs dans les romans de Romain Rolland.* Toulouse: Imprimerie du Sud-Ouest, 1931.

Levy, Arthur R. *L'Idéalisme de Romain Rolland.* Paris: A.-G. Nizet, 1946.

Liber Amicorum Romain Rolland, Leipzig: Rotapfel, 1926.

Loyson, Paul H. *Êtes-vous neutres devant le crime?* Paris: Berger-Levrault, 1916.

Machan, Helen Whitman. *The Popular Theater Movement in France: Romain Rolland and the "Revue d'Art Dramatique."* Urbana: University of Illinois Press, 1950.

Massis, Henri. *Jugements.* Paris: Plon-Nourrit, 1924.

———. *Romain Rolland contre la France.* Paris: H. Floury, 1915.

Paraf, Pierre. "Rencontres de Romain Rolland," *Europe,* CCCCXXXIX–CCCXL (November–December, 1965), 17–25.

Robichez, Jacques. *Romain Rolland.* Paris: Hatier, 1961.

Sénéchal, Christian. *Romain Rolland.* Paris: Editions de la Caravelle, 1933.

Starr, William Thomas. *Romain Rolland and a World at War.* Evanston: Northwestern University Press, 1956.

———. *Romain Rolland's Internationalism.* University of Oregon Thesis Series No. 2, 1938.

Tetu, Marcel, "Entretiens avec Romain Rolland." *Europe,* CXX (December, 1955), 176–184.

Thibaudet, Albert. *"Jean-Christophe—La Nouvelle Journée* par Romain Rolland." *Nouvelle Revue Française,* L (February 1, 1913), 316–322.
Zweig, Stefan. *Romain Rolland,* Frankfurt: Rütten, 1921.

GENERAL WORKS

Beloff, Max. *The Foreign Policy of Soviet Russia, 1929–1941.* New York: Oxford University Press, 1949.
Bonneville, Georges. *Prophètes et témoins de l'Europe.* Leyden: A. W. Sythoff, 1961.
Breton, André. *Misère de la poésie.* Paris: Editions Surréalistes, 1932.
Ceux qui ont choisi. Paris: Association des Ecrivains et Artistes Révolutionnaires, 1933.
Claudel, Paul. Préface, *Correspondance entre Louis Gillet et Romain Rolland.* Paris: Albin Michel, 1949.
Dedeyan, Charles. *Rilke et la France.* Paris: Sedes, 1961.
Deutscher, Isaac. *The Prophet Outcast.* New York: Oxford University Press, 1963.
Grenier, Jean. "L'Âge des orthodoxies." *Nouvelle Revue Française,* CCLXXI (April 1, 1936), 481–493.
Guéhenno, Jean. "Les Relations intellectuels entre la France et l'Allemagne." *Grande Revue,* IV (April, 1922), 335–343.
Naville, Pierre. *Trotsky vivant.* Paris: Julliard, 1962.
Serge, Victor. *From Lenin to Stalin,* New York: Pioneer, 1937.
———. *Mémoires d'un révolutionnaire.* Paris: Seuil, 1951.
Simon, Pierre-Henri. "Deux Hommes se rencontrent." *Le Monde,* December 30, 1964. Clipping in the Bibliothèque Doucet.
Trotsky, Leon. "I Stake My Life!" *The Basic Writings of Trotsky,* pp. 278–279. Ed. Irving Howe. New York: Random House, 1963.

Index

273

ABOUT THE AUTHOR

Frederick Harris is a graduate of Fordham College and received his Ph.D. from Columbia University. He currently teaches French and German at Fordham's College of Liberal Arts in Lincoln Center. The materials for this book were gathered during a period of concentrated research in the Archives Romain Rolland, the Bibliothèque Doucet, and other relevant manuscript collections in France.

The text of this book was set in Baskerville Linotype and printed by offset. Composed, printed and bound by Quinn & Boden Company, Inc., Rahway, N.J.